The M.E. Sharpe Library of
Franklin D. Roosevelt Studies

Volume Four

The M.E. Sharpe Library of
Franklin D. Roosevelt Studies

Franklin D. Roosevelt
and the Formation
of the Modern World

Thomas C. Howard
William D. Pederson

Editors

M.E. Sharpe

Armonk, New York
London, England

Copyright © 2003 by M. E. Sharpe, Inc.

Library of Congress Cataloging-in-Publication Data

Franklin D. Roosevelt and the formation of the modern world / Thomas C. Howard and
William D. Pederson, editors.
    p. cm.
    Includes bibliographical references and index.
    ISBN 0-7656-1030-2 (alk. paper) — ISBN 0-7656-1031-0 (pbk.: alk. paper)
    1. United States—Foreign relations—1933–1945. 2. Roosevelt, Franklin D. (Franklin
Delano), 1882–1945. I. Howard, Thomas C. II. Pederson, William D., 1946–

E806 .F6918 2003
973.917′092—dc21

2002022869

Printed in the United States of America

BM (c) 10 9 8 7 6 5 4 3 2 1
BM (p) 10 9 8 7 6 5 4 3 2 1

TABLE OF CONTENTS

ACKNOWLEDGMENTS

We would first like to express gratitude for the support provided by the History Department at Virginia Tech and the International Lincoln Center for American Studies at Louisiana State University at Shreveport.

Special thanks go to Rhonda Wills in the History Department for her preparation of successive drafts of the manuscript in addition to her many other responsibilities. Without her technical knowledge and her ability to fix the seemingly unfixable, completion of this book would not have been possible. She exceeds her resourcefulness, efficiency, and professionalism only with her care, dedication, and good-humored understanding.

More than a word of appreciation is due the able people at M.E. Sharpe. From the start, Andrew Gyory and Esther L. Clark in the Editorial Department provided enthusiastic support for the project. Thanks especially to our production editor, Henrietta Toth. She shepherded the manuscript through successive phases of the publication process, and saw to it that numerous errors were avoided.

Several contributors benefited from the generous assistance of the staff of the Franklin D. Roosevelt Library in Hyde Park, New York. Thomas Howard is indebted to the Franklin and Eleanor Roosevelt Institute for a grant funding travel and research at the Library.

Finally, Thomas Howard takes this opportunity to express his thanks to his family near and far who have tolerated his long obsession with history, his fascination with Franklin and Eleanor, and his various other idiosyncrasies. Nothing, however, counted for more throughout work on this book than the forbearance, sustenance, and encouragement of his wife, Judith.

Acknowledgements traditionally end with a ritualized disclaimer, and this will be no exception. Many have contributed to the success of this project and provided advice along the way, but only the editors are responsible for those occasions when they failed to heed it.

The M.E. Sharpe Library of
Franklin D. Roosevelt Studies

Volume Four

Introduction

Thomas C. Howard

Franklin Roosevelt's reputation as one of the great American presidents remains secure. In foreign affairs he was instrumental in moving the country from isolationism into a new era of international involvement and assertiveness that has endured since his death. During World War II he helped plan and direct the most successful military operation in the history of the nation. But while his presidency is the standard by which all his successors have been judged, it is also one of the most controversial. He provided the leadership and vision necessary to restore hope and to confront the greatest world crisis of the twentieth century, but his methods were often manipulative and deceptive. As an idealist with a coherent world vision, and a realist willing to make pragmatic deals, he was responsible for decisions and policies that were fundamentally important in the making of the world in which we live today.

The chapters in this volume provide fresh and original insights into the man who for over twelve critical years determined the foreign policy of the United States. They trace and analyze the evolution of Roosevelt's foreign policy during a time of ever-deepening involvement in world affairs in the 1930s and his role as wartime statesman. Among the numerous themes that flow through these studies, four are worthy of special mention. The first is the evolution of Roosevelt's increasingly bold internationalist thought and the profound sense of purpose that underlay his assumptions. The second is the frequently cautious nature of his leadership and the expedient means to which he was often willing to resort when he believed them necessary to achieve his greater purposes. The third is his inclination to view foreign and domestic policies as intricately bound together. Finally, there is the theme of

Roosevelt's successes and failures as "educator" of the American people on complex foreign policy issues and wartime decisions.

Chris Van Aller's chapter, "FDR's Foreign Policy Persona," centers attention on some of Roosevelt's successes as an educator by analyzing the roles and techniques that he used to "teach" the American people about the hazards of the international scene in the late 1930s. In view of the historic clashes within the American system over authority in foreign affairs and the relative absence of strong executive powers in foreign power, Roosevelt saw the need to enlighten the public and gently to persuade them to adopt his perspective on the changing international scene. Van Aller traces the strategies by which Roosevelt attempted gradually to convince a strongly isolationist public about the possible perils for the United States in the world crisis. After exploring the roots and nature of American isolationism, as well as Roosevelt's own earlier isolationist tendencies, Van Aller stresses Roosevelt's "creative uses of indirection" and his extraordinarily skillful use of the news media and manipulation of the press corps. Above all, he views Roosevelt as someone who was able to motivate the people of a democracy to action through his capacity to explain complex foreign issues in easily comprehensible human terms.

In his chapter dealing with FDR's leadership before the entry of the United States into World War II, Manfred Landecker also analyzes Roosevelt's leadership style and how it influenced his preparation of the country for the threat posed by European fascism. Echoing Van Aller's analysis, Landecker also focuses on the "indirect and unstructured" nature of presidential influence on public opinion, while broadening his analysis to include the larger circle involved in the decision-making process, including the Congress, the bureaucracy, the media, and various interest groups. Using the model of the "predominant leader" in politics, Landecker weighs Roosevelt's principles against his pragmatism and gauges the degree to which he dealt effectively with the rise of threats abroad while simultaneously handling domestic opposition to his policies. He provides many insights into Roosevelt's use of "anticipatory reaction," that is, the capacity to imagine and thus to anticipate the reactions of those affected by his actions. According to Landecker's analysis, Roosevelt did his utmost to manipulate public opinion, deliberately remaining in the background at times for tactical reasons. Landecker also concludes that Roosevelt's effort to anticipate public reaction was not only an integral part of his leadership style, but evidence of his faith in the "common man" and his belief that democratic government can only function successfully if there is reciprocal faith between leaders and followers.

David Esposito's chapter concentrates on what he views as Roosevelt's acceptance of long-standing concerns about America's strategic vulnerability to foreign invasion by a hostile military power. While both Van Aller and Landecker are mainly concerned with Roosevelt's leadership style and his efforts to "educate" public opinion, Esposito concentrates on another aspect of how Roosevelt dealt with the coming of the war by assessing Roosevelt's forward defense strategy to counter international aggression. Esposito also discusses Roosevelt's deep concern with the question of how to preserve American institutions both during and after a confrontation with aggressive foreign powers. This concern led Roosevelt to pursue postwar planning with Wilsonian ideals, modified by his far more pragmatic approach. Esposito provides a fascinating summary of late nineteenth-and early twentieth-century literature on futuristic warfare, including the advent of superweapons and mass invasions—publications that influenced the thought of national leaders in the West, including Woodrow Wilson. Esposito also describes the literature on future wars that prevailed after World War I, including new invasion scenarios that by the late 1930s focused on the possibility of an alliance between Nazi Germany and Imperial Japan. He argues persuasively that once Franklin Roosevelt moved from preoccupation with domestic issues to an increasingly interventionist position by the late 1930s, he focused on the question of how to educate the people about the possible consequences of the war in Europe. He knew he must do so without alarming them with the prospect of being dragged into it. One of his most useful strategies was use of exaggerated accounts of American strategic vulnerability in order to justify larger defense expenditures and to help arm the victims of international aggression. Roosevelt was apprehensive that even if the United States never entered the war, it might move into a state of perpetual national emergency, a garrison state in which basic American freedoms would be endangered. He also worried that loss of American access to foreign markets because of the triumph of the dictators would destroy the American economy. But it was mainly the widespread fear of foreign invasion that served the purposes of FDR as he sought to move the American public toward a more internationalist position. His concern about the survival of American institutions led him to exaggerate the dangers of foreign attack and invasion, a strategy that well served his ends. It helped also to create a continuing culture of exaggerated strategic vulnerability that was revived in a very different and dangerous context in the years of the Cold War.

In his chapter on FDR and the plausibility of a limited war in Europe, Stephen Bunch scrutinizes some of the same issues raised by Esposito, especially the conscious exaggeration by Roosevelt of the threat posed by Hitler. He asks the question why some of the more well reasoned arguments put forth by the isolationists never led Roosevelt to the formulation of a more durable and successful policy of containing Hitler by limited means. In Bunch's view such a "containment" policy was especially plausible after the Nazi invasion of the Soviet Union. He deals deftly with major objections to this scenario, and presents an intriguing study of Roosevelt's attraction to just such a war of limited means. The president's desire to avoid direct American involvement in another war led him to favor expansion of military production and the supplying of the enemies of Germany with weapons and supplies. Until after Pearl Harbor, in fact, Roosevelt continued to pursue only limited initiatives, viewing any buildup of the army in purely defensive terms. Even after entry into the war there were immense pressures to focus on a large-scale effort in the Pacific while continuing to pursue only limited objectives in Europe. These were firmly rejected by Roosevelt. In fact, once he accepted the principle of Germany as the chief enemy, he had some difficulty persuading the American people, as well as most within the administration, of the soundness of his decision. But once he decided, Roosevelt used all the skills at his command to pursue first his goal of cleansing the world of the ideological extremism of European fascism. Total victory became the only acceptable alternative. Bunch addresses many provocative questions about the evolution of Roosevelt's global thought and the reasons for his ultimate rejection of any kind of limited war or negotiated peace. He also raises the troubling question of the legacy of America's successful crusade in World War II insofar as it set the tone for American interventionist foreign policy in the Cold War years and beyond.

William Kinsella's chapter narrows the focus from Roosevelt's broad perceptions of global affairs to a consideration of the evolution of his assumptions and policies toward one foreign state. Many of Roosevelt's policies regarding the Soviet Union remain controversial, and Kinsella sheds much light on why this is so. Concentrating on the years before American entry into the war, he is mainly concerned with how FDR's perceptions of the Soviet Union influenced the evolving diplomatic relationship between the two countries. Using the correspondence of Ambassador William Bullitt, Loy Henderson, George Kennan, and other embassy personnel and state department officials, Kinsella draws a harrowing picture of the Soviet Union after the purges unleashed by Stalin following the murder of Sergei Kirov in 1935. Although Roosevelt did periodically issue protests over excesses, he was reluctant to press things too far, and was content to accept as more reliable the naively benign reports of Joseph Davies, who replaced Bullitt in

1936. Generally unpopular with the diplomatic establishment, Davies served Roosevelt's purpose of improving relations between the two countries. Events in Poland, Estonia, Latvia, and Lithuania following the Nazi-Soviet Non-Aggression Pact prompted Roosevelt's harshest criticism of Stalin's government. After the fall of France to the Nazis in 1940, such criticism was muted. After the German invasion of the USSR in June 1941, Roosevelt moved quickly to implement a program of emergency aid to the Soviets, informing Secretary of War Stimson that he considered it of paramount importance to the safety and security of America that all reasonable munitions be provided for the USSR. Despite his mistrust of the Soviets throughout the thirties, Roosevelt became convinced that Stalin was the lesser evil to Hitler and that Western military weakness and American self-interest dictated a compromise. In Kinsella's view this was an important example of Roosevelt's pragmatism and his sense of long-range purpose in foreign affairs.

The chapter by Maris Mantenieks is a major contribution to our understanding of United States policy toward the Baltic states, especially the significant role they played in great power diplomacy during World War II. By focusing on Roosevelt's thinking and actions on the subject, Mantenieks argues that the Baltic question played an important part in transforming Roosevelt from an idealist to a believer in realpolitik—much to the detriment of the Baltic states and Eastern Europe. According to Mantenieks, Roosevelt demonstrated early concern for the Baltics in his refusal to recognize Soviet annexation following the Nazi-Soviet Non-Aggression Pact. He also strongly opposed British efforts to conclude a secret agreement with Stalin on the matter. He nevertheless came to believe that because of his personal influence with Stalin he could raise the matter directly with him. In doing so, however, both at Teheran and Yalta, he implied that the United States could and would do little for the Baltic countries in the postwar settlement, therein moving far from his originally stated goals of self-determination. Mantenieks reveals some of the main weaknesses of Roosevelt's personal diplomacy and suggests that if the United States had been more forceful early in the war it is possible that Stalin would have been "unmasked" much sooner for what he really was. Mantenieks reveals much about the intricacies and frequently dangerous expediencies of Roosevelt's wartime strategies, while confirming his overriding sense of purpose.

Calvin Hines illuminates much about Roosevelt as a wartime statesman through a study of six admirals selected personally by the president for diplomatic missions. All of these senior naval officers, William H. Standley, William D. Leahy, Raymond A. Spruance, John W. Greenslade, Frederick J.

Horne, and John H. Hoover, clearly enjoyed Roosevelt's confidence and reflected his predilection for using other than career diplomats for many special assignments. After examining the missions of all six "admiral diplomats," Hines assigns most credit to those (Spruance, Greenslade, Horne, and Hoover) who operated in the "diplomatic backwater" of the Caribbean region and to Admiral Leahy, who was posted to Vichy France. Leahy was entrusted with the mission of preventing Vichy from providing military and economic aid to the Axis and securing the neutrality of the islands of the French West Indies. Leahy's personal relationship with Admiral Darlan proved especially useful. More valuable still, in Hines's view, was the work of those emissaries in the Caribbean who were charged with ensuring that French authorities there maintained neutrality, and detachment from the influence of Vichy. There was also concern that the large cache of gold in Martinique not be secretly sent by French naval vessel to Dakar in French West Africa. Hines's assessment of the short-lived term of Admiral Standley in the Moscow embassy is far less favorable. Although Standley may have served to prepare the groundwork for the much more productive mission of Averell Harriman, he seemed ill suited to the position. But Standley was the exception. In general these "admiral diplomats" served well Roosevelt's needs—and his penchant for personal diplomacy.

Elizabeth Elliott-Meisel's highly instructive chapter on the special relationship between Roosevelt and Prime Minister McKenzie King of Canada explores one of the least known yet important periods in Canadian-American relations, one that laid the foundation for bilateral cooperation between the two countries from that time on. Elliott-Meisel cites numerous examples of cooperation, such as facilitating Lend-Lease deliveries to both Britain and the Soviet Union, that are little known by either scholars or the public in both countries. By speculating on various reasons for this general ignorance, she forces us to alter many common stereotypes, and to appreciate all the more the extent to which the Roosevelt-King friendship contributed to a transition from years of suspicion and even hostility to close association amounting to actual alliance. Arguing that Roosevelt was the first and only American president to take more than a passing interest in Canada, Elliott-Meisel also provides insights into Roosevelt's style and ability to manipulate relationships to his own advantage. King played a role in facilitating Anglo-American relations, though once Roosevelt and Churchill came to know each other better, King tended to be more informed than consulted. Roosevelt and King told the public as little as possible, especially when controversial situations arose. Before entry into the war, they were concerned with domestic politics and isolationist opinion on both sides of the border. Later, despite remarkable military cooperation, there were also tensions. The American pledge to defend Canada was in effect an extension of the Monroe Doctrine to the north. Canadian concerns about sovereignty increased as thousands of Americans moved to operate on their soil in what some viewed as an "army of occupation." Canadians also resented the fact that the United States took their country too much for granted. But most of these tensions were masked by the "team approach" promoted by Roosevelt. While clearly not a team of equals, Roosevelt's capacity to charm and to get what he wanted from a generally willing partner during the war transformed a personal relationship into a comprehensive defense arrangement that forever changed Canadian relations and served Roosevelt's overarching goal of winning the war.

Turning to the question of the future of the colonial world, Thomas Howard's chapter, "Franklin Roosevelt, the Caribbean, and the Postcolonial World," explores the influence of European colonialism in the Caribbean region on the evolution of Roosevelt's plans for a postwar global settlement. Howard characterizes Roosevelt's ideas on self-determination and the future of the colonial world as a complex blend of Wilsonian idealism and pragmatic realism. Roosevelt's travels in the region, his earlier promotion of the Good Neighbor Policy, and the continued influence of several key advisors with Latin American and Caribbean interests led him increasingly to view the Caribbean as a microcosm of European colonialism. He came often to use this region as a prism through which he viewed important aspects of the world structure he desired to see put in place after the war. This vision included a permanent United Nations organization, strongly supported by the United States, that would be able to temper a world system divided into power spheres and help to maintain global peace and security. Roosevelt's underlying assumptions regarding the United Nations also included its critical role in implementing the eventual freedom and independence of all colonial peoples.

Franklin Roosevelt was keenly aware of the intricate interrelationship between foreign and domestic affairs, and invariably linked them in his planning. This was true both in terms of his desire to educate the American public to dangers abroad in order to obtain popular support for his cautiously changing policies, and his wish to express his concern about the threat to American values and freedoms from wartime conditions such as censorship and misguided patriotism. This close connection between foreign and domestic issues is explored by Julia Siebel in her chapter "Soldiers on the Home Front," in which she conveys Roosevelt's deep desire to expand and protect fundamental freedoms not only around the world but also at home.

When Roosevelt articulated his famous "Four Freedoms" early in 1941, he was anxious to find some means to protect these freedoms at home should the United States become a belligerent. His answer came in the creation of a special wartime agency designed to protect the cultural, social, and economic security of the United States so that he would be able to devote full attention to the war effort. Designated as the Civilian War Services Division (CWS) of the Office of Civilian Defense (OCD), this agency represented a fundamental effort to keep the idealism and social programs of the New Deal alive on the home front during the war. Siebel traces the formation and operation of this agency throughout the war years, documenting what she views as its overwhelming success in reducing the trauma of war on the civilian population and helping to alleviate many community problems. The president's commitment to the importance of the CWS was demonstrated by his appointment of his wife Eleanor to the post of assistant director of the OCD, with direct responsibility for the CWS division. Under her leadership, CWS volunteers worked to strengthen communities through social programs. Because they believed that community deficiencies might produce greater long-term devastation than any Axis attack, CWD volunteers came to consider themselves "soldiers on the home front." Throughout the war, the CWD reflected President Roosevelt's direct concern with protecting the Four Freedoms at home and creating a healthy nation that was strong enough to withstand any threat from within. For Roosevelt, threats from within and without were but two sides of the same coin.

In the final chapter, Carol Silverman also deals with interactions between domestic and foreign concerns in the Roosevelt administration with an examination of the administration's response to the intensifying plight of European Jewry before and during the Holocaust, and the efforts of the American Jewish establishment to influence immigration policy. It is an issue that has become one of the most controversial of the Roosevelt presidency. Silverman argues that, while no actions taken by the United States could have saved all the European Jews from systematic extermination, a major commitment could have saved many. By treating the American Jewish community as an interest group with considerable influence in the White House, she seeks to determine why it was unable to accomplish more with the president or his administration. She attributes this failure to several causes, including pervasive anti-Semitism, fear of enemy spies planted among new immigrants, widespread public indifference, and the inability of the public to comprehend the magnitude of the genocide. Silverman documents the general failure of the Jewish community to influence policy despite the number of prominent Jews in the administration. This occurred in part because of deep divisions within the community and the ironic fact that Jewish political support for the Democratic Party and the administration could be taken for granted while other constituencies that opposed more open immigration policies could not. While personally sympathetic to Jewish appeals for action, Roosevelt was reluctant to involve himself deeply in the issue. This was true as late as January 1944, when mounting pressures led him to create a War Refugee Board (WRB) separate from the State Department, which until then had played the major obstructionist role. Although the WRB played an important role in saving some 200,000 Jews, it was established too late to make a critical difference. While she acknowledges Roosevelt's very real difficulties in taking more forceful action, Silverman concludes with harsh criticism of his inaction. This stemmed in part from an administrative style that frequently led to overlapping agencies in perpetual conflict, and Roosevelt's use of the State Department as a foil to deflect criticism. Winning the war was his top priority, and the complex, controversial issue of the fate of the Jews in Europe remained marginal. The divided Jewish community was never sufficiently able to get the facts before the public or to secure enough support from other constituencies to have much impact on policy, especially during wartime. Without the backing of public opinion, there was little that could be accomplished, and President Roosevelt did not take the lead in influencing the public. A pragmatic Roosevelt, absorbed by the war, did not feel compelled to act as "teacher" on this issue to a skeptical American people in the way he had sought to educate them about the dangers of isolationism and neutrality.

From the vantage point of a new century, and over half a century since the death of Franklin Roosevelt, we are in a position to look afresh at his global vision. The chapters in this volume accomplish just this. Their substantive and often provocative arguments represent important contributions to our effort to better understand his powerful but elusive legacy. They are shaped by the conviction that continuing analysis of the foreign policies of the Roosevelt presidency will not only illuminate those years, but will also help us better to understand the times in which we live.

1

FDR's Foreign Policy Persona

Chris Van Aller

The conduct of international affairs is usually a difficult proposition for a democracy, particularly one blessed with the geographic insularity of the United States. Alexis de Tocqueville understood this dilemma only too well when he stated, "Foreign policy does not require the use of any of the good qualities peculiar to democracy but does demand . . . almost all of those which it lacks."[1] This problem is alarmingly apparent as war threatens the state, especially large-scale modern conflict that necessitates the involvement of almost all citizens. The fragmentation of power in the American system remains a final impediment. The President and Congress have feuded since the beginning of the Republic for authority in foreign policy. The "Pacificus-Helvidius" debates reveal that the Framers themselves remained divided, and challenges since that time have not ended the controversy.

Pacificus (Alexander Hamilton) could have been writing about the pre–World War II period when he stated, "In reference to the present war in Europe, it was necessary for the President to judge for himself . . . as executor of the laws, to proclaim the neutrality of the nation...."[2] Franklin Roosevelt might have agreed with the reasoning, if not the recommended option, as possible involvement in World War II loomed nearer. A number of modern authorities have felt that in times of potential emergency, the Executive, lacking strong powers in foreign policy compared to other democracies, should educate the public and Congress toward a solution to the crisis in question. The President "must put events and policies in context and must gradually prepare the public for new departures."[3]

For over half a century scholars have considered the performance of Franklin Roosevelt in foreign relations before World War II and have arrived at many different conclusions. George Kennan has suggested that the United States might have acted sooner in the 1930s, with regard to both German and Japanese expansionism. Others have gone so far as to accuse FDR of plotting American involvement from perhaps as early as 1936.[4] An examination of the accomplishments and failures of FDR at "educating" a traditionally isolationist public about the perils of the world crisis should give us greater appreciation of the obstacles that he faced and help reach a more balanced appraisal of his accomplishments. That Roosevelt considered one of his roles to be that of public educator is to be found in a number of sources. In a letter to Lord Cecil in 1937 he wrote, "I know that you are deeply disappointed, as I am, with the trends of world affairs . . . I still believe in the eventual effectiveness of preaching and preaching again."[5] He later observed that the presidency is "predominantly a place of moral leadership."[6]

Roosevelt's long political career had taught him, often through painful experience, the ability both to understand what the citizenry was thinking and to appeal to these sentiments. As assistant secretary of the Navy during the Wilson administration he was quick to assert America's rights in world affairs, and expressed disparaging views of the public's ignorance of defense matters. He advocated sometimes jingoistic policies with regard to the Mexican debt crisis in 1914. He appeared a somewhat spoiled, sometimes condescending public servant in both state and federal posts. Francis Perkins, later a member of his Cabinet, felt that before his polio attack, "I was not much impressed by him."[7]

The terrible experience with polio, in the view of some contemporaries and his wife Eleanor, helped transform the man. But he had begun to learn his "teacher" role even earlier. As Geoffrey Ward points out, FDR initially emulated his boisterous cousin Theodore Roosevelt, but later found "the creative uses of indirection."[8] Indirection is precisely the term for FDR's cautious public preparation of the country for World War II. He also displayed strong intuitive qualities from an early period, although they were not put to good political use for some years. Even his limitations would paradoxically help him in his struggle against the isolationists, such as his dislike of purely abstract reasoning revealed by his poor performance in most law school courses.[9] But this weakness helped later in his common sense explanations of complex international necessity. His lack of success on the playing fields led him to the *Harvard Crimson,* which began to prepare him for what was to become perhaps the best relationship with the press (though not the newspaper owners) in presidential history. He also revealed a concern for the welfare of the less fortunate in this early period, perhaps in emulation of his Uncle Teddy. This sympathy helped in foreign policy education, as the future President could understand the remoteness of such matters to a population in terrible economic circumstances.

The challenge of his illness propelled his communication and listening abilities beyond the social blinders of someone with his material advantages. In short, the experience taught him skills that later helped him reach millions of people, first on domestic issues and then on foreign policy. Francis Perkins pointed out "how he had walked away from bores . . . when he was in the New York State Senate. Now he could not walk away." Roosevelt amplified this point, so very important in a democracy, when he said, "everybody wants to have the sense of belonging . . . no one wants to be left out."[10] Not only did this idea imply actually helping the less fortunate; it also indicates the importance of explaining complex affairs of state to the widest possible audience. His sympathy for his fellow Americans grew to encompass other cultures and points of view, as evidenced in his Good Neighbor policy. Coping with the disease also taught him another essential lesson: patience. Just as medical treatment can often be slow and tortuous, so too is the process of citizen education in foreign affairs. Hence Tocqueville's admonition that such a society is like an enormous beast that takes a long time to anger (and to pacify).[11] Interestingly, one visitor to the FDR farm noted the pleasure the President took in solving apparently hopeless tasks.[12] He needed both optimism and patience in the years before the Second World War.

Something also should be said of Roosevelt's two great political role models, Theodore Roosevelt and Woodrow Wilson. From them he learned not only what worked to inspire or teach, but what did not. Woodrow Wilson, as a former university professor, was able to carry the country forward toward goals based on reflection and long-term political convictions. Despite his later recantation of support of the League of Nations, FDR shared Wilson's concern for basic morality governing all nations. He nonetheless remained wary of pushing the American people too swiftly toward international involvement lest another backlash occur as after World War I. Theodore Roosevelt; in contrast, "succeeded in stirring people to enthusiasm over specific events, even though these may have been superficial in comparison with the fundamentals."[13] Certainly FDR's fireside chats and inspirational addresses carried on radio were one powerful interpretation of the "bully pulpit." In a sense he combined the personal energy and warm enthusiasm of his cousin with the more studied principles of his former boss President Wilson. Particularly considering Wilson's legacy of intolerance, Roosevelt understood the importance of publicly and privately compromising with those opposed to his policies. He remained aware that shrill moralism without concession to political reality not only offended many in the present but occasioned trouble later. Needless to say, Wilson's constant idealistic proclamations of neutrality in World War I contrasted with his country's de facto support of the Allies. Roosevelt was careful not to be hypocritical on this point after 1939, as he unambiguously talked of his moral rejection of the foreign militarists. He still understood that an appeal to morality, to decency, could change public opinion; cold realpolitik would not work with an American audience.

America has always had a strong isolationist streak, often sanctioned by reference to George Washington's famous Farewell Address. A retreat from involvement in global affairs was especially strong after World War I and the resulting widespread public sense of betrayal. Woodrow Wilson had promised that if America sent her boys to fight in one last titanic war, then international relations would be transformed. The League of Nations was in some ways an attempt to organize the world according to the American constitutional principles Professor Wilson had once examined so carefully. Unfortunately the postwar world was not to be defined or governed by such principles, and the public sense of betrayal grew, aided immensely by the deprivations of the Depression. The Nye Committee, with Roosevelt's enthusiastic cooperation, attempted to find the "causes" of World War I, substituting another idealistic solution to war for the internationalist vision of Wilson. As Senator Nye stated on the committee's findings, "There may be doubt as to the degree but there is certainly none that the profits of preparation for war and the profits of war itself constitute the most serious challenge to the peace of the world."[14] Conspiracy theories, popular with both right and left down to the present, found abundant support both among the people and in their elected representatives. Hence Senator Connally wrote in his memoirs that the Committee "was probably the most effective medium for channeling American public opinion into isolationism during this period."[15]

The pressure of strong interest groups and prominent political figures also preached the doctrine of isolationism, right up to Pearl Harbor. The America First Committee was one of the most powerful anti-interventionist groups, containing some extremely influential people who voiced what many millions thought. To a large extent, they also "taught" the public ideas that supported many heretofore unfocused opinions. One of the more common themes was a deep distrust of Great Britain and British imperialism, though the smarter spokesmen were careful not to attack a now isolated Britain too completely or viciously after 1940.[16] Other spokesmen felt that any aid to the European war would enlarge the struggle and consume America's limited resources. Others pointed out the considerable inequities of the postwar treatment of Germany and the logic of her renewed place in the balance of power. Such a power would contain the Communist Soviet Union, only recently recognized by the United States. Some Cold War revisionist historians point out that many powerful groups were far less alarmed by the Nazis than the Soviets. Studs Terkel noted that those who fought against the Franco forces in Spain were termed "pre-mature anti-Fascists" tainted by association with the Communists and persecuted by the FBI for years afterward. Finally, ex-military men like General Wood doubted that Britain would fall and would eventually find a way to co-exist with a Germany dominant in Western Europe.[17]

There were other claims made as well, some of them morally reprehensible. Anti-Semitism remained unfortunately strong in the America of the late 1930s, urged on by the fanatical Father Coughlin as well as more moderate voices like Charles Lindbergh. The latter, in a famous address in Des Moines, appeared anti-Semitic in labeling those forces pushing the United States into war. His assertion that Jews were one of these major groups produced numerous denunciations and harmed his credibility, but, behind the headlines, won support from many sympathetic members of the public.[18] The majority of citizens were simply not ready to come to the aid of the Jews. There were also those who felt after the Nazi invasion of the Soviet Union that the two totalitarian powers should be left alone to cancel each other out, and that the United States should in no way aid an atheist and communistic state like the USSR.[19] America might arm itself, transform perhaps into a hemispheric fortress, but in no way export its war equipment or raw materials.[20] World War I veterans groups, such as the Catholic War Veterans (CWV), in contrast to most current ex-military groups, resolutely opposed all war through 1939. The CWV cabled FDR in 1935 that, "you have proven to the world that America loves peace . . . and desires not to become entangled in the quarrels . . . of European nations."[21]

Just how strong were isolationist sentiments as measured in Gallup polls and other forums? Did the above arguments and pressure groups speak for the nation as a whole? As late as 1939, 60 percent of those asked felt the United States should not even sponsor a conference in the interest of peace between European nations. Only 50 percent thought the United States should send a delegation.[22] After the fall of France in 1940, "approximately 80 percent of the people opposed American entry into the war. According to these polls, at no time before Pearl Harbor did a majority . . . favor a declaration of war on the Axis."[23]

The evidence, however, remains more ambiguous than the above data might imply for two separate sets of reasons. The first is that public opinion polls do not represent the last word on what the citizenry necessarily thinks. "Citizen opinions are often rife with contradictions . . . [and] some people respond to questions they know nothing about at all." Large numbers of people can change their opinions overnight, particularly if a favored candidate articulates something in a new way.[24] Furthermore, much public opinion of foreign affairs is more unfocused and primed for "education" than in more familiar domestic policy. How effectively, then, did Roosevelt provide such education? He combined a mix of elements in his efforts gently to enlighten the public, derived from his long political experience and the success and failure of previous administrations. His greatest gift was his ability to explain international crisis in terms of universal emotions, ones that everyone could understand. In his 1936 Chautauqua speech, he identified with the public's hatred of war and mixed it with his own recollections. "I have seen war . . . I have seen children starving . . . I hate war."[25] The continual use of the first person, combined with the parallel structure of the lines, helped drum home the apparent intensity of his feelings. While critics have often faulted his mid-1930s embrace of neutrality legislation, he in turn understood the powerful feelings prevalent at the time. It cannot be overemphasized that World War I and its aftermath had seared the minds of the collective citizenry of the Western world, and Roosevelt was respecting their feelings first and then moving them on from there.[26]

There is, of course, much disagreement about the famous Quarantine speech of 1937, most of which centers around what exactly he envisioned for U.S. policy. But Roosevelt was communicating a traditional and emotional theme in our foreign relations. Americans only very slowly concede the danger of conflict unless physically attacked, and war itself is seen very much as an aberration of the system, a "disease" of the world. He was warning that such a "contagion," in his words, existed and was preparing them emotionally to accept that fact. As Barbara Tuchman has stated, "Americans have shown their dislike for organized war by a desperate attachment to three principles: unpreparedness until the eleventh hour, the quickest feasible strategy regardless of [long-term] political aims, and instant demobilization, no matter how inadvisable, the moment hostilities are over."[27] Roosevelt was aware of this historical tendency all the while he signaled the need to observe the growth of a seemingly remote cancer. This warning had to precede any sort of defense mobilization. Many letters to the President also commended his references to international law, the League of Nations, and the Kellogg-Briand Pact. The public of the period tended to see international affairs more in legalistic and moralistic terms, and Roosevelt presented his warnings accordingly.[28]

His peace appeal to Hitler and Mussolini in 1939 was, at first glance, another American attempt to negotiate on moralistic terms without having the national power to influence events. Yet the President was confronting the dictators in language that the public could understand. The reaction from Hitler, which was probably anticipated by Roosevelt, was in brutal language and sarcasm that no doubt registered with the public. The American leader appeared naive and unsophisticated to the tyrants of Europe; he nonetheless unmistakably demonstrated his peace credentials to his own country. Yet his idealism was not the messianic variety of President Wilson's; it seemed to mirror the outrage, the impatience with statecraft, of the common person. It also cannot be overstated that, after 1938, the economy had again gone into a steep decline, with industrial production down by a third and wages somewhat more. During such depressing economic times, the capitulation at Munich seemed far away indeed. Simple and repeated ideas in foreign policy were the order of the day.

Roosevelt used his skills to great purpose in his fireside chat of 3 September 1939, two days after the invasion of Poland. It is uncertain how strongly he felt about the Neutrality Laws when they were first enacted; he certainly supported them publicly, but by this point perhaps the lessons of Spain and Munich had convinced him of the need to confront the Axis, though indirectly, through aid to Hitler's enemies. The President emphasized American neutrality yet went one step further by stating that "even a neutral has a right to take account of the facts." He was reflecting, accurately according to the polls, the somewhat contradictory nature of American public opinion, the majority of which supported help to the allies with no real danger of armed conflict.[29] He was preparing the people for a different sort of neutrality, one that recognized a difference between the foreign protagonists. As Dallek observes, the subsequent "cash and carry policy" helped to convince the public that it was simply foreign ships buying goods for their people. The fact that this would benefit the British much more was accepted by majority opinion.[30] FDR had reconciled two diametrically opposed feelings in the American people.

The importance of timing is evident in the gradual way Roosevelt increased criticism of the Axis powers while implying that, at each step, the U.S. was staying out as far as the national interest would permit. Some of his personal correspondence, as well as conversations with his aides, reveal that he had few illusions about the dangers that lay ahead. Communications from Churchill after his advent to power indicated the increasingly dangerous situation after the fall of France, particularly the submarine menace. But as Samuel Rosenman quoted FDR, "It's a terrible thing to look over your shoulder when you are trying to lead and to find no one there."[31] He therefore carefully stepped up preparations in terms of educating the public, and then went to Congress for legislation. By 1940, he began to reveal more alarming information about the Axis and directly confronted the isolationists about their reasoning. He attacked the idea that America could somehow continue to function in a world governed by lawlessness, in his words, "a lone island" that would eventually become a "prison, handcuffed, hungry, and fed through the bars . . . by the contemptuous, unpitying masters of other continents."[32] He then unambiguously pledged his support to the victims of Nazi aggression, and the material support of the country. According to the statistical information available, his balance of candid outrage and promise of limited help was shared by substantial majorities.[33]

Roosevelt continued to refute the objections of diehard isolationists, whose numbers Robert Sherwood estimated at one-third of the electorate.[34] Many of these maintained that Britain was either unworthy of aid because of its imperialist tendencies or would drain the U.S. of precious materials because all battles should occur on its own soil. In short, isolationists were waiting for a direct attack on the continental United States because in such a war, "we keep ourselves pure, and therefore 100 percent American."[35] In his "Arsenal of Democracy" speech in December 1940, he attacked these ideas on multiple fronts, with a combination of emotive language and common sense appeal. He had previously helped convince the majority of the public that there was a substantive moral difference between the protagonists because the polls reveal substantial support for aid to Britain by this point.[36] Then Roosevelt helped weaken the isolated fortress America concept by pointing out, in Hitler's own words, that the range of modern bombers "is ever being increased." As the 1940s were the age of air power, in terms of the supposed effects of massive aerial bombing, this was potent language. He also pointed out the continually broken non-aggression pacts made with Hitler and Mussolini, tapping again into the strong legalistic-moralistic sentiments of the public.[37]

But the feeling that America might be weakening herself for the future by giving money and material to Britain and later the USSR, still must have appeared to him formidable. Hence he used several metaphors symbolizing "square deals," in the popular vernacular, for the country. In his press conference of 16 December 1940, he explained that the U.S. was really lending material to Britain that would be returned after the war, with any damages to the leased equipment paid for after the war, and compared the transaction to the act of lending a hose to a neighbor to put out a fire. The subsequent policy known as Lend-Lease was a perfect term to counter the feeling that America was subsidizing Imperial Britain or, at worst, a lost cause. Moreover, it was backed up by a continual reiteration that this policy would enable Britain to fight without active American involvement.[38] FDR did this by gradually showing that the Axis powers were so evil, so unprincipled, that if the British Empire and later the USSR did not at least contain the fascist powers, America eventually would need to do so.

The President was also adept at appealing to historical precedent in his many forays before the public. In domestic policy, Burns notes that "Roosevelt tried to stay above the political and ideological battles that raged all around him."[39] He appealed, for example, to the legacy of the Monroe Doctrine at his Kingston speech when he asserted that the U.S. would defend Canada. Its applicability under international law was questionable; our neighbor was not being directly threatened, but it was deemed in America's interest to protect her in order to protect itself. In a sense, he was interpreting the doctrine and gently reminding everyone that the world was immeasurably more interdependent than in 1823. The fact that the doctrine was often ignored by the diplomats of the world made little difference. It was standard historical fare in every American school.

Similarly, Roosevelt invoked perhaps America's most cherished concept, individual freedom, with increasing emphasis as war drew near. He pointed out in his "Four Freedoms" speech of January 1941 how American liberty would be at stake eventually if the U.S. failed to help others defend themselves. He pointed out how small, non-imperialist countries like Norway had lost their freedom. He emphasized and defined the fourfold nature of freedom itself, thus stressing exactly what would be lost in an Axis victory. He also pointed out that with freedom comes responsibility and chastised some of the isolationist ethnic interest groups by a frank assertion that while their memories of their old lands were natural, they were now unequivocal Americans in a community of liberty.[40] As in domestic policy, FDR was concerned with the tendency of democracies to lapse into fragile coalitions of separate interests rather than finding common ground. In this speech he tapped into what political geographers call the American "melting pot" political culture. FDR had praised the historic contributions of hyphenated Americans in an earlier speech, but in both addresses, he was uniting the country in complementary ways, praising contributions of different groups but calling them together at the same time.

As a former newspaperman, and as someone who liked to meet and talk with all kinds of people, FDR knew that the newer mediums of communication could reach many millions. Denton has stated "[how] it has always been important to manage the medium of the era." He also noted "that film allowed a short Wilson to appear tall, just as radio permitted a disabled Franklin Roosevelt to sound powerful. . . ."[41] Radio allowed the President to talk directly to the people, without the press or hostile congressman distorting his views. He knew that unlike his predecessor Herbert Hoover his voice and ideas carried very well over radio. One of his critics admitted, "Roosevelt possessed a golden voice and a seductive and challenging radio technique."[42] His continued use of personal and direct language endeared him to many even if they might disagree with his views on foreign policy. He utilized other media as well, being very careful that only flattering images appeared of himself both in still pictures and in newsreels. People need a strong, vital person to protect them in a time of danger. Movies and famous movie stars that promoted aid to the Allies were also encouraged, both officially and through behind-the-scenes funding.

Finally, the stories of the President's relationship with the press are legendary. He developed a special rapport with the White House press corps. His personal relations with individual news people to some extent short-circuited their natural skepticism and ensured him good coverage, although individual newspaper owners often disliked him.[43] As John Gunther wrote, FDR's ability to charm the media by a myriad of facial and verbal expressions was so effective that "he said almost nothing" when he wished to do so.[44] Finally, Samuel Rosenman notes that the President, after the fall of France, never appeared frightened; in his words, "I do not ever recall seeing the President scared at any time."[45] This image was a formidable feat given the many people Roosevelt met every day.

Of course, as private conversations and letters reveal, the President was very concerned and worried, especially after 1939. Yet his public optimism and simplifications were a subset of what FDR's critics have called his politics of deceit. Some have said that he paved the way for presidential use of selective information in foreign policy leading, for example, to LBJ's lies about Vietnam. There is no doubt that often the exact details of dangerous incidents, like the destroyer *Greer* episode, or the precise nature of what went on behind the scenes, such as the training of British pilots by 1941, was not officially announced to the public. But, unlike LBJ in Vietnam, Roosevelt had to prepare the country for a total war that required huge preparation. As William Hodson wrote, "But let's think back to . . . 1940: Who among us, except the President . . . really saw the job ahead. . . . None of us—not one that I know of, except the President—saw that we might be fighting Germany and Japan all over the world."[46]

Given the opposite problems of unprecedented danger and anti-interventionist sentiment, the President had to weigh the competing goods of complete openness and of preparation for potential threats. While he broke the letter of the law in terms of information availability in a democracy, he still acted in the spirit of what he and the public desired—to avoid war if at all possible. Many of his behind-the-scenes orders were designed to aid the British without necessarily pulling the U.S. into hostilities. Several authorities remain convinced that Roosevelt was hoping in the end to preclude total U.S. involvement.[47] The public is sometimes wrong in a democracy, but as John F. Kennedy noted, foreign policy can kill us, while domestic policies can only set us back. In short, FDR had to act to protect the public from its own inconsistency and ignorance. This was a time when the President used his best judgment to educate the public and prepare the country for the onslaught of modern war.

This examination has sought to highlight some of the roles and techniques Roosevelt used in teaching the American people about the hazards of the European war. Through idealistic invocation, non-intellectual explanations, trading metaphors, legalistic and moralistic terminology, repetition of historical precedents, symbolic personal optimism and heroic imagery, undeniable deceit, and unmatched mastery of the media, he made decided progress. As scholars such as Ryan and Cole point out, the President had defeated the isolationist's arguments short of directly fighting for the Allies. This analysis is not the place for an examination of whether Roosevelt could have pursued a different, perhaps faster, course; its emphasis is on "teaching" in foreign policy. Yet a partial answer to this question can be found in some of the points previously discussed. One can certainly make a case, as Secretary Stimpson often did, that the Allies were in desperate shape and that the public needed total honesty. Other advisors such as Secretary of State Hull and William Bullitt, however, were not nearly so sanguine about the need for frankness.[48]

In terms of Roosevelt's qualities revealed in this study, one stands out. Roosevelt's unique talents were made possible because he was part of the body politic; he could sense its fears, comprehend its limited understanding of remote events. These qualities perhaps limited FDR's own understanding of what in more theoretical terms, more realistic terms, could have been done to prepare the public for war. Another leader convinced of the need for urgency might have pushed the public too quickly. Roosevelt's character prevented this, and demanded an approach that was precisely what was necessary given the public's aversion to involvement. Moreover, the President had to be a realist about the nature of an idealistic, ill-informed public. He therefore attempted, in the most difficult position possible, to reconcile "his noble objectives and the tactics of the feasible."[49]

Whether or not some of Roosevelt's educational methods can be replicated in current foreign policy is hard to discern. The news media have lost most of the inhibitions about exposing the personal flaws of U.S. leaders. The public's faith in the honesty of its leaders in foreign policy has been declining since Vietnam. Roosevelt's ebullient personality, which Churchill compared to opening a bottle of champagne, could not today be manufactured or merely imitated. But the patient education of the public in foreign policy can be emulated, and integrated more completely into domestic considerations. In this sense, there needs to be more education of the public from the very beginning of an administration, something Roosevelt himself might have attempted earlier in the 1930s. Presidents need to invoke the humane idealism necessary to motivate a democratic people, but not the sort that promises a utopian future. Democracies need leaders who are able to explain complex international issues in human terms. Roosevelt was able to do just this.

Notes

1. Alexis de Tocqueville, *Democracy in America* (New York: Anchor Books, 1969), 228–229.
2. Alexander Hamilton in the *Gazette of the United States* (Philadelphia) June 29, 1793.
3. Edwin C. Hargrove, *Presidential Leadership* (New York: Macmillan, 1966), 2.
4. Robert Smith Thompson, *A Time for War* (New York: Prentice Hall, 1991), is one of the many studies that take this position.
5. Letter from Roosevelt to Viscount Cecil, cited in Eliot Roosevelt, ed., *FDR: His Personal Letters* (New York: Duel, Sloan, and Pierce, 1946), 671–672.
6. Frank Freidel, *Launching the New Deal* (Boston: Little, Brown, 1973), 5.
7. Francis Perkins, *The Roosevelt I Knew* (New York: Viking Press, 1946), 39.
8. Geoffrey Ward, *A First-Class Temperament* (New York: Harper and Row, 1989), 160.
9. Ibid., 162.
10. John B. Moses and Wilbur Cross, *Presidential Courage* (New York: W.W. Norton, 1980), 195.
11. Tocqueville, 649.
12. Ward, 769.
13. FDR to Edward M. House, cited in John Milton Cooper, *The Warrior and the Priest* (Cambridge: The Belknap Press of Harvard University, 1983), 351–352.
14. Wayne S. Cole, *Roosevelt and the Isolationists* (Lincoln: University of Nebraska Press, 1983), 151.
15. Ibid., 161.
16. Wayne S. Cole, *America First* (Madison: University of Wisconsin Press, 1953), 36.
17. Ibid., 37–38.
18. In a U.S. poll taken in July, 1939, 40 percent of those polled felt Jews were like other Americans, 51 percent felt that to some degree Jews should be restricted, with 10 percent advocating humane deportation. Cited in Hadley Cantrill, ed., *Public Opinion 1935-1946* (Princeton: Princeton University Press, 1951), 383.
19. Harry S. Truman once made this point when he served in the Senate.
20. Cole, *America First*, 84–85.
21. Ibid., 97–101.
22. Cantril, 372–373.
23. Cole, *America First*, 53.
24. George C. Edwards, *The Public Presidency* (New York: St. Martin's Press, 1983), 9–10.
25. Edgar D. Nixon, ed., *Franklin D. Roosevelt and Foreign Affairs*, vol. 3 (Cambridge: The Belknap Press of Harvard University, 1969), 380.
26. Hitler was so concerned about the memories of the Great War that he had banned all pacifist and anti-war literature such as Erich Remarque's *All Quiet on the Western Front*.

27. Barbara Tuchman, "The American People and Military Power in Historical Perspective," *International Institute for Strategic Studies* (Spring 1982): 5.

28. Cited in Patrick Maney, *The Roosevelt Presence* (New York: Twayne Publishers, 1992), 110.

29. Ibid., 118.

30. Halford R. Ryan, *Franklin D. Roosevelt's Rhetorical Presidency* (New York: Greenwood Press, 1988), 142.

31. Samuel Rosenman, *Working with Roosevelt* (New York: Harper & Brothers, 1952), 167.

32. Address of 10 June 1940 at the University of Virginia in *The Public Papers and Addresses of Franklin D. Roosevelt* (New York: Macmillan, 1941), 261.

33. Ryan, 144.

34. Robert E. Sherwood, *Roosevelt and Hopkins: An Intimate History* (New York: Harper & Brothers, 1948), 128.

35. Ibid., 134.

36. Cantril, 970–971.

37. Ryan, 145.

38. Ryan and Maney both point this out.

39. James MacGregor Burns, *The Lion and the Fox* (New York: Harcourt, Brace, 1956), 183.

40. Ryan, 54–55.

41. Robert E. Denton, Jr., *The Primetime Presidency of Ronald Reagan* (New York: Praeger, 1988), 69.

42. Betty H. Winfield, *FDR and the News Media* (Chicago: University of Illinois Press, 1990), 105.

43. Ibid., 117.

44. Elmer E. Cornwell, *Presidential Leadership of Public Opinion* (Bloomington: Indiana University Press, 1965), 144.

45. Rosenman, 196.

46. Sherwood, 159–160.

47. Maney, 134.

48. Rosenman, 280.

49. Bruce Kulick, *The Good Ruler* (New Brunswick, NJ: Rutgers University Press, 1988), 75.

2

FDR's Leadership before World War II: The Concept of Anticipatory Reaction

Manfred Landecker

The enormous recent expansion of scholarly interest in the foreign policy of Franklin Roosevelt has highlighted the lack of consensus on his alignment of U.S. policy with that of those European nations facing Axis aggression. Analysis of Roosevelt's leadership style and his use of anticipatory reaction helps to explain the policies he formulated to prepare the nation for the growing fascist threat long before this danger was recognized by the public.

At first glance the concepts of anticipatory reaction and presidential leadership appear unrelated. This is not the case. As Carl J. Friedrich, who provides a most thoughtful discussion of the interconnection between presidential influence and the rule of anticipated reaction, writes, anticipatory reaction is based "upon the capacity of human beings to imagine and thus to anticipate the reactions of those who are affected by their actions."[1] He notes that the impact of influence "is a kind of power, indirect and unstructured,"[2] and very difficult to trace. Although the concept is an imprecise device, it has the potential to provide insights not otherwise available.[3] Aaron Wildavsky has also wrestled with the idea of anticipatory reaction and observes that a president's involvement with foreign and defense policies influences the manner in which he calculates his power base. He agrees with John F. Kennedy that "Domestic policy . . . can only defeat us; foreign policy can kill us."[4] Emmet John Hughes effectively defined the issue when he wrote, "The Presidency . . . depends on, and responds to, the political climate all around it."[5]

There is wide agreement among historians that FDR exuded a tremendous "confidence in himself and the American people."[6] Of course, the anticipatory reaction syndrome does not just relate to public opinion, but the whole circle involved in the decision-making process. This includes members of Congress, the bureaucracy, the media, and interest groups. With reference to public opinion, Morton H. Halperin writes, "Arguments about public mood play a role in internal debate about foreign policy proposals and shift as that reality becomes manifest."[7]

Roosevelt possessed strong communication skills, despite his often quoted remark after the Quarantine speech that "It's a terrible thing . . . to look over your shoulder when you are trying to lead and to find no one there."[8] In truth, he is in many ways the perfect fit for the political science model of the "predominant leader." He dominated the White House staff and members of the Cabinet, and he was the "master of the self-created deadline and of self-directed networks of intelligence," according to Richard E. Neustadt, who also notes that "competitive personalities mixed with competitive jurisdiction was Roosevelt's formula for putting pressure on himself."[9]

The "predominant leader" faced with a given problem, according to Margaret G. Herman, "seeks to maximize the information in the context of making a decision—he wants to use the situation to move toward his goals if possible while keeping his important constituencies satisfied and supportive. Thus, if the leader has a position, he will probably check to see how broadly the option he favors is supported by the relevant constituencies—he will seek to build a consensus for his position." Herman continues, "if the leader cannot gain legitimacy for his position or build consensus around the position of one of his constituencies, he is likely to stall and not to act." In this process, she says, "timing is all important."[10] This description accurately presents Roosevelt's perception of the public opinion landscape.

The central argument in the literature focuses on interpretation of the strength and importance of the opposition to the president's foreign policy. Neustadt believes that "the main thrust of New Deal innovation was long past by 1939. The emergency had lost its cutting edge. In Congress, the anti–New Deal coalition had become a formidable act of life. In the executive, sails were trimmed accordingly."[11]

The crucial question of this inquiry is: "How do we decide when a leader is more principled or more pragmatic—that is, relatively unresponsive versus responsive to contextual clues?"[12] The majority of Roosevelt scholars conclude that the president accurately and properly perceived the threat from the Axis dictators and that he was a "predominant leader." There is consensus that FDR was restrained by the rule of anticipatory reaction in "maximizing United States influence in deterring dictators without enhancing opposition to his foreign or domestic agenda in the media or public opinion."[13] The key issue is whether FDR accurately assessed the potential strength and influence of his opposition or whether that opposition was exaggerated in his own mind.

In confronting the heightened Axis threat, FDR was faced by two major challenges. One was the deep-set public opposition to U.S involvement in overseas affairs; the other was public ignorance about the threat emanating from abroad. Despite the great victory that he won in the 1936 election, there was widespread opposition to his foreign policy. For this reason his speeches and policies were predicated on the rule of anticipatory reaction as he maneuvered for a greater role for the United States in world affairs.

The anticipatory response role is not inconsistent with the president's vision of himself as the clarifier of events. FDR certainly would have agreed with V.O. Key's conclusion that "a President who abdicated the duty of leadership of opinion leaves the country rudderless."[14]   Doris Kearns Goodwin has expressed similar thoughts with respect to Roosevelt: "Throughout his long political career, Roosevelt worked hard to fathom the unfathomable force of public opinion. From long experience, he had learned that in a democracy one man alone cannot guide tens of millions of people without following (and shaping, as far as one could) that intangible force called the spirit of the country."[15]

Despite the voluminous information available, it is difficult to document FDR's attitude concerning the relationship between public opinion and leadership and his views on the role of the individual in a democracy. A letter he wrote to Carl Sandburg in 1940, however, is pertinent in this regard. "'It is amazing,' Roosevelt said, 'that the independent voters of America— an increasing number of them—many of them without a real education—do have that final ability to decide our and the country's fate.'"[16] In the same year Mrs. Roosevelt also commented on the president's attitude about the relationship between leadership and public opinion when she told a group of young people that "the President is willing to lead, but never too far in advance of public opinion, because that is the way things work in a democracy as understood by a politician and a democrat."[17]

With respect to FDR's leadership role, there are two dominant interpretations. For the most part, earlier scholars believed that anticipatory reaction was utilized effectively by the president for strategic purposes to further his foreign policy agenda. Over and over they describe the president's personality as confident, determined, and persuasive.

According to this interpretation, FDR fits the Herman model of a "predominant personality." The President's rule of anticipatory response was not one characterized by waffling and delay. Neustadt interprets FDR's character as follows: "Roosevelt's methods were the product of his insights, his incentives, and his confidence. No president in this century has had a sharper sense of personal power, a sense of what it is and where it comes from; none has had more hunger for it, few have had more use for it, and only one or two could match his faith in his own competence to use it."[18] Barbara Farnham also stresses the president's leadership when she notes that after Munich, "although nearly all of the political incentives pointed in the direction of isolation, Roosevelt chose to aid the democracies, not only pushing against the domestic constraint but attempting to change it, leading policy in a different direction than a domestic politics perspective would have predicted."[19]

William E. Leuchtenburg, a prolific scholar of the Roosevelt years, has emphasized the idiosyncratic judgments in the literature about whether the president was a dynamic leader or procrastinator. He notes that "historians have . . . disagreed about whether Roosevelt should be hailed as a master of the art of compromise or faulted as a vacillator." His critics, Leuchtenburg concludes, "see FDR as too often the fox rather than the lion, too unwilling to impose the national interest on parochial groups, too much a temporizer rather than a leader."[20] Neustadt's judgment describing Roosevelt's tactic as one that "shunned fixed positions" and that "characteristically kept fire-exits open" rings true.[21]

On the other hand, many contemporary revisionists, much like Charles A. Beard and Charles Tansill before them, believe that FDR demonstrated a lack of leadership, decisiveness, frankness, and honesty. Robert Shogan, in his 1995 book, *Hard Bargain*, for example, concludes that, "what FDR's behavior called into question was not the quality of democracy, but the quality of Roosevelt's leadership, which much of the time made the avoidance of 'an uproar' its supreme objective. His zeal to suppress disagreement often led him to conceal realities because they were bound to be disturbing."[22] He further argues that Roosevelt lacked the courage to promote his convictions and that he followed "his long-established pattern of calculated ambiguity."[23] Frank Freidel reports that in 1941 the interventionists still "despaired over his caution."[24] Frederick Marks III concludes that he refused to carry the case for re-armament "until opinion polls showed him lagging well behind Congress and the public."[25]

Public opinion data for the 1938-1939 period bear this out. Hadley C. Cantril, whose office at Princeton University provided pre-publication Gallup data to the White House,[26] once suggested that "by and large, public opinion does not anticipate emergencies; it only reacts to them."[27] News of Hitler's occupation of Austria and the Munich crisis, for example, seems to have had considerable impact on public opinion. In March 1939, 66 percent expressed support for the sale of military equipment to England and France; only 34 percent expressed this same sentiment in September of 1938.[28] Congress, however, was not in step with this change in attitude; the president wanted the repeal of the Neutrality Act, but because of the isolationist bloc in the Senate he asked only for the revocation of the arms embargo. Even this request was not supported by Congress. In the fall of 1938, President Roosevelt began to pay more attention to shoring up the national defense, but he wished to do this without provoking public controversy. The Democrats had not fared well in the congressional elections of 1938, and the isolationists remained a powerful group in Congress.

In the Roosevelt literature there is a common refrain on the president's style. This is well summarized in Doris Kearns Goodwin's *No Ordinary Time*. In reference to the mobilization effort, she writes, "While claiming that the American people would do anything asked of them provided they fully understood what they were being asked, Roosevelt was afraid of asking too much. Despite the swelling demand for preparedness, he did not trust the people's willingness at this juncture to make sacrifices in order to speed up the mobilization process."[29]

Page and Shapiro, in their fine summary of public opinion data for the period immediately prior to World War II, argue that "Roosevelt's opinion leadership was mostly indirect. It depended heavily on taking actions that shaped events—some of which actions were concealed from or misrepresented to the public—as well as uprooting publicity campaigns by people outside of government."[30] They conclude that "the president balanced his overt statements and actions rather carefully so as not to offend prevailing opinions, to stay only one step ahead. Roosevelt showed great skill (with Cantril's assistance) at interpreting foreign policy polls and at tailoring his political strategy and his messages accordingly; he is probably the most skillful president at this we have had, at least until Reagan."[31] The contemporary revisionists claim that "too little attention has been paid to his manipulation of public opinion or to the troubling questions it raises."[32] The "why not tell the truth" approach is based on two fallacious assumptions. The first assumption is that the president's policies were promoted through "deception," and, second, that he underestimated the persuasiveness of his "bully pulpit." Shogan believes that "the President had more strength than he realized, or was willing to use."[33]

Two older studies also conclude that Roosevelt was reluctant to enunciate the issues and alternative policies for the American people. Langer and Gleason carefully note that "the question has often been raised and debated why, if the president was aware of the dangers inherent in the European situation after Munich, he did not state them publicly and use his tremendous influence and prestige to induce a change in American opinion."[34] The answer to this question, the authors conclude, is a complicated one because the administration, although well aware of the danger of war, did not envision the possibility of future American intervention. Therefore, the problem was not one of preparing public opinion for such an eventuality, but was instead one of bolstering American defenses and building up an arsenal upon which European democracies could draw. "This," Langer and Gleason observe, "Mr. Roosevelt apparently hoped to accomplish without provoking too much public controversy, avoidance of which seemed to him at the time to be absolutely essential."[35] Donald Drummond is somewhat less charitable in his observations. He suggests that the president did not fully appreciate the importance of Munich and observes that "the American government dabbled in appeasement through most of 1938."[36] A careful reading of the historical record, however, does not bear this out. Basil Rauch, to name one source, presents sound evidence that Roosevelt fully appreciated the dangers of appeasement and explains how the timing of Roosevelt's intervention in the Munich crisis gave rise to the later accusation that the president "implicated himself in Chamberlain's appeasement of Hitler at Munich."[37] It is true, however, as Drummond writes, that Roosevelt continually "balanced one statement against another" and thereby canceled any advantage made in gaining support of public opinion for a more active foreign policy.

A good example of this is the president's bitter and repeated denial of his alleged statement at an executive session of the Military Affairs Committee, 31 January 1939, that the American frontier was on the Rhine. Asked at a press conference whether he thought that this catch phrase summed up the situation, the president replied, "Of course not."[38] On the other hand, one of his important themes in the annual message to the

Congress, delivered on 4 January 1939, was the promotion of the idea that our spiritual frontier was the Rhine. In this speech the president emphasized the need for a close relationship with the other democracies and noted that there would be no intervention with arms to "prevent acts of aggression."[39]

The point is that, after severe criticism in the press and attacks by isolationists in and out of Congress, the president seemed to make a hasty retreat from the dramatic statement attributed to him. Yet despite his most vehement denials, a little more than a year later he delineated in the clearest way what he had been saying to the Military Affairs Committee. Addressing members of the Business Advisory Council on 23 May 1940, the president said that he had told the Committee over a year before that there would be war and, he continued, "not that our 'frontier was on the Rhine,' but that the continued existence of, for example, Finland, or the Baltic states, or the Scandinavian nations—did have a pretty definite relationship to the defense of the United States. And there was a most awful howl of protest all over the country, as you know, at that time."[40] After Munich the president was more anxious than ever to give encouragement to the democracies. He felt that the time had come to take a more active stand against the Axis and to let the struggle for domestic reforms take second place. The most effective way America could help the Allies was to repeal the all-embracing arms embargo and to replace it with a discriminatory embargo against the aggressor nations.

The president also referred to the Munich agreement in his annual address to Congress in 1939 as no guarantee that world peace was assured, and stated that there were many methods short of war bringing home to aggressor governments the sentiments of our people. He spoke more forcefully than ever about the need for a strong defense, adding that it was at times necessary to protect other nations from lawless acts, and that danger from abroad was no less to be feared than problems at home.

The response to the president's address, particularly in Congress, emphasized the divided views on the subject of neutrality. Again Roosevelt was dismayed by the strong reaction to his speech; he decided that the best way to fight was to withdraw from the scene, letting his congressional lieutenants wage the battle for revision. When he was questioned in his news conference about his reference to means other than war to let the aggressor nations know our sentiments, he said that he had no specific actions in mind at that time.[41] Perhaps if the president had been able to exert a little more leadership at this point, his warnings would have been heeded. But he was in a precarious position: first, there was the strategy of restraint to win the fight for revision of the Neutrality Act; second, with every word of warning he let fall, he was accused of warmongering.[42]

There is no question that there was considerable resentment of the administration at the time. This feeling stemmed not just from recent administrative action in foreign affairs, but was a residue of many New Deal measures. Rauch refers to the "accumulated distempers of the six strenuous New Deal years."[43] The president, who was usually magnificent in handling the press, showed the strain of constant attack and criticism when he lashed out at the press on 3 February 1939. Emphasizing the point that there was nothing new about his foreign policy, he told the assembled reporters that "a great many people, some of the House, some members of the Senate and quite a number of newspaper owners, are deliberately putting before the American people a deliberate misrepresentation of fact—deliberate."[44] He summarized the principles of U.S. policy this way:

1. We are against any entangling alliances, obviously.
2. We are in favor of the maintenance of world trade for everybody—all nations—including ourselves.
3. We are in complete sympathy with any and every effort made to reduce or limit armaments.
4. As a nation—as American people—we are sympathetic with the peaceful maintenance of political, economic and social independence of all nations in the world.[45]

In spite of this succinct statement of the four major policy aims, people who supported the Allied cause and who appreciated the nature of the totalitarian menace were not satisfied. They were becoming exceedingly restless about the lack of leadership of public opinion. One of the bluntest of these people was Clyde Eagleton, professor at New York University, who wrote to Stanley K. Hornbeck, political advisor to the State Department, on 16 February 1939:

> [The] American people have been confused through irresponsible leadership and . . . would welcome a clear statement, and follow it with relief. In various meetings we discussed this, and everywhere I have found this belief. And when I ask who could furnish such leadership, the answer is always: "Only the President could do it; if only he would give a fireside chat!" It has been my experience that when the matter is explained to people, they turn against the policy

in the neutrality legislation. How far they may be willing to go after that varies; but they can be easily convinced that the policy is wrong.[46]

Roosevelt obviously had good information, but he was not using it to alert the American people as some thought he should. On 18 February 1939, for example, as he was preparing for one of his departures from Warm Springs, he was quoted as saying, "I'll be back in the fall, if we don't have a war."[47] In connection with this statement, the president indicated his approval of an editorial titled "The Collective Pronoun," that had appeared in the *Washington Post*, by making it available at a subsequent press conference.[48] Because of the special effort made by Roosevelt to focus public attention on the article, it is quoted here in part:

'I'll be back in the fall, if we don't have a war.' These words, spoken by the President to the group assembled at Warm Springs to see him off for Washington, were seemingly wholly unpremeditated. Actually it is proper to surmise that serious consideration preceded their utterance. No one knows better than the President that his office makes his most casual public observation subject to interpretation as a matter of national policy. And no President was ever more skillful than Mr. Roosevelt in making the most of every opportunity to give a positive direction to public thinking on important issues. Most Americans realize today that the sweep of events has now brought Europe to the very verge of war. What is insufficiently realized is the tremendous implication of the impending catastrophe for every citizen of the country.

These comments point to the dilemma Roosevelt faced, one which Robert E. Osgood assesses in clear, accurate terms:

Roosevelt, like his cautious Secretary of State, Cordell Hull, was acutely conscious of the force of traditional attitudes toward American foreign policy and, perhaps, too little aware of the transformation of the American outlook being wrought under the impact of revolutionary circumstances. Consequently, he defended America's step-by-step in the world struggle for power too much in terms of neutrality, nonintervention, and altruism at a time when these traditional considerations were becoming increasingly irrelevant to the real issues which troubled the American public. Thus, in order to appease an isolationist minority he muddled the public's perception of the hardheaded case for American aid to the anti-Fascist powers and weakened its will to act upon that perception. Whether this was an inevitable result of necessary domestic political expediency is another matter.[49]

At the time, this issue was summed up well by A.A. Berle in a memorandum on 24 April 1939. He wrote, "Americans want two inconsistent things at once: to stay out of war, and to damn the side they disagree with."[50]

Many sources of information were available to the president and he was particularly interested in reports from informed observers traveling around the country. As far back as 1933 Roosevelt had suggested to Cornelius Vanderbilt, Jr., journalist and lecturer, that he send him occasional comments while on tour.[51] Writing at the time when Congress was in special session to consider the neutrality revision (26 September 1939), Vanderbilt reported to the president that his heaviest opposition was in the farm districts. Father Coughlin was causing a lot of harm, and neither Herbert Hoover nor the president's son Elliott was helping the cause.[52] By early October, Vanderbilt found growing opposition in the Midwest to changes in the Neutrality Law, and he wrote to the president that "there seems to be a strong feeling that you personally have sold out to Wall Street and the Munition Makers." He also expressed doubt about the president's ability at that time to win a third term.[53] Later in the month in a confidential survey that Vanderbilt periodically submitted to the White House, he estimated that 51 percent of the people in the section of the Middle West that he had visited favored revision while 49 percent were opposed. As others before him had advised, he wrote, "Recommendation: Putting into the field as fast as possible competent authorities to lecture, to be interviewed, to talk over the radio of the vital need to the world for Revision."[54]

The external developments, which served as background for the bitter revision debate on the floor of the Congress in July 1939, were volatile and contentious. Hitler occupied Austria in March 1938. The Munich agreement concerning the Sudetenland had been signed on 30 September 1938. On 15 March 1939, the Germans occupied Czechoslovakia, and on March 22 they incorporated Memel. France and Great Britain had pledged themselves to defend Poland on March 31; a week later, on April 7, Italy occupied Albania. On April 28, Germany denounced the 1935 naval agreement with

Great Britain and a ten-year non-aggression treaty with Poland and made new demands on that country. Summer came, and in America the battle for neutrality revision was in full swing. After having already defeated revision in the House of Representatives and approved postponement by a vote of twelve to eleven in the Senate Foreign Relations Committee, the Congress received a presidential message on July 14. In an obviously last-ditch effort destined to fail, the administration asked the Senate to override its own committee.[55] Every effort was made to win support within the political arena. Leading members of both parties attended a special conference called by the president. During this conference, Senator Borah made his often quoted remark: "I have my own sources of information which I have provided myself and on several occasions I've found them more reliable than the State Department."[56] Later, on the floor of the Senate, Borah presented the opinion of many that there would be no war in Europe unless the United States encouraged the democracies to be aggressive.

By 30 July 1939, Congress had decided that neutrality revision could wait. The public mood seemed to be shifting constantly; it was torn between sympathy for Great Britain and France and the desire to stay out of the war at all costs. This indecision made itself felt in Congress by a stalemate. The president for political reasons had adopted the strategy of remaining in the background in order not to alienate possible supporters of revision. Contemporary observers point to the politicians' deep distrust of the president. Roosevelt's strategy did not work, but whether "bold and precise executive leadership might have won over many wavering congressmen and stimulated a public ground swell in behalf of the arms-embargo repeal" is difficult to determine.[57]

The battle for neutrality revision was not won until 4 November 1939, when the president signed the new Neutrality Act of 1939. Compromises were made to achieve this final goal, and the "cash and carry" concept was one of them. But the well-known battle for revision in the special session of Congress was fierce. The isolationists massed their total strength and put up a stubborn fight. Matching the isolationists' all-out drive (which included major addresses to the American people by Charles A. Lindbergh,[58] Herbert Hoover, and a whole roster of senators), the president made strenuous efforts to counter their highly successful propaganda.[59] Again the president limited his appeals, but he did attempt to win bipartisan support from the congressional leaders. In this struggle the administration had the backing of some prominent business leaders. The president also called on two well-known Republicans, Alfred M. Landon and Frank Knox, for support.

In another effort to halt the isolationists, the president asked Clark Eichelberger to organize the public fight for revision. At the latter's suggestion, William Allen White, the widely known Republican editor of the *Emporia Gazette*, was summoned to head a group called the Non-Partisan Committee for Peace through Revision of the Neutrality Act. On an organized basis all the isolationists' statements and speeches were rebutted, and once the campaign to repeal the isolationists' charges had been embarked on, a majority for the repeal of the arms embargo was attained.

Perhaps the most fascinating analysis of the "great agitation in the United States . . . over the President's leadership" is to be found in an article by Raymond Gram Swing for the *London Sunday Express*, dated 11 May 1941.[60] Swing pointed out that the president was in a difficult position: on the one side were his closest friends who were impatient with his leadership and particularly with his reluctance to tell the nation the whole truth; on the other side were his opponents who were "ready to close in on him like wolves and rend him for hesitancy, inconsistent drifting and inability to lead." Acknowledging that he had no firsthand information about the president's strategy for winning the necessary public support for American involvement on the Allied side, Swing still felt confident of the accuracy of his analysis because "President Roosevelt has a sense of history, of the nature of democracy, and of deep responsibility, so that the inside of his mind is hardly a secret."

What then was the basis, in Swing's view, for the president's reluctance to press for American intervention in the European war? Swing felt that Roosevelt was very conscious of the difference between the presidential and the parliamentary system in a crisis situation. In the latter system, if leadership proves inadequate, a Chamberlain can be replaced by a Churchill. Under the presidential system, the leader must attempt to carry on the affairs of state even if his position has been undermined by his opponents and public criticism, and other obstacles hamper his efforts at policy formulation. Swing emphasized Roosevelt's recognition of his own limitations in the following words:

> What is important, in its deepest historic meaning, is not American entrance into the war, but American effectiveness. And the shape of that contribution is being moulded . . . by the character of the entry. America must come in, if it comes, after full discussion, with a feeling of having known the facts, and having been allowed to make up its mind. That is the democratic way. It is the way which

Roosevelt understands and values, not only as an ideal, but as the hardest kind of political realism. He cannot gamble with such precepts. The life and safety of the nation depend on his most scrupulous loyalty to them. He must choose a time for assuming leadership which makes for strength and reliability later on.

The impatience with Roosevelt's leadership, documented in the literature, "paradoxically becomes part of the Roosevelt strategy," Swing wrote. The more impatience the president could muster, the sounder his position. Swing continued:

The more his friends are in anguish about his inscrutable delay, the better they serve him. The more vocative the protests in newspapers and at public meetings, the safer the future and the sounder the President's leadership when it comes. That is not to say that he is egging his associates on to create a demand, which is not an accurate way to describe the situation. He feels that the public is not yet aware enough of the dangers and the gravity of the hour for him to move now. That being his view, he still does not undertake to instruct the public himself. That is for others to do, and do with all eloquence and alacrity. They are doing it. Hull, Knox, Stimson, and Willkie, the four most authentic secondary leaders in the country, are hammering and teaching. [61]

Swing concluded that May 1941 was not yet the "occasion for the President to organize and educate, to cajole and to threaten." A decision to stand with the Allies must be an American decision to be worthwhile, he believed. It must be a national decision "before it can be Roosevelt-led."

Swing's challenging account of the forces that motivated the president enables us to see his actions in a positive and constructive light. But his analysis also presents Roosevelt as a better tactician than he really was and makes him a better statesman than even a great politician in a democracy can be. The political maneuvering during 1939, 1940, and 1941 indicates a desire to avoid direct confrontation with public opinion on the issue of America's role in world affairs. The record shows that during the four years between the Quarantine speech and the Pearl Harbor attack, the president made no further speeches to promote the idea of collective security. The standard explanations for Roosevelt's position are well known: The administration could not afford a serious political defeat in the Congress on the issue of American interventionism, nor could the president afford to deepen the bitter divisions of opinion that were current in the country before World War II.

Studies of this period, however, do not agree in their appraisal of Roosevelt's role. Selig Adler, for example, writes that an evaluation of the president's leadership cannot be based on the historical evidence alone; it involves a value judgment concerning the effective strength of the isolationists if the United States had been drawn into a declared war in Western Europe without the attack on Pearl Harbor.[62] Langer and Gleason conclude that an out-and-out proposal to declare war would certainly have been defeated, even on the threshold of the Pearl Harbor attack. Adler notes that the president would have had to contend with partisan dissent.[63] Another study finds that without the attack on Pearl Harbor the "United States' entry into the war would have been postponed—possibly indefinitely."[64] These conclusions underestimate the support in the country for the concrete measures that had been taken by the president to aid the Allies, and particularly they evince a lack of appreciation of the leadership role of the president, whose potential had not yet been fully employed to alert the American people.

The rule of anticipatory reaction is the crucial link in analyzing the relationship between the president, the public, and the Congress. Sensible judgments regarding the president's character, his motivations and judgments must be made with respect to the president's state of mind. What did he know, what were his perceptions, who were his advisors, what was their advice, and what advice did he follow? What were the real goals and strategies of the president? We are working here with intangibles, the inherent weakness of anticipatory reaction as an analytical tool. Our primary sources are "whatever observations journalists, government officials, and others may have recorded at the time, and on subsequent recollections of people who participated in the event."[65] We can attempt to psychoanalyze the president and evaluate all the potential influences we can locate, but at best the scholar can recreate only partially the multiple forces that influenced him. Theoretical formulations (beyond the one that it is easier to pursue a particular foreign policy with public and congressional support than without it) are extremely difficult.

President Roosevelt appreciated the importance of laying the groundwork so that the general public and the Congress would accept his recommendations. Because the president was associated with sympathy for the Allies, he sometimes resorted to silence in order to de-emphasize his role with regard to policies for which he was seeking public support and legislative approval. The record indicates that Roosevelt was always wary of his political opposition. Concerned with leading opinion, he modulated his position according to the pace of his followers. As important as these political manipulations were for the purpose of attaining legislative victories, the record demonstrates that Roosevelt's lack of frankness profoundly disturbed some of his advisors and supporters. The deliberate blurring of issues to gain political advantage in the legislature made it more difficult to gain public confidence.

Sumner Welles offers a partial explanation for President Roosevelt's reluctance to issue forthright public appeals prior to Pearl Harbor for a policy of assistance and firmness in support of the anti-Nazi coalition. Welles observes that, while the president did not have a "one-track mind," he preferred "to segregate the urgent from the not-so-urgent." He was inclined to "devote himself to the task which was immediate rather than to the task which could be undertaken later on."[66] Accepting, therefore, the state of negative public opinion toward the dangers of involvement in a war and fearing a political setback on any one of the several important measures he wanted Congress to approve, the president set his sights on getting each required legislative item approved one by one. As a policymaker, he was convinced that "policy had to stay within the bounds of toleration set by opinion."[67]

Roosevelt fully understood the potential impact of a German victory. The primary problem that confronted him was how and when to provide assistance to the Allies. Many, but not all, contemporary scholars of this period fault the president not for the means but the method employed in providing aid to Britain. The strongest critics suggest that the "destroyer for bases" agreement provided the precedents for the latter-day "imperial presidency." The interpretation of these events has everything to do with a depiction of the president's method of leadership and the interpretation of his perception of what was achievable by taking Congress into his confidence.[68]

Robert Shogan writes that Roosevelt's "determination to avoid 'scaring the people' as he had termed it to William Allen White, inhibited the President from spurring the pace of the military buildup." Shogan concludes that "Roosevelt's gravest sin as a leader was not that he was too political but that he lacked the courage to use his political skills to promote his own convictions."[69] This view is the key issue to the revisionist dilemma. Roosevelt was either a procrastinator, a liar, a deceiver, or a keen strategist with an incisive appreciation for the possible and achievable in politics.

Congress presented formidable opposition to the administration's foreign and defense policies. Shogan acknowledges that "the personal antagonism against Roosevelt which had mounted, during two terms, in both parties" created difficulties. The president could not count on the support of his own party on crucial issues. As Shogan again notes, "On the critical vote to extend selective service, members of Roosevelt's own party cast 64 of the 202 opposition votes."[70] Comparison of polls with congressional attitudes indicated that on a number of important issues, such as the elimination of the Neutrality Act and conscription, the people were favorably inclined before the Congress reluctantly took action.

In the final analysis, it is almost impossible for a chief executive to promote a consensus in support of a policy if he cannot count on the Congress for dispassionate, frank consideration of the issues. On some issues (the change in the Neutrality Law, the repeal of the arms embargo, the extension of the draft), the administration needed legislation from the Congress. The aim was to win congressional support without strengthening opposition there. Roosevelt certainly had no intention of taking on the Congress with respect to the destroyer-base deal. Shogan asks, "What accounted for the President's unwillingness to match his power, prestige and skill against the forces of isolationism?"[71] The response is that Roosevelt was probably convinced he would be defeated.

In a review of the growing body of Roosevelt literature, especially the studies that dwell on the president's perception of the isolationist opposition to his policies, J. Garry Clifford concludes that "most scholars still assume that FDR could not have led the country more directly into the war. . . ." [72] Yet he believes with others that the president could have exerted more leadership. He is convinced that at this late date the last word has not been written on the acuity and judgment demonstrated by the president with respect to his "anticipatory reaction." Echoing a pervasive theme in the contemporary literature, Shogan says, "What FDR's behavior called into question was not the quality of democracy, but the quality of Roosevelt's leadership, which much of the time made the avoidance of 'an uproar' its supreme objective."[73] Clifford correctly notes that "evaluating FDR's foreign policy performance on the home front means widening the lens to illuminate the interaction between the leader and his would-be followers."[74] But the interpretation of how FDR viewed this information and how it influenced his policies is very difficult, and ultimately it is based on the analyst's instincts and values. Michael Leigh, having analyzed polling data, writes that "although public confidence in the viability of American insulation was on the decline and public sympathies with victims of Axis aggression were on the rise, large segments clung to the belief that direct American involvement would be avoided."[75]

Clifford notes that "using PSF and OF files at Hyde Park, one can find polls, roll calls, and analyses of editorial opinion, and understand why Roosevelt thought he should rely on events and his own manipulative ability to educate public opinion before he placed measures before Congress and risked public debate."[76] There is convincing evidence that the president appreciated that he served as a lightning rod for isolationist opposition to his policies and that for tactical reasons he deliberately stayed in the background.

The president firmly believed that democratic government can only function successfully if there is a reciprocal faith between leaders and followers. Ernest R. May also believes that the chief reason for the influence of public opinion on foreign policy is our knowledge that "American statesmen have traditionally thought themselves responsible to, and supported or constrained by, some sort of general will."[77]

President Roosevelt's dependence on the anticipatory reaction syndrome was part of his leadership tactic, but it is also evidence of his faith in the "common man." Perhaps Robert Dallek summed it up best when he wrote that "too much has been made of Roosevelt's shortcomings and too little of the constraints under which he had to work in foreign affairs."[78]

Notes

The following abbreviations have been used in the notes which follow: FDRL: Franklin D. Roosevelt Library, Hyde Park, New York; PPF: Post-Presidential Files; PSF: President's Secretary Files.

1. Carl J. Friedrich, *Man and His Government: An Empirical Theory of Politics* (New York: McGraw Hill, 1963), 201.
2. Ibid., 199.
3. Ibid., 206.
4. Aaron Wildavsky, "The Two Presidents," in Aaron Wildavsky, ed., *The Presidency* (Boston: Little, Brown, 1969), 242.
5. Emmet John Hughes, *The Living Presidency* (Baltimore: Penguin, 1940), 115.
6. Doris Kearns Goodwin, C-Span, 22 April 1995.
7. Morton H. Halperin, *Bureaucratic Politics and Foreign Policy* (Washington, D.C.: Brookings Institution, 1974), 15.

8. Samuel I. Rosenman and Dorothy Rosenman, *Working with Roosevelt* (New York: Harpers, 1952), 167, quoted in Elmer E. Cornwell, Jr., *Presidential Leadership of Public Opinion* (Bloomington: Indiana University Press, 1965), 141.

9. Richard E. Neustadt, *Presidential Power: The Politics of Leadership from FDR to Carter* (New York: John Wiley, 1980), 132.

10. Margaret G. Herman, "How Leaders Affect Foreign Policy Decisions: The Impact of Predominant Leader Decision Units on Foreign Policy" (paper presented at the annual meeting of the International Studies Association, St. Louis, Mo., March–April 1988), 18.

11. Richard E. Neustadt, "Presidency and Legislation: The Growth of Central Clearance," in Aaron Wildavsky, ed., *The Presidency*, 614.

12. Herman, 8.

13. Albert E. Gollin, "Polling and the Newsmedia," *Public Opinion Quarterly* 51, 4 (1989): 586.

14. V.O. Key, Jr., *Public Opinion and American Democracy* (New York: Alfred A. Knopf, 1961), 284.

15. Doris Kearns Goodwin, *No Ordinary Time: Franklin and Eleanor Roosevelt, The Home Front in World War II* (New York: Simon & Schuster, 1994), 236.

16. FDR to Carl Sandburg, 3 December 1940, quoted in Basil Rauch, ed., The *Roosevelt Reader* (New York: Rinehart, 1957), 268.

17. Eleanor Roosevelt, transcript of FDR's meeting with a segment of American youth, Conference 649-A, FDRL.

18. Richard E. Neustadt, *Presidential Power*, 118–119.

19. Barbara Farnham, "The Impact of the Political Context on Foreign Policy Decision-Making" (paper presented at the annual meeting of the International Studies Association, Chicago, Ill., February 1995), 30.

20. William E. Leuchtenburg, ed., *Franklin D. Roosevelt: A Profile* (New York: Hill & Wang, 1967), xv.

21. Neustadt, *Presidential Power*, 130.

22. Robert Shogan, *Hard Bargain: How FDR Twisted Churchill's Arm, Evaded the Law, and Changed the Role of the American Presidency* (New York: Scribner, 1995), 267.

23 Ibid., 264.

24. Frank Freidel, *Franklin D. Roosevelt: A Rendezvous with Destiny* (Boston: Little, Brown, 1990), 368.

25. Frederick W. Marks III, *Wind over Sand: The Diplomacy of Franklin D. Roosevelt* (Athens: University of Georgia Press, 1988), xi.

26. Michael Leigh, *Mobilizing Consent: Public Opinion and American Foreign Policy, 1937-1947* (Westport, CT: Greenwood Press, 1976), 16.

27. Hadley Cantril, "America Faces the War: A Study in Public Opinion," *Public Opinion Quarterly* 4, 3 (1940): 405.

28. Nancy Boardman Eddy, "Public Opinion and United States Foreign Policy, 1937-1956," *American Project, Working Paper* 1 (Cambridge: Massachusetts Institute of Technology, n.d.), 14.

29. Doris Kearns Goodwin, *No Ordinary Time*, 57.

30. Benjamin I. Page and Robert Y. Shapiro, *The Rational Public: Fifty Years of Trends in America's Policy Preferences* (Chicago: University of Chicago Press, 1992), 192.

31. Page and Shapiro.

32. Page and Shapiro, 192–193; Shogan, Chap. 14, "Breach of Trust," 259–279.

33. Shogan, 267.

34. William L. Langer and S. Everett Gleason, *The Challenge to Isolation, 1937-1940* (New York: Harpers, 1952), 38.

35. Langer and Gleason, 39.

36. Donald F. Drummond, *The Passing of American Neutrality, 1937-1941* (Ann Arbor: University of Michigan Press, 1955), 81.

37. Basil Rauch, ed., *The Roosevelt Reader* (New York: Rinehart, 1957), 79.

38. Franklin D. Roosevelt, Press Conference 523, 3 February 1939, in Franklin D. Roosevelt, *The Public Papers and Addresses of Franklin D. Roosevelt*, collated by Samuel Rosenman, vol. 8 (New York: Macmillan, 1941), 115. Hereafter cited as Papers and Addresses.

39. Franklin D. Roosevelt, annual message to Congress, 4 January 1939, *Papers and Addresses*, pp. 1–12. Subsequent quotes from this message are from these pages.

40. Franklin D. Roosevelt, conference with members of the Business Advisory Council, Executive Office of the White House, Conference 645-A, 23 May 1940, p. 23, FDRL.

41. Franklin D. Roosevelt, Press Conference 18, Executive Office of the White House, 17 January 1939, FDRL.

42. Typical is the angry reaction to the suggestion by the president that he might have to return to Washington earlier than he had expected because "information that continues to be received with respect to the international situation continues to be disturbing. . . ." Press Conference 526, Civilian Conservation Corps Camp, West Summerfield Key, Florida, 18 February 1939, FDRL.

43. Rauch, ed., 211.

44. Franklin D. Roosevelt, *Papers and Addresses*, 110.

45. Franklin D. Roosevelt, *Papers and Addresses*, 111.

46. Clyde Eagleton to Dr. Stanley K. Hornbeck, political advisor to the State Department, 16 February 1939, Group 13, PPF 1820, Box 24, FDRL.

47. For what the president actually said, see Press Conference 526 (excerpts), at a Civilian Conservation Camp in Florida, 18 February 1939, quoted in *Papers and Addresses*, p. 140.

48. Franklin D. Roosevelt, Press Conference 538, Executive Office of the White House, 11 April 1939, FDRL.

49. Robert E. Osgood, *Ideals and Self-Interest in America's Foreign Relations* (Chicago: University of Chicago Press, 1963), 412.

50. A.A. Berle, Jr., Assistant Secretary of State, 1938-1944, memorandum for the president, 24 April 1939, Group 13, PPF, Box 24, FDRL.

51. Cornelius Vanderbilt, Jr., to Marvin H. McIntyre, 27 September 1933, PPF 104, 1933-1945, FDRL. A large file of correspondence and detailed reports from Vanderbilt to the president is available at Hyde Park. Many of these reports are addressed to the president's personal staff, such as Margaret LeHand, secretary; Colonel Edwin Martin Watson, personal aide; and Marvin H. McIntyre, member of the secretariat. The president probably saw a number of these reports through the years.

52. Cornelius Vanderbilt, Jr., report to President Roosevelt, 26 September 1939, PPF 104, FDRL.

53. Vanderbilt, Jr., 5 October 1939.

54. Vanderbilt, Jr., 24 October 1939.

55. Robert A. Divine, *The Illusion of Neutrality* (Chicago: University of Chicago Press, 1962), 281. See pp. 281–285 for an excellent analysis of the failure to achieve revision of the Neutrality Act before the outbreak of the war.

56. As quoted House in Kenneth S. Davis, *FDR into the Storm, 1937-1940: A History* (New York: Random, 1993), 457–458.

57. Divine, 284.

58. Charles A. Lindbergh, *The Radio Addresses of Col. Charles A. Lindbergh, 1939-1940* (New York: Scribner's Commentators, 1940), 1–7. Lindbergh delivered two remarkable speeches during the fight against neutrality revision.

59. One of the most effective organizations fighting neutrality revision was the Citizens National "Keep America Out of War" Committee under the chairmanship of Hamilton Fish. In a subheading of their newsletter, this organization referred to itself as "A Consolidation of Patriotic Organization Leaders and Citizens Representative of Every Phase of Our National Life, Banded Together to Fight to Keep America Out of Foreign Wars." PPF 1561, 2 September 1939, FDRL.

60. Raymond Gram Swing, editorial, PPF 1820, Group 3, 1941, Box 7, File 5/31/41, FDRL. Subsequent quotes from this source.

61. Wendell L. Willkie provided vigorous leadership for all-out support to England after the 1940 presidential elections. A fine presentation of his views ("I feel that perhaps the American people have not yet fully grasped the extent of the crisis, or of their responsibility with regard to it" [870].) may be found in hearings before the Committee on Foreign Relations, U.S. Senate, Seventy-Seventh Congress, First Session on S. 275, A Bill Further to Promote the Defense of the United States, and for Other Purposes. Part 3, 11 February 1941: 870–903.

62. Selig Adler, *The Isolationist Impulse: Its Twentieth Century Reaction* (New York: Collier Books, 1961), 288.

63. Ibid., 288.

64. Bernard Fensterwald, Jr., "The Anatomy of American 'Isolationism' and Expansionism," *Journal of Conflict Resolution* 2, no. 1 (1958): 125.

65. W. Phillips Davison, *The Berlin Blockade: A Study in Cold War Politics* (Princeton, N.J.: Princeton University, 1958), 381.

66. Sumner Welles, *Where Are We Heading?* (New York: Harpers, 1946), 19.

67. John W. Masland, "Pressure Groups and American Foreign Policy," *Public Opinion Quarterly* 6 (Spring 1942): 122.

68. J. Garry Clifford, "Both Ends of the Telescope: New Perspectives on FDR and the American Entry into World War II," *Diplomatic History*. 13, 2 (1989): 215.

69. Shogan, 269.

70. Shogan, 266.

71. Shogan.

72. Clifford, 228.

73. Shogan, 267.

74. Clifford, 229.

75. Michael Leigh, *Mobilizing Consent: Public Opinion and American Foreign Policy, 1937-1947* (Westport, CT: Greenwood Press, 1976), 45.

76. Clifford, 229.

77. As quoted in William H. Nelson, ed., *Theory and Practice in American Politics* (Chicago: University of Chicago Press, 1964), 122.

78.   Robert Dallek, *Franklin D. Roosevelt and American Foreign Policy, 1932-1945* (New York: Oxford University Press, 1979), 529.

3

Franklin D. Roosevelt and American Strategic Vulnerability

David M. Esposito

> At what point shall we expect the approach of danger? By
> what means shall we fortify against it? Shall we expect
> some transatlantic military giant to step across the ocean
> and crush us at a blow? Never! All the armies of Europe,
> Asia and Africa combined, with all the treasure on earth
> (our own excepted) in their military chest, with a Bonaparte
> for a commander, could not by force take a drink from the
> Ohio or make a track on the Blue Ridge in a trial of a
> thousand years.
>
> —Abraham Lincoln, 1837

Historians have long debated how Franklin Roosevelt dealt with the coming
of the Second World War, and how decision makers in Washington
perceived the growing danger to peace in the 1930s posed by dictatorial
powers. New scholarship increasingly suggests that Franklin Roosevelt's
view of Nazi Germany and Imperial Japan reflected pre-established patterns
of American exaggerated strategic vulnerability: American leaders feared
foreign invasion of the U.S. by a hostile military power. Although it may
seem odd to the modern reader, this belief was reflected in contemporary
popular culture and personal behavior. In the 1940s many Americans feared
that someday Hitler's legions (or the Japanese hordes) would come
marching down Main Street, USA. More importantly, FDR held that even if
foreign enemies did not invade the continental United States (or even

penetrate the Western Hemisphere) that America would be forced to take measures of defense that would prove fatal to democratic government. Freedom would not long last in an armed camp and liberalism would find no home in a garrison state. Thus, much like his mentor Woodrow Wilson in 1917, Roosevelt opted for a forward defense strategy and joined a world war in progress.[1]

The case of the First World War deserves special attention. Imperial Germany did not pose any direct military threat to the U.S., as most American statesmen, journalists, and military officers of the day knew well. What people overlooked then, and overlook now, was the threat to American institutions and ideals implicit in a German victory. No invading army would have had to cross the seas in order to force the U.S. to adopt defensive measures that liberals feared would put an end to the great experiment in democracy. A permanent state of unlimited national emergency—the garrison state—would destroy the U.S. as certainly as any foreign invasion. Wilson was the first American president in this century to face this alarming possibility, although virtually every U.S. president since 1939 has shared this nightmare in one form or another. The question Wilson, Franklin D. Roosevelt, and others faced was how to preserve American institutions against rampant and aggressive powers without suspending the constitution, sinking the nation under the weight of its own military expenditures, crushing organized labor, and turning the government over to illiberal super-patriots. In time, both Wilson and Roosevelt found their answer in aggressive defense to counter international aggression, and both found it incumbent upon the nation to enter a global war already in progress. Wilson is unique because he apparently believed that intervention would be a one-time affair, and that thereafter the affairs of nations would yield to the organized opinion of mankind. FDR's postwar plans included many Wilsonian features including collective security, but with characteristically "pragmatic" changes.[2]

Invasion and hypothetical war novels have a long and distinguished lineage in utopian (or anti-utopian) literature, with examples going back to Napoleonic times. However, taking advantage of the new mass literacy and inexpensive media, the "new" fiction of futuristic warfare began a generation before World War I. The genre developed several interesting conventions: real locations, famous casualties, and well-known monuments destroyed. By 1914, the major combatants had been fighting each other furiously, on paper, for over a generation.[3]

American authors wrote in this genre long before the Great War began. H. Bruce Franklin observes that they added several uniquely American elements to the literature, especially by predicting the advent of superweapons. In these writers' fevered imaginations America was invaded by, in different stories, Britain, czarist the USSR, the "Yellow Peril" Japan, Imperial Germany; even China was envisioned as a potential conqueror. In these tales the U.S. is saved in its hour of peril by the advent of some Thomas Edison-type inventor with a devastating superweapon that annihilates the enemy and leaves America in a position to dictate world peace.[4]

The only known plans for an invasion of the United States were written between 1898 and 1905 by junior officers of the kaiser's Admiralty Staff. Thereafter, changing military alignments in Europe forced the Germans to shelve hypothetical attacks on America and concentrate work on more likely adversaries. As Holger Herwig observed, "Even the most anti-American officials of the Reich could not fail to recognize the frivolity of a contingency war plan that called for full-scale operations" against the continental United States. Unquestionably, the balance of naval forces between Germany and its enemies in World War II was even more unfavorable than before the First World War. If Germany could not invade in 1910, such operations were even less likely thereafter.[5]

H.G. Wells helped popularize future war books in America with his 1908 novel *War in the Air*. In it, the United States is attacked by Imperial Germany. The German navy decimates a divided American fleet, followed by Zeppelin bombardment and invasion of New York City. Fighting eventually spreads to engulf the entire world, leading to the collapse of Western civilization. At the end of the book, the world is wracked by famine, plague, and political chaos. Although obviously innocent of insight into contemporary German strategic calculations, the work contains visions of strategic bombing of civilian targets and an ominous warning to those who were blasé about great power conflict in the twentieth century. Unlike so many lesser writers, Wells warned that "the next war" could result in the complete destruction of human progress and a mass return to barbarism. Wells returned to the same theme before World War II, again stressing the dire consequences for civilization in his *Things to Come* (1936).

Of course, Americans could not decide if they were more threatened by developments in the Atlantic or the Pacific. Author Homer Lea (sometime military advisor to Chinese President Sun Yat-sen) was more responsible than anyone for introducing Americans to "The Yellow Peril." He gave prescient warning of Japanese expansionism in *The Valor of Ignorance* (1909), and explained how all Asians were deeply offended by America's frankly racist immigration policies. His work is interesting, not only for acknowledging Japan's emergence as a great power, but for its attempt to reckon the parameters of transoceanic amphibious operations. Lea estimated that Japan could land a fully equipped first-wave invasion force of 200,000 soldiers on the California coast and have an army of one million fighting on U.S. soil inside a year.[6]

In fact, his figures were preposterous. Nevertheless, subsequent "experts" civilian and military would revisit this scenario (or a German, later Soviet, invasion) and come to similar, and equally misguided, conclusions. For point of reference, his imagined invasion is approximately the size of the Anglo-American landing in Normandy in June 1944. There the Allies were able to stage a large amphibious landing, but only across the very narrow waters of the English Channel and after two years of intensive preparations. Transoceanic invasion scenarios have always been, despite all disclaimers, mere moonshine.

Admiral Alfred Thayer Mahan, high priest of American navalism, reviewing the international politico-military situation in 1910, noted the growing power of Germany in Europe and Japan in Asia as cause for national concern. His public professions of anxiety contrast markedly with his views expressed privately. He wrote Captain Henry Taylor somewhat earlier, "In considering possible wars with the great nations of the world it seems to me inconceivable that any one of them should expect seriously to modify, or even weaken, our position in this hemisphere."[7]

Nevertheless, the Great War portended serious changes in the international balance of power. In August 1914, presidential advisor Edward M. House wrote President Wilson to argue that no matter which side won, the war did not augur well for the future. If the Allies won, the USSR would dominate the European mainland; if Germany won it would mean "the unspeakable tyranny of militarism for generations to come." A German success would "ultimately mean trouble for us" because it would force the U.S. to create "a military machine of vast proportions." In a meeting with the president a week later, House was interested to hear Wilson agree with his assessment. Wilson asserted that if Germany won "it would change the course of our civilization and make the United States a military nation."[8]

In a well-known conversation with British Ambassador Sir Cecil Spring Rice in September 1914, Wilson expressed sympathy for the British cause and explained how the war could harm America. Spring Rice quoted the president to Foreign Secretary Sir Edward Grey as saying "If they [the Germans] succeed, we shall be forced to take measures of defense here as would be fatal to our form of government and American ideals."[9] In fact, Wilson had defined one of the cardinal principles of American strategic interest regarding the Great War. He was not so much in favor of the Allies as he was opposed to German domination of Europe. Unlike the nascent preparedness advocates, he was not afraid of some hypothetical invasion. Instead he feared a German victory would force the U.S. to become a "garrison state" in which liberty would not long survive. The threat to American values posed by a German victory in Europe remained a constant, if somewhat infrequently expressed, concern in the president's mind. His worries were mitigated by the fact that after a few weeks the war seemed destined to end in a stalemate—a solution to the war Wilson found preferable to any other. While his enthusiasm for Britain waned, his definition of American strategic interests did not change significantly.

By 1915, Wilson found himself under attack by the Preparedness Movement. These "patriots in pinstripe" were usually Anglophile Eastern businessmen with progressive political credentials. They enthusiastically favored the Entente alliance and although some thought the U.S. should enter the war over Germany's unrestricted submarine warfare, few demanded American intervention in the war. Instead, they argued for expanding the armed forces to protect the U.S. *after* the war in Europe was over. Their propaganda was inflammatory, yet profoundly isolationist. Assistant Secretary of the Navy Franklin Roosevelt sympathized with the movement and leaked confidential government information to it, in order to help bolster its case with the public. At the time, FDR was more in tune with his "Uncle Ted" than he was with Woodrow Wilson.[10]

Concern over American national defense was an important issue in 1915, and this fear was reflected in popular culture. Americans already had been given the tabloid treatment of German *Weltmacht* philosophy when American publishers discovered that German militarists such as General Bernhardi or the ominous fulminations of Nietzsche and Treitschke sold newspapers. During the summer of 1915 the invasion motif became a common theme in popular media. Serious works such as Hudson Maxim's *Defenseless America* were supplemented with dozens of lesser literary works and movies including *The Battle Cry of Peace* and a play titled *The Fall of a Nation*. The common link in all these works, and dozens of lesser efforts, was the idea that military weakness made the U.S. ripe for foreign invasion. Muckraker Ray Stannard Baker, Wilson's future biographer, wrote one of these stories, but only to pillory the genre. His story ends with Americans laughing German invaders out of the country. *Life* (a period humor magazine not to be confused its later picture-packed namesake) also played the theme for fun by publishing a spurious map of America after hypothetical German conquest.[11] This device, the future map of a defeated U.S. with all the cities renamed and boundaries re-drawn, became a regular staple in invasion literature.

After America entered the war in 1917, Wilson explained the nature of the German threat in his Flag Day address. He argued that the avowed purpose of Germany's military masters was continental domination, that the start of the war was "a mere single step in a plan which encompassed Europe and Asia, from Berlin to Baghdad." Germany had seized "political control across the very center of Europe and beyond the Mediterranean into the heart of Asia." The Central Powers were, he argued, "but a single power." If the Germans were checked, they would fold. "If they fall back or are forced back an inch, their power both at home and abroad will fall to pieces." If they failed, they would have to accept democratic reforms. If they succeeded, the U.S. would be menaced and have to remain armed to resist the "next step in their aggression." Wilson did not use the analogy of dominoes falling, but if the metaphor had occurred to him it would have illustrated his argument perfectly. Liberal democratic political institutions were at risk, even without the possibility of actual invasion of the continental United States.[12] Wilson elaborated a strategic rationale that would become a staple of American geopolitical calculation, and eventually the "Domino Theory." Enemy forces gain momentum from conquest, until the United States, left without allies, has its very survival threatened.

After the Great War, European authors who addressed the possibility of future wars did so with trepidation. The war had swept away romantic notions of chivalry, and war as a kind of adventure. Having experienced the horror of industrialized slaughter, European authors almost invariably characterized the next war in terms akin to H.G. Wells. Interestingly, American authors generally addressed future conflicts without regret.[13]

In *The Great Pacific War* (1925, reprinted 1931), military expert Hector Bywater predicted a Japanese-American war over the Pacific. His scenario begins with a Japanese sneak attack on a forward U.S. military base; not Pearl Harbor, but the Panama Canal. The book ends with American victory in a clash of dreadnoughts in the style prescribed by Admiral Mahan. Although tempted to include a Japanese invasion of Hawaii or the Pacific Coast, the author noted dryly that such plot devices were sufficiently improbable as to bring professional ridicule upon a writer. The reviewer for the *New York Times*, Nicholas Roosevelt (FDR's cousin) pronounced the story quite good. In a strange twist of fate, Bywater is credited by some historians with putting the idea of a Japanese carrier-based air attack on the American fleet at Pearl Harbor into the mind of his Japanese friend, naval attaché (later Admiral) Yamamoto. The Roosevelt-Bywater-Yamamoto connection, though tenuous, is the stuff from which marvelously elaborate conspiracy webs can be spun.[14]

Former war correspondent Floyd Gibbons wrote the all-time best-selling America-gets-invaded novel in 1929. *The Red Napoleon* tells the story of the evil genius Karakhan, a lineal descendent of Genghis Khan, who rises in the Soviet Army (unlikely) and seizes power after the assassination of Josef Stalin in 1932. He mobilizes the hordes of Asia under the rainbow flag and sets out to conquer the world while the U.S. remains determinedly neutral. With the aid of newly communist Japan and "Red" Britain, Karakhan invades unprepared America from east and west. Through unprecedented sacrifice, the United States is preserved and defeats the oriental despot.[15] Although clearly indebted to prior invasion works, Gibbons developed a new plot device based in part on American experience in the Great War. His geopolitical calculations are reminiscent of Wilson's 1917 Flag Day address.

The international political turbulence of the 1930s brought new invasion scenarios. In 1937's *Is America Afraid?* political scientist Livingston Hartley called America "the ham in the world sandwich." Predicting an alliance between Nazi Germany and Imperial Japan (which was signed later that year), he envisioned their joint attack on the nation. According to his scenario, the U.S. would be overcome rapidly. His book ends with a refugee American government holding on grimly in Topeka as German and Japanese generals coordinate their final offensive using polyglot armies of subject peoples. He intimated that America's fate at the hands of such a horde would not be kind.[16]

In an atmosphere of official encouragement it is not surprising that stories using the invasion myth experienced a resurgent popularity. Perhaps the most interesting (and certainly the most prophetic) work of this genre was a series written by journalist Fred Allhoff for *Liberty* magazine shortly before America entered World War II. "Lightning in the Night" begins with a Japanese attack on Pearl Harbor and ends with the detonation of an atomic bomb. Despite his clairvoyance in some matters, Allhoff did not see the future in its full complexity. He envisioned a perpetuation of the de facto Soviet-German-Japanese alliance; thus the planes bombing Pearl Harbor were Soviet and not Japanese. Likewise, the destructive power of the atomic bomb is demonstrated on the vast wasteland of the Soviet steppes and not on a large Japanese city such as Hiroshima.[17] Nevertheless, there is an eerie plausibility to "Lightning" not always found in works of this kind.

So how does FDR fit into all of this? Franklin Roosevelt was a child of the Progressive Era and the living embodiment of the policy fusion between archrivals Theodore Roosevelt and Woodrow Wilson. He imbibed American popular culture and reflected its peculiarities; it informed his thinking. Many of the ideas, conventions, and plot devices of the future war novelists worked their way into his speeches and policy proposals. He was aware of the nascent Domino Theory and shared its view of liberal democracies as weaker than illiberal dictatorships. Despite his brush with Wilsonian internationalism, his basic inclination in the 1930s was isolationist. When he was not focused on the New Deal, he expected America's limited military buildup in the period to deter foreign aggression.

A quick review of FDR's major speeches from 1933 to 1941 illustrates clearly what scholars already know: until 1938 he had little to say about defense and foreign affairs. A typical example from the period is his 1935 rejection of an initiative to rename the army's chemical weapons unit as "The Gas Service." In a classic piece of progressive political posturing, Roosevelt refused the new euphemism for what he considered a barbaric business.[18] His public persona was not particularly different from that found in his private correspondence. When New York City Mayor Fiorello LaGuardia wrote in 1938 to express concern about potential conflict between the U.S. and the dictatorships, FDR wrote back jauntily: "Don't stay up nights thinking of drums and bombs. The Navy program is having an excellent effect in Berlin, Rome and Tokyo. Enough said!"[19] In fact, American rearmament programs made little impact on the dictators because the U.S. (read FDR) was firmly committed to isolationism.

As William Manchester explains, the United States was protected by the British Royal Navy "as surely as any crown colony." In 1932, when Lloyds of London offered 500–1 odds against an invasion of the U.S., there were very few takers. Most Americans expected, without saying so explicitly, that no matter how fast ships would sail or airplanes fly, their hemisphere would remain safe from foreign danger. At the time, and for years after, it did not seem that Roosevelt viewed the situation any differently.[20]

When the Second World War broke out in September 1939, the president's proclamation of neutrality was passionately isolationist. He averred, "Let no man or woman thoughtlessly or falsely talk of America sending its armies to European fields." He said, "I trust that in the days to come our neutrality can be made a true neutrality." In his most memorable peroration of the speech, he noted, "I have seen war. I hate war. I will say that again and again. I hope the U.S. will keep out of this war. I believe that it will." And he promised to make every effort, "as long as it remains in my power."[21]

The question of when Roosevelt turned from isolationist to interventionist remains unsettled. His public sentiments of September 1939 contrast vividly with what he supposedly told a group of U.S. Senators privately in January: "the United States' frontier lies along the Rhine." When one of his confidants leaked FDR's statement to the press, the president repudiated it flatly. The irreconcilable distance between the public and private pronouncements of the president unsettled old allies such as journalist William Allen White. "As an old friend," he chided, "let me warn you that maybe you will not be able to lead the American people unless you catch up with them. They are going fast."[22]

FDR had already explained his dilemma to White. "My problem is to get the American people to think about the possible consequences of this war without scaring the American people into thinking that they are going to be dragged into this war."[23]

As the war in Europe turned against Britain and France, FDR turned to the tradition of exaggerated American strategic vulnerability to justify increased expenditures on defense and, eventually, as a justification for arming the victims of international aggression. As early as April 1939 he warned a group of newspaper editors that the development of long-range bombing aircraft by foreign powers presented a potential threat to the American heartland. Although he admitted that even modern bombers could not cross the 3,000 miles of the Atlantic Ocean, he asserted "they" had 1,500 planes that could reach the U.S. in three jumps: from central Europe to Brazil and from Brazil to Mexico. "Enemy" planes based in the Yucatan could flatten New Orleans in less than two hours or raid Kansas City in a little over three. He made much the same point to the same audience the next year, only raising his estimation of the foreign danger. The "unnamed country" in Europe could move 5,000 bombing planes to the Western Hemisphere and could have done it "three or four years ago."[24]

FDR's exaggerated estimation of Germany's force structure, capabilities, and intentions, is understandable given the situation in 1940. American foreign intelligence was, by modern standards, absolutely primitive. No one in Washington had reliable numbers on Germany's military production, and "trustworthy" estimations were off by an order of magnitude. It also illustrates a problem regarding technological capability that Cold War survivors remember: the contradiction between aircraft top speed, full weapons load, and greatest range. In brief, aircraft can *either* fly very fast, go a long way, or carry a heavy load. They cannot do two of those at once. No plane ever made can carry its maximum load at full throttle to its maximum range. Certain tradeoffs are inescapable. The president's whole point was not to analyze airframe capabilities, but to invigorate public concern over nation defense. He wanted his countrymen to worry about their safety, *and* to help him do something about it.

FDR took his case to the public using "common sense" and raised disturbing historical parallels. As he pointed out in 1940, Alexander the Great did not begin with a plan to conquer the known world nor did Napoleon start with the expectation of dominating continental Europe, but that is what they accomplished. If Hitler defeated the French army and the British navy, what would stop him from attacking the New World? In his fireside chat justifying Lend-Lease to the public in December 1940, the president claimed that the menace to American civilization was unprecedented. The Nazis had made it clear that they intended "not only to dominate all life and thought in their country, but also to enslave the whole of Europe, and to use the resources of Europe to dominate the rest of the world." Even if the United States were not invaded, it would be living "at the point of a gun."[25]

In July 1941, Roosevelt said unequivocally that Hitler's aim was "the political and physical control of the whole world." In his Navy and Total Defense Day address in October, he brandished a map "made in Germany by Hitler's government." On it, all of Latin and South America were divided up into conquered principalities loyal to the Third Reich. The map was, of course, a fake cobbled together by British intelligence. Even at the height of his power, Hitler apparently did not even fantasize about conquering the Western Hemisphere. This did not stop FDR from believing, and telling the American public about, even more fanciful German plots south of the border.[26]

As the Nazi juggernaut rolled over Europe unimpeded, the president's scenarios became increasingly implausible. In December 1940, he told an audience that the latest German bombers could hit American cities from bases in the British Isles and return without refueling. Needless to say, the Germans had no planes of this kind. Usually, the president acknowledged the limitations on modern aircraft and explained that they would have to move by stages to the New World before they could hit America. However, he never addressed the charges made by isolationists such as Charles Lindbergh that the large-scale production of modern interceptor aircraft could render the nation virtually invulnerable to foreign attack. Indeed, as late as November 1938 FDR had proposed building a large "striking force" of bombers to deter foreign aggression, however the admirals and generals prevailed in their demand for a more balanced force structure.[27]

An objective assessment of American national security in 1941 would find the continental U.S. comfortably safe from foreign conquest, as FDR probably knew well. After June 23, the bulk of German forces were tied down in the Soviet campaign. Although some claimed that a quick Nazi victory over the Soviet Union would make Germany an even greater menace, allowing Germany to access all the resources of the conquered USSR, by December 1941 it was clear that the Soviet Union was not going to collapse as Poland and France had.[28]

The danger was not that enemy hordes would soon descend on America's coastlines, but that the nation would sit safe behind its great ocean barriers and let the world go to hell while it turned itself into a gigantic armed camp. FDR had more to fear from a permanent state of unlimited national emergency than from hostile invasion. War, once begun, would someday end and life would return more or less to normal. The garrison state could last generations, and by the time it was over Americans would forget that there ever was such a thing as freedom. As he explained in May 1941, to maintain America's crippled independence in the face of Nazi hegemony "would require the conscription of our manpower, curtail education funds, housing, public works, flood control and heath. All would go for armaments year in and out, standing watch."[29]

The president made a similar case in economic terms to Bill White. He argued that if foreign conquest went unchallenged, Americans would find their economic prospects clouded. The American way of life depended on access to foreign markets and resources, but the dictators were establishing exclusive economic zones and stifling U.S. competition. If their campaign was not arrested, entire industries would be put out of business and American farmers would have trouble selling produce abroad.[30]

Revisionist historian Patrick Hearden seized upon statements such as this to argue that Roosevelt saw fascism primarily as a threat to U.S. global *economic* hegemony. His case is reminiscent of revisionist treatments explaining American entry into World War I; in short, America entered the Great War at the command of gold to ensure its commercial supremacy.[31] Although scientific materialist interpretations of Wilson have known considerable popularity, Hearden's work stands far outside the mainstream consensus on FDR. Obviously there was a capitalist engine pulling Roosevelt's train of thought, but few believe it was carrying all that freight alone.

After years of public warning from authors, journalists, and statesmen, it should come as no surprise that there was massive public hysteria about enemy invasion during the early days of American involvement in the Second World War. The pointless preparations were nonetheless impressive: the Capitol was ringed with anti-aircraft guns; militia squads trained for guerrilla warfare in Oregon; gas masks were distributed to the public; artillery and mines were placed to defend every major harbor; millions of citizens enrolled as air raid wardens; residents of one city after another reported sighting enemy planes that only existed in their overwrought imaginations. As the war years passed without enemy invasion, and the Germans and Japanese were beaten back and finally defeated, FDR dismantled the massive Civil Defense apparatus.[32]

If Americans behaved hysterically during World War II and did things they later regretted (such as interning Japanese-Americans), one root cause was the culture of exaggerated strategic vulnerability. FDR did not create the invasion myth, although he certainly flogged it for his own political purposes. In the twentieth century, few presidents have been able to look out at the world with the kind of innocent confidence Lincoln expressed in 1837. Technology has made the world smaller. Starting with World War I, U.S. leaders fought to reconcile nineteenth-century isolationism with the reality of being the world's leading industrial power. Tugged into world affairs by American missionary idealism, commercial realities, questions of neutral rights in wartime, and national prestige, they have also felt threatened by realignments in the world balance of power. The serious implications for American national security of a foreign power achieving hegemony in Eurasia have unsettled virtually every U.S. president in the twentieth century. Concern about the survival of American liberal institutions in a world gone mad have led more than one president to exaggerate the danger of foreign attack and to promote a concomitant forward defense strategy as an alternative to geopolitical disaster.

Notes

1. For an exceptionally thoughtful treatment of the transformation of U.S. strategic culture from Theodore Roosevelt to Lyndon Johnson, see Frank Ninkovich, *Modernity and Power: A History of the Domino Theory in the Twentieth Century* (Chicago: University of Chicago Press, 1994).
2. Thomas Knock claims that advocates of unilateral American globalism are the illegitimate heirs of Wilson—in his felicitous phrase, Wilson's "bastard children." Thomas Knock, *To End All Wars* (New York: Oxford University Press, 1992), 269.
3. I.F. Clark, *Voices Prophesying War, 1763-1984* (New York: Oxford University Press, 1966),1–3.
4. H. Bruce Franklin, *War Stars: The Superweapon and the American Imagination* (New York: Oxford University Press, 1988), 29–39.
5. Holger Herwig, *Politics of Frustration: The United States in German Naval Planning, 1889-1941* (Boston: Little, Brown, 1976), 91, 193–194.
6. Homer Lea, *The Valor of Ignorance* (New York: Harper & Bros., 1909), 2–5, 231.

7. Richard Turk, *The Ambiguous Relationship: Theodore Roosevelt and Alfred Thayer Mahan* (Westport, CT: Greenwood Press, 1987), 95, quote on page 50.

8. House to Wilson, 22 August 1915, and diary 30 August 1915, House papers, Yale University Library Archives.

9. Sir Cecil Spring Rice to Sir Edward Grey, 3 September 1914, Arthur Link et al. (eds), *The Papers of Woodrow Wilson* (Princeton: Princeton University, 1969), XXX, 472–473. Hereafter PWW.

10. John Finnegan, *Against the Spectre of a Dragon* (Westport, CT: Greenwood Press, 1974), 9–11.

11. Robert E. Osgood, *Ideals and Self Interest in American Foreign Relations* (Chicago: University of Chicago Press, 1953), 132–133.

12. Wilson's Flag Day Address, 14 June 1917, PWW XXXVI, 278–280.

13. Clarke, 213.

14. Hector Bywater, *The Great Pacific War* (Boston: Houghton Mifflin, 1925), vi, 22, 278–286, *New York Times*, 13 September 1925.

15. Floyd Gibbons, *The Red Napoleon* (New York: Jonathan Cape & Harrison Smith, 1929), 1, 77, 322.

16. John Thompson, "The Exaggeration of American Vulnerability: The Anatomy of a Tradition," *Diplomatic History*, 5 (1993), 13.

17. Fred Allhoff, *Lightning in the Night* (Englewood Cliffs, NJ: Prentice-Hall, 1979), 58–63, 193–194.

18. Samuel Rosenman, ed., *Public Papers and Addresses of Franklin D. Roosevelt* (New York: 1934-1943), VI, 331. Hereafter PPA.

19. Don B. Schewe, ed., *FDR and Foreign Affairs* (New York: Clearwater Pub., 1979), VIII, 211, 239.

20. William Manchester, *The Glory and the Dream* (Boston: Little, Brown, 1973), I, 3.

21. Russell Buhite and David Levy, eds., *FDR's Fireside Chats* (Norman, OK: University of Oklahoma Press, 1992), 149.

22. Robert Dallek, *Franklin D. Roosevelt and American Foreign Policy, 1932-1945* (New York: Oxford University Press, 1979) 181. William Allen White to Franklin Roosevelt, 10 June 1940, PPF 1196, Franklin D. Roosevelt Library, Hyde Park. Here after FDRL.

23. FDR to White, 14 December 1939, PPF 1196, FDRL.

24. Thompson, "Vulnerability," 28.

25. Buhite and Levy, 166-167.

26. FDR did have at least one report that suggested that Hitler intended to "settle accounts" with the "Dollarjuden" after reorganizing Europe. However, the source, an anti-Nazi scion of the Hapsburg family, may be considered less than authoritative. William Bullitt to FDR, 12 March and 16 September 1939, PSP 2, FDRL. The president had reports from several sources regarding Nazi politico-economic penetration of South America. See Bernard Baruch to FDR, 29 April 1938, PSF 10, FDRL.

27. Buhite and Levy, 167; Dallek, 172–173.

28. Bullitt to FDR, 1 July 1941, PPF 1124, FDRL.

29. Buhite and Levy, 177.

30. FDR to William A. White, 17 February 1940, PPF 1196, FDRL.

31. Patrick Hearden, *Roosevelt Confronts Hitler* (DeKalb, IL: Northern Illinois University Press, 1987).

32. James Chiles, "How We Got Ready for a War We Never Fought," *Smithsonian* 19 (1988), 175–177, 204.

4

FDR and Limited War in Europe: A Plausible Middle Course?

Stephen G. Bunch

There has developed over the last two decades a broad consensus among historians of international relations that American policymakers exaggerated to a greater or lesser degree the Cold War Communist threat, especially that issuing from the military power of the Soviet Union. This exaggeration was both rhetorical and substantive; there were associated costs, often immense. Yet at the same time the principle of Containment that served as the guidepost for U.S. foreign policy in Europe in these years appears to have been generally sound.

The question raised here is whether the similar phenomenon of exaggeration of threat used in the struggle with Hitler and Nazism, coupled with the geopolitical map in 1941, also allows for a policy of containing Hitler? On national security grounds, did Hitler and his armed forces truly constitute a deadly threat to America and its vital interests, a threat so severe that it warranted the costs associated with the U.S. participation in a total war for absolute victory?

The answer is by no means obvious. Behind the hyperbole and political ax-grinding, isolationists put forth some serious and well-reasoned arguments for staying aloof from the European struggle. They went, of course, too far. To have dismissed the German threat as largely benign was mistaken, especially for the months between the fall of France and the German invasion of Soviet the USSR. But was there perhaps a less costly middle alternative to a war aim of total victory? Might Roosevelt have considered continuing with his limited, defensive policies, especially after the Pearl Harbor attack? That is to say, should he have considered a durable policy that continued, and augmented somewhat, his policy of containing Hitler by limited means while still providing material aid and naval support for the allies? This option seems superficially plausible because early on it balanced response to threat. But it seems especially plausible after June 1941 when it became increasingly clear to FDR and his advisors that Hitler may well have stubbed his toe in his effort to kick in the many doors that led to Moscow.

After Hitler launched operation Barbarossa in June 1941, there was time for FDR to take stock. Consider the set of likely military outcomes from the perspective of late summer, 1941, to Pearl Harbor. Had Germany defeated the USSR or reached some kind of settlement in 1941 or 1942, an Allied invasion of the continent anytime thereafter would have been prohibitively costly, and probably disastrous. A major invasion to "save" the USSR in 1942 was out of the question. Not even the American Chief of Staff General George Marshall, a consistent proponent of an Allied assault on the continent, believed this was physically possible. A lengthy and exhausting Russo-German struggle, ending in either a Nazi "victory" or Nazi-Soviet stalemate, very possibly would have minimized the German threat, despite the additional resources that might have fallen into Nazi hands. As FDR was to learn, the Soviet leader Joseph Stalin was determined to fight from bases east of the Ural mountains if necessary, and with much of his industrial capacity at hand. A rough equilibrium of power (Great Britain and the USSR, with limited U.S. aid, opposing Germany and her satellites) was at least a possibility, making any Nazi threat to the Western Hemisphere quite manageable.

Before any attempt to make this case stronger by briefly examining important developments after Barbarossa, it is first necessary to respond to two obvious objections to the notion of containing Nazi Germany, two objections that are to some degree ahistorical and yet psychologically powerful. The first deals with the Nazi atomic program.

This is not as debate-stopping as it first appears, for atomic weapons were utterly theoretical and unproven in the early 1940s. And there was every reason to assume that an Allied program based in the United States would be safe from Nazi penetration or physical attack, while any German program would be forced to build facilities that eventually would come within range of allied bombers. Nevertheless, had Hitler's leftover scientists succeeded in developing atomic weapons as quickly as the Allies, a state of deterrence was quite possible. This might seem like faint assurance, but it must be recalled that Hitler was not the first to engage in strategic bombing; Britain was. Nor did Hitler once resort to the use of poison gas, in part because he knew the Allies would retaliate in kind. Finally, if deterrence failed, the United States had another edge: it could deliver aerial bombs to Germany from Britain, but Germany for many years would be unable to reciprocate effectively. In retrospect, of course, we know Hitler had little interest in atomic research. Consequently the German atomic program was underfunded and far behind the Allied effort.

Second, the Holocaust. And here the stubborn and unpleasant fact is that FDR and his advisors did little to rescue its victims. In the 1930s and the early phases of the war, the President could have opened American borders to ethnic and political victims of Nazism and pressured other countries to do likewise. But he was unenthusiastic about measures that doubtless would have proved unpopular, and as the war dragged on the State Department was obstructionist. The notion of specific bombing targets in and around the Auschwitz complex in 1944 has been revived by David Wyman.[1] Though of debatable life-saving value, bombing was also vetoed by U.S. military officers who were absorbed with day-to-day demands and with the overall aim of achieving military victory as soon as possible.

But the important point to be made is that, given the strategic realities evident early on, a limited war to contain Germany no more excluded the possibility of rescuing Holocaust victims than did a total policy. The only exception might have been the bombing of Auschwitz and its rail lines from bases in Italy. But here, too, there may have been other military or bombing options (from other bases or from aircraft carriers, for example), especially since news of mass deaths, without a full-scale U.S.-German war in progress, might have become more publicized in the United States and placed more pressure on the White House to act. In short, invoking the specter of atomic weapons or the Holocaust remain analytically weak objections to the concept of a limited policy.

FDR was clearly attracted to the idea of such a war of limited means. Like Winston Churchill—who during World War I had been an outspoken critic of trench warfare—Roosevelt also was repelled by the thought of another bloody conflict on the continent of Europe. He witnessed firsthand the carnage of the Great War, which, though leaving the United States citizenry largely unscathed, had been a demographic catastrophe for Britain and the belligerent states of Europe. The ruling classes had lost the flower of their youth. Moreover, in the 1930s, the American people and the Congress were becoming increasingly isolationist. Any future war, Roosevelt realized, must be avoided if at all possible, or fought by methods that promised fewer casualties. One method was to provide the enemies of Germany with the weapons and supplies to fight for both themselves and the United States. Another was to substitute, as much as possible, machines for men. For an equivalent destructive power, machines required fewer men than did an army of infantry. This held true for warships and, especially, for warplanes.

As early as 1938, FDR's advisor Harold Ickes noted that the President believed Germany could not protect itself from the combined air power of England, France, and the USSR. In the President's optimistic view, "the morale of the German people would crack under aerial attacks much sooner than that of the French or the English." The President, said Ickes, believed "that this kind of war would cost less money, would mean comparatively few casualties, and would be more likely to succeed than a traditional war by land and sea." Shortly after the appeasement at Munich, FDR told his key civilian and military chiefs that he wanted 10,000 planes in the American inventory, with the capacity to produce an additional 20,000 a year. He told the chiefs that an American army would do little to deter Hitler, "whereas a heavy strike force of aircraft would."[2]

Soon after the outbreak of war in Europe, Roosevelt objected when he learned of War Department plans to equip an expeditionary force, explaining, "we don't send troops abroad. We need only think of defending this hemisphere." This was indicative of an expanding divide between FDR and the U.S. Army in 1941 over Grand Strategy in the event the United States entered the war. Though self-serving, the Army chiefs were becoming firm in their opinion that Germany could not be defeated without a large contribution by American ground forces in an invasion of the continent. But Roosevelt preempted the generals by endorsing Churchill's strategy, as eloquently set forth by the Prime Minister at the Argentia conference in August 1941, that sea and air power should carry the weight of offensive operations, and in fact in the end would win the day, with ground forces largely limited to providing support for insurgencies and resistance movements on the continent. Accordingly, until the Pearl Harbor attack, FDR's major initiatives were limited in nature, comprising a buildup of the Army for largely defensive purposes in the Western Hemisphere, the destroyer-bases deal, Lend-Lease, and aid to the Soviets, Atlantic naval patrols, and eventually the escorting of supply convoys in route to Britain.[3]

Domestic politics played a dominating role in determining Roosevelt's partiality for limited measures. Isolationism was a powerful force in the electorate and in Congress right up to the Pearl Harbor attack. Polls consistently showed that most Americans disapproved of sending an expeditionary force to Europe. Early in 1940 FDR denied that any public consent was necessary for American youth to fight in Europe, "for nobody expects such an undertaking." In July, and again in the heat of the 1940 election campaign, he reaffirmed his promise by publicly endorsing the relevant language of the Democratic Party platform: "We will not participate in foreign wars, and we will not send our Army, naval, or air forces to fight in foreign lands outside of the Americas, except in case of attack." Feeling the pressure of late campaign warmongering charges from the Republican challenger Wendell Willkie, the President uttered his best remembered disclaimer in a Boston speech just days before the election: "I have said this before, but I shall say it again and again and again: Your boys are not going to be sent into any foreign wars. They are going into training to form a force so strong that, by its very existence, it will keep the threat of war far away from our shores. The purpose of defense is defense." These campaign assurances were not altogether disingenuous. After the election he repeated his pledge, and until Pearl Harbor steadfastly held to the proposition that the dispatch of American ground forces to Europe was both politically undesirable and strategically unnecessary. A German defeat could be achieved without them.[4]

But in the autumn of 1941 the President found himself in a mounting predicament. On the one hand he had assured Americans of limited U.S. participation in the war. On the other he increasingly had used alarming and inflammatory rhetoric about the United States' strategic vulnerability and the absolute necessity for the utter conquest of Germany and Nazism. Yet General Marshall had spelled out for the President in September that the Allies could not obtain a sure and total victory without a massive assault on the European heartland by enormous British and American ground forces. This was the Army's famous Victory Program, which called for a buildup to 215 U.S. ground divisions. The Navy chiefs had by now grudgingly acceded to the Army's conventional logic. Stalin had also called for a Second Front on the continent as early as July and was unimpressed with any "peripheral" strategy by the Western powers. How was the President to extricate himself from this dilemma?[5]

One track—the one taken—was to muddle through and hope Hitler would lose patience with American naval escorts and precipitate a high seas crisis, which in turn could lead to full U.S. belligerency. Another option, which was becoming increasingly viable during the months of July to December, was quietly to consider a possible second track: to extend his present strategy of war by limited means into a war of limited means and limited aim. Politically, it would have been unnecessary for Roosevelt to announce any additions to his list of policy options, and he was most comfortable with ambiguity in policy. A rhetorical stress on defense, on the steady buildup of the armed forces, and on war production and material aid, coupled with a quiet policy of wait-and-see would have been sufficient, especially given the Army's inability to conduct major offensive operations—according to the War Plans Division of the War Department—until mid-1943.

What made a policy of containing Hitler conceivable was the Wehrmacht's difficulties in the Soviet Union. Though initially blitzkrieg warfare appeared as effective in the East as in the West, the USSR was not France, where encircled troops had acknowledged their hopeless condition and surrendered. The Soviets, deprived of central direction and having in hand the standing order to "attack the invader whenever and wherever he be encountered," continued to resist, to the amazement of German officers. Army Chief of Staff General Franz Halder noted the remarkable energy of the forces opposing Army Group Center and complained that "his endless flank and frontal attacks are causing us heavy losses." General Manstein described a trapped German patrol as having been "gruesomely mutilated," and the Soviet practice of infantry "throwing up their hands as if to surrender and reaching for their arms as soon as our infantry came near enough."[6]

Perhaps more important, hubris had plagued the German high command since their easy victories in the West. Thus Hitler and his generals never thought it necessary to reach an understanding on precise strategic aims. The armed forces high command (OKW) wished to rely on the great railroad line from Warsaw to Moscow for supplies, and hence expected to conduct major operations on either side of that line. The army high command (OKH) concentrated their attention on tank combat and the Soviet road network. The roads were better and more numerous north of the Pripet marshes, but terrain more favorable for tank combat was to be found south of the marshes and into the Ukraine. Hitler concerned himself with an Eastern empire and with ideology; in the south were oil and wheat, in the north the symbol of Bolshevism, Leningrad. General Halder wished to capture Moscow. The outcome of these conflicting aims was directive number 21, which provided for three army groups to proceed in general fashion toward all these objectives, along lines eventually to be separated by thousands of miles. The stated strategic aim was to destroy the Soviet forces before they could withdraw to the interior and to reach a line extending from Archangel to the

Caspian. The generality of this directive would lead to disagreements and indecision between panzer and infantry commanders, while the enlargement of the theater of operations would present intractable logistical problems.[7]

The General Staffs in Washington and London should have taken more notice of German logistical problems, both immediate and expected. Barbarossa was immense, involving 3.5 million German troops and hundreds of thousands of horses and vehicles. Supporting this mass required not only food, fuel, clothing, ammunition, spare parts, and other supplies, but also sufficient numbers of trucks and railroad cars to deliver them to the front. Yet it was well known that Soviet roads were few and poor; available trucks were also in short supply, and Soviet rails had to be converted to standard European gauge before use by German rail cars. In retrospect, only if the Wehrmacht had penetrated no more than 300 miles into the USSR and achieved victory within four to six weeks would logistical planning have been barely adequate. Otherwise the delivery problems (which came to include guerrilla raids and wet weather) would necessitate eventual retrenchment and a much longer war than planned. Resources from Romania and the Ukraine could not be exploited so soon.[8]

Meanwhile, early assessments of long-term Soviet chances by the War Department and the U.S. and British embassies in Moscow were largely negative. Yet even with the news of a rapid Soviet retreat, there were promising signs. On July 3, the U.S. Ambassador to Moscow, Laurence Steinhardt—no friend of the regime—reported on Stalin's public address of the day before, describing it as "reflecting a determination to fight to the bitter end, no matter what the cost." Muscovites were in good fighting spirit, he said. The Ambassador to Vichy France, William Leahy, sent word that French officials saw the invasion as an act of desperation and weakness, with Berlin fearing American involvement and failing to work its will in Europe without war. Even a retreat to the Urals, said one official, "would constitute a constant threat." Even at this early date FDR probably shared this kind of optimism. He quickly became receptive to proposals for aiding the Soviets, and he wrote to Leahy on July 26: "Now comes this Soviet diversion. If it means anything more than just that it will mean the liberation of Europe from Nazi domination."[9]

Some have in part explained Roosevelt's confidence about Soviet chances by pointing to the influence of his friend Joseph Davies, by now a Special Assistant to the Secretary of State.[10] Learning of the attack on the USSR, Davies told reporters that though Hitler might occupy portions of the Ukraine, "his troubles would then just begin." Indeed, "the Red Army would amaze and surprise the world." In early July Davies buttonholed Harry Hopkins, the President's closest advisor. He urged American material aid for the Soviets, promised to deliver "objective" reports on the Soviet military that he had written while in Moscow as U.S. Ambassador, and pointed on a map to the location of Soviet military factories behind the Ural mountains.[11]

As June faded into July the weight of informed opinion on Soviet fortunes began to deviate from a kind of self-satisfied pessimism. At the end of June the American embassy in Berlin contended that according to Nazi propaganda the Red Army was exerting "stubborn and even desperate opposition"; German tactical difficulties were "enormous." In Washington, Adolf Berle admitted that "no living thing can tell what will wash out of this." More important, Joseph Davies delivered his promised memorandum to Hopkins in mid-July. In it he conceded that if the Luftwaffe could dominate the skies, then Moscow could fall and White the USSR and the Ukraine would lose up to 60 percent of their agricultural resources and industrial production. Nevertheless, he wrote, there were situated in the Far East and the interior large, self-sufficient armies at Stalin's disposal; "enormous steel and aircraft plants" are about 1,000 miles east of Moscow; and the "Ural and Caucasus mountains afford a very strong natural barrier to a mechanized attack." If finally Stalin were compelled to withdraw to the interior, Hitler would face "three major problems": guerrilla warfare, sabotage by a nationalist population, and "the necessity of policing conquered territory and making it produce." In the end, he argued, the Soviet leadership could fight indefinitely from behind the Ural mountains.[12]

In fact by mid-July the German offensive was slowing considerably. Tough Soviet resistance, difficult terrain, and the slower-than-tanks infantry contributed. But telling were the vast spaces and the inadequate German supply system. The Wehrmacht was far from quitting, but the same could be said for the Red Army, which seemed continually to confront the Germans with fresh divisions.[13]

Through newspaper headlines and Soviet communiqués, Roosevelt and the rest of the world learned of the new blitzkrieg-without-the-blitz. As the *New York Times* wrote: "Nazi tanks go where the Golden Horde once ruled but the mud and dust may swallow them up too." Adolf Berle now believed the invasion was "already a failure."[14]

Even some in the War Department were having second thoughts. On July 28, Marshall, Major General Henry "Hap" Arnold of the Army Air Forces, and others on the General Staff met with Stimson and high War Department civilians to brief them on recent global developments, including the German offensive. The Germans had "stubbed their toe," recorded Stimson; the Wehrmacht had been stalled for a week and casualties were estimated at up to one million. The Soviets were "fighting very stubbornly," part of their success stemming from guerrilla action behind the lines that had "been very carefully prepared for beforehand." Marshall also kept the President up to date, informing him that inferior lubricating oil was responsible for a particular German aircraft engine wearing out after 120 hours of operation, and that "all the German tanks used the airplane engine." The tank engines should therefore wear out after only 200 hours, or about 40 days of campaigning. On August 1, FDR's confidence burst out publicly at a press conference. Soviet resistance, he exclaimed, "is magnificent, and frankly, better than any military expert in Germany thought it would be."[15]

In the coming months good news from the Soviet front would wax and wane. But buoyed by upbeat reports by Hopkins and Averell Harriman on their visits with Stalin, and by the continuing Soviet resistance that appeared ever more likely to last through the winter, FDR remained optimistic for all but brief periods. Then, finally, on the night of December 4, seventeen Soviet corps, many containing fresh troops from the Far East, went on the offensive all across the Moscow front. The Germans were forced to withdraw to positions sixty miles west of the city, where they eventually took up winter quarters. In the south General Timoshenko drove General Rundstedt's forces to positions forty miles from Rostov. A long war in Eurasia was all but certain.[16]

At the same time, as FDR and his military chiefs had observed on numerous occasions, the security of Great Britain and the British Navy were the linchpins to United States security. But by autumn it was clear that a German invasion of the islands in 1942 or 1943 would have presented Hitler with insurmountable difficulties, even if one had assumed a quick Soviet collapse. In November Churchill assured his military chiefs that if Germany prepared for an invasion, aerial photography would reveal the certain buildup of landing craft and other vessels in rivers and harbors. Local British air superiority would then permit daylight bombing attacks on these targets for two weeks or longer. If invasion craft survived and disembarked, then it was "reasonable to expect that naval resistance will be available in a very high form." If the Soviets did not collapse, then "the threat of invasion to our Island was removed."[17]

Nevertheless, Churchill believed that Hitler attached "more importance to starving us out than to invasion," and that British success in the Atlantic war was critical to final victory. Here also the Prime Minister viewed British chances with "solid reassurance." True, more U-boats were in operation, but British anti-submarine ships and aircraft were growing in number and their tactics were improving. More help came on September 16 when Roosevelt issued orders to the Navy to provide escort to British convoys. By autumn, "shipping losses were greatly reduced"; indeed, shipping losses for November in the North Atlantic were the lowest since May 1940.[18]

Clearly, on the eve of the Japanese aerial assault on the U.S. naval base in Hawaii, in fact for months previous, the Nazi threat to the Western Hemisphere had diminished substantially from that obtaining in the months before Barbarossa. Although a re-examination of the European policy aims of the United States was warranted, it did not occur.

That day, December 7, the President was presented with yet another opportunity to reassess America's strategic position and follow through on his avowed preference for a war of limited means in the European theater. Pearl Harbor could have served not simply as a release from official American nonbelligerency in the war against Hitler, but as a release from the constraining power of Roosevelt's previous public rhetoric, a rhetoric that demanded total victory. In short, he now had the opportunity to acquiesce in the public's hostility toward Japan, conduct a large-scale war in the Pacific, and shift his war aim in Europe from one of total victory to one of containment of German Nazism.[19] An armistice in Europe, once declared taboo, was again conceivable.

Doubtless a shift in war aims would have met with some resistance from within the Executive branch, segments of the Democratic party and Congress, and the more militant interventionist groups. But such resistance would hardly have been decisive. The Pearl Harbor attack was such a galvanizing event that it could have been exploited by the President to force his will on any holdouts. Certainly the Navy would have soon fallen into line since it was the Navy that would assume the principal role in fighting Japan. General Marshall and many of the Army chiefs would have been reluctant to restore the Army largely to a posture of hemisphere defense, but they too would have yielded, especially when it became clear that Britain was in no hurry to cooperate with a U.S. Army Grand Strategy that featured a massive cross-channel invasion of Europe. Moreover, the U.S. armed forces as a whole had lost some bargaining leverage after the debacle in Hawaii. Had he needed it, the failures at Pearl Harbor would have provided a convenient club for Roosevelt in any disagreements with the military.

Civilian interventionists, too, would have been displeased with any shift in Roosevelt's European war aims. Stimson and perhaps others in the administration (some of whom FDR had chosen in part for their hawkish views) might have resigned in protest if the shift had been mishandled. But FDR had made a career out of using ambiguity and of having subordinates work at cross purposes. For the moment it was needless to announce a clear-cut policy or strategy that might have risked precipitating a minor internal crisis. The Declaration of War against Germany, for example, still might have been issued, but could have been written in wooly and limited language. Then too, one should not exaggerate the power of the warhawks. Though one of their number, Roosevelt had often resisted their demands for all-out measures, whether over issues of war production, follow-up after inflammatory speeches, convoy escorts, neutrality repeal, indeed, over whether to declare war in the previous months of 1941. Finally, and perhaps most important, the overwhelming public anger toward Japan would have kept most dissenters quiet. Indeed, once Roosevelt in fact decided to hold fast to the principle of Germany as the chief enemy, he had some difficulty in persuading the American people of the soundness of his decision.

For several months polling results showed public dissatisfaction or apathy with the conduct of the war. In February 62 percent of those polled preferred a military concentration against Japan, whereas only 26 percent wished to see a concentration of military effort against Germany while holding Japan in check. In March, 88 percent of respondents hoped the United States would fight an all-out war against the Japanese wherever they could be attacked, and 62 percent versus 21 percent still believed it was more important to fight Japan than Germany. Almost half said they did not know what the United States was fighting for, though by July almost two-thirds believed they did know; of these, 27 percent believed the United States was fighting for ideological aims, while only 16 percent believed the nation was fighting a war for survival.[20]

Although FDR made attempts to counter these attitudes, he was up against news of military setback after setback in the Pacific and, in addition to public dissent, considerable dissent in the press. Criticism burst forth among both isolationist and internationalist newspapers in mid-January when Navy Secretary Knox held a press conference in which he attempted to reverse the public's obvious lack of enthusiasm for a war against Hitler. Germany was the principal power behind the Axis, Knox insisted; to conquer the Nazis was tantamount to conquering the entire Axis alliance. Therefore Germany must be defeated first, not Japan. The press reaction, however, was unfavorable, with most newspapers objecting that the war against Japan was at least as important as that against Germany. After the

Arcadia conference declarations to fight to the finish, and now Knox's speech, *Time* wondered in print if the two indicated "some kind of private war, Winston Churchill and Franklin Roosevelt against Adolph Hitler?" If so, it "would be a shock to U.S. civilians who had picked the Japanese as their enemy." There was also much editorializing about the lack of presidential military leadership and the need for offensive action, by sources that had been both hostile and friendly to the President. FDR felt the sting of these views, and they reaffirmed his belief that an offensive somewhere in the European theater was necessary to quell these rumblings of discontent and to redirect public attention toward Germany.[21]

Nor did the military and political realities in the European theater stand in the way of a thoroughgoing reassessment and shift in war aims. Nationalism had been an outstanding feature of European political and social life for well over a century and had arisen over most of the globe in the twentieth century. In early 1942 a European empire was no longer possible without Germany imposing a ruthless, totalitarian grip on all its subjects. But such a grip would have required not only enormous physical resources but also a unity of purpose and spirit, in conjunction with high morale, on the part of the Nazis and the German people. In the late twentieth century, and out of bitter experience, Western elites and especially professional soldiers have acknowledged and feared the demoralizing effect on a powerful nation of coping with endless insurgency and guerrilla warfare in foreign lands.[22] But such adversities were not alien from the thinking of British and American officials, especially that of Churchill and Roosevelt. Armies of occupation had always encountered difficulties with indigenous populations, and indeed Britain's preferred strategy—which FDR readily embraced at Argentina—relied on insurgent resistance on the continent for victory.

But more important, by early 1942 FDR need not have relied on nationalist resistance to ensure American safety. As mentioned, the Red Army had counterattacked all along the Eastern front, forcing the Germans to abandon most of their advance positions. There was some concern in Washington and London about a German spring offensive, but for the moment Roosevelt and Churchill were elated with the Soviets' success. Within two weeks of Pearl Harbor, British Air Chief Marshall Portal informed General Arnold that the Soviets were now producing 1,500 combat aircraft a month and had achieved air superiority over the entire Eastern front. What defeated the Germans, he said, was the Soviet ability to bring up reserves, a luxury the Wehrmacht lacked. The Prime Minister was sufficiently confident of Soviet staying power that he considered encouraging Moscow to begin hostilities against Japan, and in January expressed the opinion to his chiefs of staff that the degree of German suffering on the Eastern front might be enough to threaten the Nazi regime by spring.[23]

Britain also could look to the future with some assurance, whether or not the United States chose to support London's aim of total victory. Writing in his memoirs about those days after the Pearl Harbor attack, Churchill exuded confidence about the U-boat war and Soviet resistance. He believed Britain could maintain the security of her sea communications and "felt sure [the armed forces] could defeat Hitler if he tried to invade the island." Then too, even a limited American contribution would have been important. Limited options were numerous, but with only the addition of defensive air, sea, and ground forces in the Atlantic and British Isles, Germany stood little chance of infringing on British sovereignty. And without a massive U.S. ground army buildup, additional Lend-Lease resources would have been available for both Britain and the USSR.[24]

To be sure, from the statesman's perspective a defensive strategy of containing Germany might have eventually brought problems. One can speculate that after the defeat of Japan and the successful containment of Germany, a kind of treaty-less "cold war" might have ensued, with little hope of immediate resolution, and perhaps requiring American vigilance for years. But this is precisely the point. Other alternatives warranted consideration; costs and benefits needed weighing. It is conceivable that an "early day" George Kennan would have drawn conclusions similar to those of the real Kennan several years later when the United States confronted the USSR. That is to say, perhaps it was too costly to vanquish Germany militarily, but given the nature of Hitler and Nazism, political victory was probable if the United States could simply have mustered some patience. Hitler, the Nazi philosophy, and their totalitarian government needed enemies to conquer, as both Roosevelt and Churchill had acknowledged. Without them, the party's legitimacy would eventually suffer, possibly enough to result in the party's fall from power.

In 1942 Nicholas Spykman, a professor international relations at Yale, authored a book entitled *America's Strategy in World Politics*. In its pages Spykman was the first to give a scholarly and thoroughgoing exposition of the threat posed by Nazi Germany and the need to defeat it, framed in terms of geopolitics and the balance of power. Yet, paradoxically, he also acknowledged that so long as Great Britain and Soviet the USSR remained fighting, with their armed forces intact, Europe would "remain balanced."

The seeming paradox vanishes when the reader realizes that Spykman and later most "Realists" assumed that the war must end with a clear victor and a clear loser, and that the USSR and Britain had inadequate strength to achieve a decisive victory. There was no middle ground. If Germany were not crushed, then, inevitably, the United States faced eventual encirclement by hostile empires. On its face this assumption seems remarkable in retrospect, for many had spoken or written of a negotiated peace, and the famed British strategist B.H. Liddell Hart had even written a book extolling the advantages to Britain of conducting a defensive war of "limited liability." But after the war the all-or-nothing and "restore-the-old-equilibrium" assumptions became the prevailing dogma among Realists in the United States.[25]

As already observed, by the autumn of 1941, and especially by mid-December, there was actually an excellent probability that Europe would remain "balanced," or roughly balanced, without United States military intervention. If so, the Nazi threat to the Western Hemisphere—whether narrowly conceived as economic and military, or more broadly conceived as this plus the danger of political and ideological penetration—could have been readily controlled by the Americans through a limited war designed to contain German expansion.

Roosevelt and his advisors understood, or should have understood, these realities. Yet there is no evidence that they at any time stopped to take stock and reconsider war aims and Grand Strategy. Why? Because for Roosevelt and ardent interventionists, maintaining the balance of power in Europe was not the true aim. In truth Roosevelt's purpose became, as he had publicly pronounced, to "cleanse" the world of ideological extremism on the Right. From the outset of the war and certainly after the defeat of France, total victory was the only acceptable alternative, whatever the nature of the United States participation.

Well before June 1941, the President's mind had closed to the large questions. Barbarossa for him was not an opportunity to reassess interests and aims, but an opportunity to think more seriously about the ways to achieve total victory. The implications of the Victory Program were brushed aside. The Pearl Harbor attack also was not an occasion for careful reflection; instead it served as a release from much congressional and public opinion, perhaps a release from personal reservations about the evils of ground warfare, and thus as an opening for the United States to participate fully in total war. It served, too, as a release from his mounting policy predicament. In the months after the American war declarations, Roosevelt eagerly embraced Eisenhower's plan for a cross-channel attack and promised Soviet Foreign Minister Molotov a Second Front in Europe sometime in 1942.

For apologists to speak of FDR's concern for the security of the United States as an important reason for America's participation in total war is to ignore chronology and to confuse cause with what eventually became conscious or subconscious rationalization. Since the mid-1930s Roosevelt clearly was concerned about U.S. security, and for the thirteen months or so beginning in May 1940, concern was warranted. But from the outset of the war these concerns increasingly were fed by ideological and moral factors, not from any careful analysis of vital U.S. interests. Then too, concrete U.S. interests perhaps eventually took a back seat to Roosevelt's agenda of global collective security by means of the Four Policemen.[26] In any case, if even broadly conceived United States security interests had been of first importance, then a dispassionate and continuing reassessment would have occurred after 22 June 1941, and certainly after Pearl Harbor.

But what about the moral and ideological question? How can one seriously suggest the consideration of a limited policy that might have allowed a demon such as Hitler, and his philosophy, to have survived even for a short time? And what about global collective security? Was this ideal not worthy of the supreme effort?

In fact, the case for America's total war against Hitler and Nazi Germany was not so morally crisp as has been commonly assumed. First, the cost in blood and treasure of ensuring the destruction of the Nazis was going to be immense. For Nazism to have been in stark opposition to the American liberal ethos was not enough to justify full U.S. participation in a total war, unless perhaps the American people viewed Europe's "redemption" as the most worthy of aims and worth the necessary sacrifices. But this was not the case. Notwithstanding the rough ideological consensus among the public (and especially among the nation's elite), no consensus was reached by the early months of 1942 on just how far or in what way American ideals should affect the nature of the antagonism with Germany. A consensus was achieved only through the passions of war and by much domestic propaganda that finally persuaded most Americans not only of absolute Axis iniquity but also of the concrete Axis threat to the homeland.[27]

But for the sake of argument, even had the citizenry been fanatically idealistic, because of the near anarchy of the state system and America's still limited power, true leadership still demanded a healthy dose of political courage and dispassionate judgment. Even in the American democracy, the president, as first statesman and commander-in-chief, has an obligation to leaven any endemic ideologies that can result in policies harmful to the general welfare. In this vein, and in addition to the costs of the war proper, by autumn of 1941 the prospect of crushing Germany held out little hope that postwar Europe could be made to conform to American moral and political sensibilities. Would Americans, with their penchant for periodic and self-righteous isolationism, have proved willing to maintain a "redeemed" Europe long after the war, let alone the world?[28] Would Roosevelt's enforcement partners—Britain, the USSR, and China (or the Great Power members of a United Nations Security Council)—cooperate and act in accordance with American liberal standards and the demands of global collective security? The Soviet Union's likely status as a powerful postwar victor, coupled with its 1941 and 1942 territorial demands leveled at Britain, its political culture, and Stalin's history of realpolitik, suggested not; would an already weakened Britain and a divided China likewise have fallen short of Roosevelt and the public's expectations? If so, the United States government and its people would ultimately have proven unwilling and unable to alone enforce American standards everywhere.

This is not to argue that the consideration of a middle course would have come easily and naturally to Roosevelt, to the American military, or to Americans generally. Their political culture and traditional ethos often led Americans and their leaders instinctively to gravitate toward all-or-nothing solutions to the problems of war and peace, especially since the experience of Wilson after World War I. Limited war and policies for containment were largely unexplored concepts in academia, the press, and intellectual circles generally. Doubtless the mentality of the times helps explain FDR's single-mindedness before and during official American belligerency.

Neither is this intended to be an unabashed endorsement of limited war in the 1940s, nor, ultimately, an outright indictment of the content of Roosevelt's decisions. But to understand these realities is not to absolve Roosevelt for his narrow vision of statesmanship in 1941. A negotiated peace had been widely discussed, and Liddell Hart at least had reintroduced the notion of limited war to military men and statesmen alike. Many wars fought by the United States had been limited in both means and aim. Moreover, in his years as President, FDR demonstrated a fondness for fresh ideas and the unconventional. In other diplomatic contexts, one can envision Roosevelt seizing on the concept of a limited war for the containment of an aggressor. Indeed, the United States was engaged in a de facto defensive war of limited means after the passage of the Lend-Lease bill and the commencement of Atlantic naval patrols in the spring of 1941. The contention here is not that the President needed to reinvent the theory of limited war but merely that he should have at least considered a continuation of his limited means policy and a corresponding adjustment of his war aims.

Finally, the legacy of Roosevelt's policies is palpable and also must not be ignored. The World War II precedent of successful crusade and absolutism, boosted by America's historical self-image as moral and political savior, set the tone for American foreign policy in the Cold War years and beyond. Now communism replaced Nazism as the scourge of humanity. The emotive word appeasement, the symbolism of falling dominoes, the inflammatory and universalist rhetoric (though little could compare to Roosevelt's from 1940 to 1942), and the exaggeration of American ideological, military, political, and economic vulnerability were dusted off to justify another costly effort.

But in the end, and with the aid of faulty Communist economic doctrine, the Containment policy was successful. We should now acknowledge that a similar policy just might have been a wise one for the United States in its struggle with Hitler. At the very least it deserved a serious look. There were risks, as with any policy, but Franklin D. Roosevelt never gave it a thought.

Notes

1. See David Wyman, *The Abandonment of the Jews* (New York: Pantheon Books, 1984).
2. Harold Ickes, *The Secret Diary of Harold Ickes* (New York: Simon and Schuster, 1955), vol. 2, 213; Michael Sherry, *The Rise of American Air Power* (New Haven: Yale University Press, 1987), 78-80; Mark Watson, *Chief of Staff: Prewar Plans and Preparations* (Washington DC: Department of the Army, 1950), 136-139; H.H. Arnold, *Global Mission* (New York: Harper, 1949), 171-180.
3. Sherry, 91; Watson, 342–344, 400; Charles E. Kirkpatrick, *An Unknown Future and a Doubtful Present: Writing the Victory Plan of 1941* (Washington DC: Center for Military History, 1990), 77–102, passim; Arnold, 252; Theodore Wilson, *The First Summit: Roosevelt and Churchill at Placentia Bay, 1941*, rev. ed. (Lawrence: University of Kansas Press, 1991), 94–95.
4. Hadley Cantril, ed., *Public Opinion, 1935-1946* (Princeton; Princeton University Press, 1951), 267, 1128; George H. Gallup, *The Gallup Poll: Public Opinion, 1935-1971* (New York: Random House, 1972), 307; Robert Dallek, *Franklin D. Roosevelt and American Foreign Policy, 1932-1945* (New York: Oxford University Press, 1979), 310–311; Samuel I. Rosenman, ed., *The Public Papers and Addresses of Franklin D. Roosevelt* (New York: Random House, 1941-1950), vol. 8, 462, 557; and vol. 9, 415, 517.
5. A quick examination of Roosevelt's speeches will reveal his alarmist public discourse. For a discussion of this in a broader context, see John A. Thompson, "The Exaggeration of American Vulnerability," *Diplomatic History*, 16 (Winter 1992), 23–43; Watson, 354; see the Joint Board Strategic Estimate of September 1941 in Robert E. Sherwood,

Roosevelt and Hopkins: An Intimate History (New York: Harper, 1948), 413–417; for a copy of Stalin's message to Churchill on July 19, see Winston Churchill, *The Second World War: The Grand Alliance* (Boston: Houghton Mifflin, 1950), 383–384; also see U.S. Department of State, *Foreign Relations of the United States* (Washington, DC: USGPO), vol. 1, 1941, pp. 655–657.

6. Alan Clark, *Barbarossa: The Russian-German Conflict, 1941-1945* (New York: Morrow, 1965), 49–50, 54–56.

7. Ibid., 46; Martin van Creveld, *Supplying War: Logistics from Wallerstein to Patton* (London: Cambridge University Press, 1977), 148–149.

8. Ibid., 149–157.

9. FRUS, 1941, vol. 1, 628; Leahy to Sec. of State, 22, 23 June 1941, 740.0011 European War/12304, 12400, Record Group 59 (State Dept. Decimal file, National Archives, Civil Reference Branch); Elliot Roosevelt, ed., *FDR, His Personal Letters: 1928-1945* (New York: Duell, Sloan, and Pearce, 1950), 1177.

10. See, for example, William L. Langer and S. Everett Gleason, *The Undeclared War, 1940-1941* (Gloucester, MA: Peter Smith, 1953), 540; and Elizabeth MacLean, "Joseph Davies and Soviet-American Relations, 1941-1943," *Diplomatic History* 4, 1 (1980).

11. Joseph E. Davies, *Mission to Moscow* (New York: Simon and Shuster, 1941), 475–476, 487–489.

12. Morris to Sec of State, 30 June 1941, EW/12649, 13078, RG 59; Adolph Berle Diary, 23 July 1941, Franklin D. Roosevelt Library; Davies, *Mission*, 493–497.

13. Clark, chaps. 4–6; van Creveld, 160–180.

14. *New York Times*, 21, 24 July 1941; Berle Diary, 31 July 1941.

15. Henry Stimson Diary for 28 July 1941, microfilm edition from Yale University Library, Manuscripts and Archives, 1973; Morgenthau Presidential Diary for 4 August 1941, microfilm edition, University Publications of America, 1981; *Complete Presidential Press Conferences of Franklin D. Roosevelt* (New York, 1972), 1941, vol. 18, 72–73.

16. Clark, 172; Waldo Heinrichs, *Threshold of War: Franklin D. Roosevelt and American Entry into World War II* (New York: Oxford University Press, 1988), 213; Morgenthau Diary, 26 November 1941.

17. *Grand Alliance*, 513, 515, 537.

18. Stephen W. Roskill *The War at Sea, 1939-1945*, 4 vols. (London-Collins: 1955-62), 18; *Grand Alliance*, 516–523.

19. On concrete security grounds, the United States could also have fought a limited war in the Pacific, and given time this might have become a realistic possibility. But politically, the attack on U.S. territory would have made such an option a difficult one for any president to pursue.

20. Cantril, 1077–78, 1174–76.

21. *New York Times*, 15 January 1942; *Time* magazine, 26 January 1942, 12–13; for a discussion of public and press dissatisfaction, see Richard W. Steele, *The First Offensive, 1942: Roosevelt, Marshall and the Making of American Strategy* (Bloomington: Indiana University Press, 1973), 81–93.

22. This has almost grown into an article of faith among Western, especially American, statesmen, soldiers, and policy analysts so far as it pertains to popular morale. Sometimes overlooked, however, is the greater demoralization that eventually afflicts the counter-insurgency fighter and his organization. As pointed out by Martin van Creveld, *The*

Transformation of War (New York: Free Press, 1991), it is psychologically debilitating for any conventional army to grapple repeatedly with an outwardly weaker foe. According to van Creveld, the British victory in Malaya after World War II, and after a decade of low-intensity fighting, has been the only example of a successful counter insurgency.

23. *Grand Alliance*, 624, 627–628; FRUS, *Conferences at Washington and Casablanca, 1941-43*, 66–67, 224.

24. *Grand Alliance*, 641.

25. See Nicholas Spykman, *America's Strategy in World Politics: The United States and the Balance of Power* (New York: Harcourt Brace, 1942), especially pp. 11–40, 194, 450; Liddell Hart, *The Defence of Britain* (New York: Random House, 1939).

26. By 1944, however, and in the face of increasing public and bureaucratic excitement, FDR again was on record as supporting an international organization to preserve the postwar peace. In all likelihood electoral and Washington bureaucratic politics lay behind his decision to soft pedal Great Power collective security and instead publicly (and in his diplomacy) advocate a United Nations Organization. For the changing public and bureaucratic sentiment, see Robert A. Divine, *Second Chance: The Triumph of Internationalism in America during World War II* (New York: Atheneum, 1967). For the related role of domestic politics, see William C. Widenor, "American Planning for the United Nations: Have We Been Asking the Right Questions?" *Diplomatic History* 6, 2 (1982).

27. See Allan M. Winkler, *The Politics of Propaganda: The Office of War Information, 1942-1945* (New Haven: Yale University Press, 1978); John Blum, *V Was for Victory* (New York: Harcourt Brace, 1976), 15–52; and Clayton R Koppes and Gregory D. Black, *Hollywood Goes to War: How Politics, Profits, and Propaganda Shaped World War II Movies* (New York: Free Press, 1987).

28. At the Crimea conference in February 1945, FDR told Churchill and Stalin that American troops could remain in Europe for no longer than two years after the war's end. See Churchill, *Triumph and Tragedy* (Boston: Houghton Mifflin, 1953), 308.

5

Franklin D. Roosevelt and the Soviet Union 1933–1941

William E. Kinsella, Jr.

Millions of innocent victims perished in the Soviet Union during Stalin's terror in the 1930s. This chapter documents information recorded by American diplomats and military intelligence about these events that was sent to Washington in the years before entry of the United States into the Second World War. It also raises and analyzes three important questions: What knowledge did President Franklin Roosevelt have of these events in the USSR? What were his perceptions of the Soviet Union's domestic and foreign policies before 1941? How did these perceptions and other factors determine the evolving diplomatic and military relationship between the United States and the Soviet Union?

A wave of arrests and executions swept over the USSR months after William Bullitt, America's first Ambassador to the Soviet Union, arrived in Moscow. Sergei Kirov, Leningrad Party chief, was murdered on December 1, 1934, marking the beginning of Stalin's Great Terror. John Wiley noted how precipitously the leaders in Moscow departed for Leningrad after the shooting. A law was passed immediately stating that in terrorist cases there would be no clemency, and executions would be carried out without delay. Sixty-six persons were shot by December 6, and within a month that number had risen to one hundred seventeen. The OGPU, later known as the NKVD (People's Commissariat for Internal Affairs, 1934-1943), under Genrikh Yagoda arrested eight hundred of its personnel in Leningrad. Wiley noted that the trials were conducted in secrecy and were based largely on confessions. It was obvious to Wiley that "the murder has been used by the Kremlin as an excuse to liquidate the dying adherents of communism."[1]

William Bullitt's views of the underlying facts concerning the Kirov murder were contained in a dispatch to Secretary of State Cordell Hull dated April 26, 1935, which was then forwarded to President Roosevelt. The murder of Kirov, Bullitt reported, resulted from a personal affair involving his wife and her relationship with the assassin. Stalin, who had selected Kirov as his successor, was not only angered but saw the murder as a pretext that could be used to rid himself of those he perceived to be his rivals and adversaries. Bullitt concluded his comments noting that "the arrest and exiling of innocent human beings in all quarters of the Soviet Union continues apace." Roosevelt responded, "That was a fascinating story. Do write me often." A month later Bullitt observed that "the terror, always present, has risen to such a pitch that the least of the Muscovites, as well as the greatest, is in fear."[2]

The extent of this first phase of the terror was more fully presented in dispatches filed with the State Department. John Wiley noted that the regime was determined to stamp out oppositionist ideology at all costs after the Kirov affair. Reports circulated of 20,000 arrests in Leningrad and 60,000 in Moscow. Ambassador Bullitt reported that deportations to Siberia and Central Asia were increasing every day. He described the Orenburg rail station as a concentration camp with hundreds of deportees arriving daily. The Ambassador also noted that the death penalty for terrorism included children from the age of twelve. Loy Henderson observed, "probably in no country of the world has such a large percentage of the population served prison sentences at some time or another during these postwar years." [3]

The Seventh All-World Congress of the Communist International convened in Moscow from July 25 to August 20, 1935. Ambassador Bullitt considered the Comintern proceedings a flagrant violation of Litvinov's pledge to the President not to conduct propaganda against the United States. He urged Roosevelt to give him advance notice "so that I can send out of the country by courier our code books, confidential dispatches, and telegrams before our Soviet friends grab them. They are entirely capable of behaving like Bolsheviks." Ambassador Bullitt cautioned against breaking diplomatic ties. America required an organization in Moscow "to measure and report on the increasingly noxious activities and breach of faith of the Soviet Union." President Roosevelt approved a note of protest issued on August 23, 1935, warning of serious consequences should further acts violate the solemn pledges given to the United States government. Assistant Secretary R. Walton Moore told Bullitt that the President had reached the conclusion that it was best to do nothing further at this moment, adding that Roosevelt had acted "very independently" and was not swayed by any individual.[4]

William Bullitt departed the USSR in the spring of 1936. He summarized his views on the Soviet Union in a dispatch dated April 20, 1936, which was sent to President Roosevelt. He described communism as a militant faith intent on the liquidation of all non-believers, and the Kremlin as presiding over the murder of millions. He cautioned that the United States should never be do deluded as to think that genuinely friendly relations would ever be possible with the Soviet Union. The Ambassador was more succinct in a letter to Judge Moore. Bullitt noted that the Soviet government was again exiling people on a grand scale; he added that "Russia is a good country for pine trees, St. Bernard dogs, and polar bears, and I must say frankly that I long to be at home again."[5]

The purges intensified with the trial on August 19, 1936, of sixteen prominent Party officials, including Zinoviev and Kamenev, allegedly members of a terrorist organization. R. Walton Moore sent a dispatch written by Loy Henderson describing the trial to Franklin Roosevelt on September 22, 1936. Moore noted that this was the "best brief description I have seen of what was certainly one of the most remarkable trials that ever occurred. So far as I can recall, there is no record in either sacred or profane history of defendants charged with crime vying with each other in a very dramatic and eloquent way, not only to confess guilt, but to claim priority in doing what was done or sought to be done." He added that Ambassador Troyanovsky "seemed to be about as much at a loss as anyone else in explaining the attitude of the defendants, some of whom he knew well and rated very highly." Henderson wrote that the trial was beautifully staged with the Prosecutor, Andrei Vyshinsky, exceedingly well-groomed and highly theatrical in manner. Vyshinsky reminded Henderson of Lionel Barrymore acting in one of his favorite roles as a criminal lawyer. Henderson wrote, "I began to feel that I was looking at a circus director putting a group of well-trained seals through a series of difficult acts." The prisoners, watching the prosecutor during their confessions to make sure they made no mistakes in addressing the court, confessed to conspiring to kill Stalin, Kirov, Voroshilov, and prominent Party leaders. Henderson described their confessions as "carefully memorized orations" given "with all the fervor of collegians engaging in an oratorical contest." The defendants appeared to expect the death sentence and not a one displayed any sign of emotion when the court announced it. Henderson doubted the existence of any plot, or that Trotsky was involved, or that the German police had any connections with the defendants. Henderson concluded by noting that the immediate execution of all sixteen defendants had made a profound impression, and that a wave of fear, almost equal to that following the assassination of Kirov was sweeping over the country. Hundreds of individuals had been arrested on charges of disloyalty and were being tried in secret.[6]

Judge Moore forwarded a second memorandum by Loy Henderson to Franklin Roosevelt. Henderson, described by Moore as "one of the most intelligent men in our service," reviewed Soviet-American relations on the third anniversary of recognition, November 16, 1936. Moore concluded from the document, and so advised the President, that while it was wise to recognize the Soviet Union in support of the cause of world peace, "we are compelled to proceed very slowly in placing our relations with that Government on an approximately satisfactory basis, because of so many obstacles being encountered, due to the novelty of the political system that has been set up in Russia, and the peculiar mentality of those who are in charge of it." Henderson discounted the value of a more tolerant policy. The ultimate objective of the Soviet Union was the creation of a Union of World Soviet Socialist Republics, a "factor not to be ignored in any discussion of Soviet-American relations." Its immediate objective, continued Henderson, was "the establishment of Moscow as the capital of the foremost world Power and as the director in peace or war of the activities of the world revolutionary forces in all countries." [7]

U.S.-Soviet relations were strained during these early years of the evolving relationship. Visiting Washington briefly in 1935, Ambassador Bullitt wrote John Wiley saying that the executions in the USSR had produced an "astonishing effect" in the United States; that he had not met a single American who had offered a "good word" for the Soviet Union; and that even the enthusiasts for recognition would not support it now. Recognition "unquestionably would be disapproved by the entire nation," predicted the Ambassador. He noted that "thank God" the feeling against tyranny and summary executions remains in the United States. Bullitt concluded in saying "Litvinov probably doesn't know it, but a snotty policy toward us now would be resented by this country much more violently that at any time since recognition."[8]

Franklin Roosevelt's efforts to improve relations with the Kremlin began with the selection of an ambassador to replace William Bullitt. Bullitt had written R. Walton Moore saying that Joe Davies, the likely candidate, could not be counted on to handle the Soviet situation in a serious manner, and that Robert Kelley, presently Director of the State Department's Division of Eastern European Affairs, was the only man in the entire diplomatic service capable of directing the Embassy in Moscow. President Roosevelt appointed Joseph Davies as Ambassador to the Soviet Union in November 1936.[9]

Roosevelt directed Davies to assess the Soviet Union's strength and to determine what side it would join in the event of conflict. He was told to approach the USSR from a position of dignified friendliness and definite reserve. These instructions were later revised by the President as he urged Davies to pursue a "Good Neighbor Policy" toward the USSR. Davies interpreted this policy as one "based not upon a critical and intolerant attitude that induces irritation, but upon an attitude of tolerant understanding of the difficulties under which the officials here are laboring."[10]

Davies's appointment was not favorably received by professional diplomats knowledgeable about conditions in the Soviet Union. Charles Bohlen thought Davies to be sublimely ignorant of the most elementary realities of the Soviet system and its ideology. George Kennan saw the Davies appointment as a political plum in return for campaign contributions. Kennan believed that if the President had wished to slap down the diplomatic officers in Moscow, he could have done it in no better way than by sending Davies. The Embassy staff considered resigning in protest.[11]

The selection of Ambassador Davies was one action designed to improve relations with the Soviet Union. The Eastern European Division was also to be merged with the Western European Affairs Division. Criticism of negative reporting about the USSR first appeared in 1936. Arthur Bliss Lane complained about the Soviet specialists in Riga who "have come to think in terms of Russia as a separate entity, rather than in terms of Russia's relationship to Europe and to the rest of the world." He thought that "these specialists, through the very nature of their research work, acquire an academic attitude, akin to that of a student preparing a doctor's thesis, and, as a result, they tend to become unfitted for the substantial duties with which the Service as a whole has to deal. Short assignments to Latin America, for instance, would give these officers a valuable sense of perspective which I fear many of them now sadly lack, and would likewise give them an opportunity to tackle practical problems." R. Walton Moore criticized the "unnecessarily voluminous" reporting from Moscow, asking Bullitt how it might be curtailed. Loy Henderson wrote to John Wiley on June 30, 1936, stating that "internally things are sizzling" in Moscow, but the Embassy lacked a reporting staff. He regretted that interest in the Soviet Union was at a very low point in Washington so that the reports were not quite as frequent and thick as they were "in the good old days." The decision to merge the Eastern European Affairs Division with the Western European Affairs Division in June 1937 was taken six months after a Soviet official notified Ambassador Joe Davies that certain quarters in the State Department were opposed to working out any agreement with the

USSR. Loy Henderson warned of Moscow's campaign against the Division of Eastern European Affairs and against diplomats who failed to present a true picture of the situation to their superiors because of what Soviet officials deemed their reactionary outlook. William Bullitt regretted the decision to eliminate Robert Kelley's division. He described the division as a source of profound knowledge and "by far the most efficient agency in any government" for understanding the Soviet Union. The division's books, periodicals, and newspaper files were moved to the Library of Congress by department officials hurriedly attempting to save their valuable research.[12]

The arrival of Ambassador Davies in the USSR coincided with the beginning of the second show trial. The defendants were alleged to have organized the Anti-Soviet Trotskyite Center. They were accused of terrorism, sabotage, wrecking, and espionage. Davies was convinced that the government had overwhelmingly established its case because all defendants confessed to the charges, and had done so in an open courtroom. He found it extraordinary by Western standards that there should have been a trial. Prosecutor Vyshinsky offered a scholarly and able presentation, said Davies. The Ambassador was convinced of a widespread conspiracy and plot. There was a ruthlessness and cruelty in the application of the laws, but also a fine idealistic humanitarian purpose to aid and bring up the standard of living of the underprivileged, wrote the Ambassador. Davies stated that "they will continue to make men free even if they have to kill every man in the country to do it."[13]

Ambassador Davies instructed George Kennan to make a "brief formal abstract" of the trial proceedings, with a description of each crime not to exceed one sentence. Davies wrote as an example, "Three mine explosions by blank, blank, blank." Kennan noted that the trial was based not on evidence, but confessions, and that the testimony seemed incomplete, conflicting, and ambiguous. He doubted that there was ever a terrorist organization, and believed that the conspiracy charge rested on very shaky foundations. He thought that the accused had confessed to save their own lives or persons near to them. Kennan added that the police had no shortage of raw material to force confessions. Davies, referring to Kennan as an exceptionally able man, noted that certain references to testimony were contrary to his own memory of the trial record. George Kennan would soon be sent to Washington at the request of Ambassador Davies for health reasons.[14]

Henderson reported a wave of arrests in April 1937, including Yagoda and many members of the NKVD. No one knows, he said, who will be the next to disappear, or whose head will be the next to fall. Writers, historians, security personnel, government and Party officials were targeted for arrest. By June, the purges were affecting every field of Soviet politics, government, education, science, literature, and the fine arts. Lists of victims numbering in the hundreds were sent to the State Department. Whole commissariats, wrote Henderson, were being ripped to pieces. Hundreds of thousands were disappearing in the Soviet republics, while thousands of Party, Komsomol, and trade union members were being purged. Henderson reported that every department head in the law school at Moscow University had disappeared. Lecturers were afraid to appear before their classes, fearful of arrest for a misguided statement.[15]

Ambassador Davies and Military Attaché Philip Faymonville were shocked when on June 11, 1937, it was announced that eight senior army commanders, including Marshal Tukhachevsky, were being charged with plotting a coup against Joseph Stalin. Germany, it was alleged, had recruited the Soviet generals for this purpose. These men, said Faymonville, devoted their adult lives to the Soviet state. This plot, he continued, was beyond the dreams of even German espionage. He believed it was a Party-Army conflict, as the latter resisted demands for submission to Party discipline. Henderson thought that Stalin intended to eradicate all persons endeavoring to acquire too much personal power and prestige. Henderson added that no foreign observers accepted their guilt. Stalin had begun a purge that would eliminate tens of thousands of army and navy officers.[16]

Rumors circulated that Stalin was the "sick man in the Kremlin" behind the terror. These rumors were discredited by Ambassador Davies. Stalin was a healthy, normal, clean-living, modest, retiring, and single-purpose man with a one-track mind. He was an "easy Boss" devoted to communism and the elevation of the proletariat. Davies said that Stalin was not held personally responsible for the purges, and was the driving force behind the secret ballot, universal suffrage, and freedom of religion articles in the new constitution. Loy Henderson's description of Stalin was noticeably different: extraordinarily vain, loving of flattery, vengeful, never forgetting real or imagined slights, jealous, suspicious, crafty, and hot-tempered. Stalin directed Yezhov's NKVD in the expanding purge operations.[17]

In October 1937, Henderson reported that the purges were seeping into all nooks and corners of the Soviet state and Party structure. Tens of thousands had disappeared; the overwhelming majority had passed off the scene and would never return. He attached a list of two hundred victims to the dispatch, including 41 Central Committee members, 9 Politburo members, 14 Union commissars, 44 assistant commissars, 23 army officers, 16 ambassadors, and names of statisticians, writers, professors, scientists, engineers, heads of industry, directors of factories, telegraphic agency and State Bank employees, and members of the Komsomol youth organization and trade unions. Loy Henderson noted that the purges were also sweeping away the leadership of the Soviet Republics. Davies regretted that "their many fine ideals are being besmirched by this horrible blood letting." The Ambassador agreed that thousands had been executed and hundreds of thousands arrested, but that dangerous elements existed. Industry would gain by removing many malefactors. However, he noted that the purges "undoubtedly removed a greater proportion of innocent from office than guilty."[18]

Henderson sent an additional list of one hundred purge victims to the State Department in January 1938. He noted that the provincial press listed five hundred executed in October 1937, three hundred in November, and two hundred in December, but that these numbers were only a fraction of those executed. Attaché G.B. Guenther reported that 35 percent of the officer corps had been eliminated including 2 marshals of 5; 3 first category army commanders of 6; 10 second category army commanders of 13; 57 corps commanders of 85; 110 division commanders of 193; and 207 brigade commanders of 406. In later dispatches, Guenther asserted that the purge of the navy was as deep, with the execution of commanders of the Baltic Sea, Black Sea, Pacific, and Arctic fleets, the Amur Flotilla, and leaders of the Naval Academy.[19]

The third show trial began on March 2, 1938. It included three members of Lenin's Politburo—Bukharin, Rykov, and Krestinsky—the former head of the NKVD, Yagoda, and other prominent communists. Their crimes were espionage, wrecking, terrorist activities, and plotting to kill Lenin and Stalin. Ambassador Davies noted the calm and lack of passion in the proceedings; the credibility of the confessions and witnesses; and the reasonableness of the testimony. He was convinced of their guilt. He added that although the terror was nothing new in Russian History, everyone felt its present horror. He noted that some Russians actually apologized on behalf of their leaders who they maintained regretted the deaths and were themselves suffering from "tired hearts."[20]

The purges continued throughout 1938. Alexander Kirk conservatively estimated that 80 percent of the Soviet government, Party, and military leaders had been executed, arrested, or dismissed in the past two years. There was a growing fear of being liquidated, especially in the higher ranks of the Party. He noted that there were no ex-commissars in the Soviet Union. Personnel in Machine Building, Food Industry, Trade, Light Industry, Agriculture, Water Transport, the Komsomol, NKVD, and in the Party and state institutions of the Republics continued to suffer in large numbers. Kirk attended the Eighteenth Congress of the Communist Party in 1939 and reported that of 71 Central Committee members in 1934, only 16 remained; and of 139 candidate members, only 24 returned. There had been a reduction of 285,636 Party members.[21]

The mass terror began to subside in the early months of 1939. Alexander Kirk stated that no outstanding official had been arrested since the removal of Nikolai Yezhov in December, and his subsequent arrest and replacement by Levrentia Beria. He reported many arrests of NKVD officials. He predicted, however, that leniency would not be extended to those who opposed Stalin, and that NKVD procedures would not be modified in the slightest degree. Ambassador Steinhardt, Davies's successor after his departure in June 1938, notified the State Department on August 14, 1939, that the USSR had returned "more or less" to normal after a wave of purges and arrests.[22]

Several days later, the USSR and Germany signed the Nazi-Soviet Non-Aggression Pact, and within weeks German and Soviet troops invaded Poland. Red Army troops and NKVD units moved quickly into Poland, Estonia, Latvia, and Lithuania. Arthur Lane wrote that events in Poland were similar to those in the early days of the Russian Revolution. Landlords, clergy, intelligentsia, white-collar workers, military officers, and government officials had been arrested and either sent to concentration camps or executed. Guenther reported executions of Ukrainians and Poles, and the mass deportation of Poles in locked cars and trucks. Kirk urged the Red Cross to use its influence to free interned Polish doctors. Steinhardt reported that large numbers of Poles were being sent to Siberia, Kazakhstan, and Archangel, and that many were suffering from malnutrition and starvation. Kirk gave the number of deported Poles as more than 200,000. John Franklin Carter wrote to Roosevelt saying that "many thousands" of Polish professors, scientists, army officers, police officials, and judges had been arrested. The President expressed concern about the safety of Foreign Minister Jozef Beck, believing that he could be executed by either German or Soviet authorities. The Vatican, in a detailed report that included explicit descriptions of tortures inflicted by Soviet authorities on Catholic ecclesiastics, informed President Roosevelt of the deportations and executions of clergy taking place in the Soviet-occupied Baltic countries and Poland.[23]

Numerous dispatches filed with the State Department offered extensive coverage of the Soviet Union's terror in Estonia, Latvia, and Lithuania. John Wiley in Riga noted the wave of arrests, and predicted purges and public trials in the Moscow manner. Owen Norem in Kaunas and Steinhardt depicted similar events in Lithuania. Reports of repression in Estonia were filed by Lewis Gleek in Helsinki and Hershel Johnson in Stockholm. Gleek described mass arrests, prisoners forced into freight cars for deportation, and the execution of political prisoners and professional specialists. By the time the Soviets evacuated Estonia on November 23, 1941, 58,000 inhabitants had been arrested and deported. Mass murders were reported in Dorpat, Arensburg, and Narva. Leland Morris wrote that the economies in the Baltic countries were devastated. Practically all merchandise had disappeared. Machines, woolen and cotton clothing, textiles, butter, and cheese had been sent to the USSR.[24]

In the Soviet Union by 1941, the dictatorship of the Communist Party and its security forces had achieved the complete submission of societal and state institutions by force and violence. Military attaché Ivan Yeaton wrote that "the entire USSR is simply one large concentration camp from which there is no escape and control lies in the NKVD, locally known as the People's Commissariat for All Affairs." Attaché Joseph Michela described the NKVD as the check and balance weapon of the government with agents to be found in all institutions. He depicted the ruling hierarchy as cunning, shrewd, cruel, and unscrupulous with policies based on expediency only. He suggested that any approach to the Soviet Union must be accompanied by a forceful, decisive, blunt, almost rude, and even contemptuous personal demeanor.[25]

A retaliatory and hostile approach to the Soviet Union would not serve America's vital interests. Franklin Roosevelt's aim of defending America's security, given the threat posed by Germany and Japan, depended on the survival of the Soviet Union. The President's task was extraordinarily difficult for he was dealing with a ruthless and opportunistic regime. America's diplomats assessing Soviet foreign policies, including the Soviet Union's limited involvement in the Spanish Civil War, its discredited promises of support for Czechoslovakia during the Munich crisis, the neutrality treaties signed with Germany and Japan, and the invasion of Estonia, Latvia, Lithuania, Poland, and Finland did not view the Soviet Union as a collaborative force in the Western coalition. Stalin's aim was to advance the Soviet Union's strategic interests either by aggression against weaker nations, or by engaging the armed forces of the major powers in conflicts that would not initially include Soviet armed forces.[26]

German and Japanese aggression shaped the course of U.S. foreign policy toward the Soviet Union before the Second World War. President Roosevelt was steadfast in his determination to convince Stalin that the

Kremlin's security would best be achieved if the USSR joined the democratic coalition against fascism. Roosevelt's support of Stalin's request for battleships to be built in the United States, his offer of a military liaison with Soviet authorities, and his secret message urging the Kremlin to join Great Britain and France during the Moscow negotiations in August 1939, were intended to influence the Soviet Union's future alliance decisions.[27]

The Nazi-Soviet Pact and the Soviet invasion of Finland prompted President Roosevelt's harshest criticism of the Stalin regime. He denounced its "indiscriminate killings of thousands of innocent victims," and described the Soviet government as a dictatorship as absolute as any other dictatorship in the world. When the Soviet government failed to respond to Roosevelt's warning about bombing raids in Finland, denied Embassy officials access to the American crew of the *City of Flint* merchant ship in Murmansk, and forced U.S. diplomats to be searched by customs officials, the President issued a formal remonstrance. He termed the actions "a complete disregard for the ordinary politeness and amenities between civilized governments." He suggested that "we should match every Soviet annoyance by a similar annoyance here against them." Roosevelt cautioned, however, that "when it comes to the larger questions of downright rudeness on the part of Stalin, Kalinin, or Molotov we cannot afford to repay such rudeness with equivalent rudeness over here." Steinhardt was advised to communicate "that the President honestly wonders whether the Soviet Government considers it worthwhile to continue diplomatic relations."[28]

Germany's offensive in Europe and the fall of France in the spring of 1940 muted Washington's official criticism of the Soviet Union. Undersecretary of State Sumner Welles and Ambassador Oumansky began negotiations in July 1940 to restore a more friendly dialogue. Predictions of a German invasion of the USSR came from reliable sources. Roosevelt assumed these reports were credible and informed Oumansky in early 1941. The attack on the Soviet Union commenced on June 22, 1941. The President, rejecting State Department guidelines stipulating a reserved response to the USSR based solely on reciprocity, followed the counsel of Winston Churchill and promised America's support to the Soviet Union in the common struggle against Hitler.[29]

Franklin Roosevelt, uncertain of the outcome in the USSR, fearing a separate peace between Hitler and Stalin, and concerned about a possible Japanese attack on the USSR, embarked on a program of emergency aid to the Soviet Union. Harry Hopkins was sent to Moscow to inform Stalin on behalf of the President that he considered Hitler the enemy of mankind and therefore wished to aid the Soviet Union in the fight against Germany.

During the Atlantic Conference in August 1941, Churchill and Roosevelt agreed on sending a British-American mission to determine Soviet military requirements. Averell Harriman and Lord Beaverbrook arrived in Moscow in September 1941. Roosevelt, with Lend-Lease aid to the USSR approved by Congress, urgently pressed responsible government agencies to fulfill Soviet requests as enumerated by Harriman. The President had earlier told Secretary of War Stimson, "I deem it to be of paramount importance for the safety and security of America that all reasonable munitions help be provided for Russia, not only immediately but as long as she continues to fight."[30]

Germany's attack on the USSR brought a troublesome and truculent ally into the democratic coalition. FDR explained his decision to aid the Soviets in a letter to Pope Pius XII. The President believed that the Soviet Union was governed by a dictatorship as rigid as the dictatorship in Germany, but that the Soviet dictatorship was less dangerous to the safety of other nations. Germany, said Roosevelt, had embarked on a program of military aggression outside of its borders for the purpose of world conquest by force of arms. The survival of the USSR, concluded Roosevelt, was less dangerous to humanity in general than would be the survival of the German form of dictatorship. Averell Harriman thought that the President's decision to help the Soviets was a simple matter of American self-interest. George Kennan described collaboration with Soviet Russia in 1941 as one of the tortured compromises of the democracies made necessary by Western military weakness. Franklin Roosevelt would have agreed with both statesmen.[31]

Notes

1. Wiley, 12/3/34, 861.00/11572; 12/24/34, 861.00/11576; 12/26/34, 861.00/11586 (decimal notations hereafter refer to Department of State files in the National Archives).

2. Hull to FDR, May 16, 1935, enclosing Bullitt to Hull, April 26, 1935, no. 552, President's Secretary's File, Diplomatic Correspondence, Russia, Franklin D. Roosevelt Library (hereafter cited as PSF, DC, FDRL); and FDR to Bullitt, June 3, 1935, Orville H. Bullitt, *For the President Personal and Secret: Correspondence between Franklin D. Roosevelt and William Bullitt* (Boston: Houghton Mifflin Co., 1972), 121; and Bullitt to FDR, May 1, 1935, PSF, DC, Russia, FDRL.

3. Wiley, 1/19/35, 861.00/11589; 3/22/35, 861.00/11599; Bullitt, 4/29/35, 861.00/11602; 4/24/35, 861.108/15; Henderson, 11/20/35, 861.108/17.

4. Bullitt to Moore, July 15, 1935, and Moore to FDR, August 1, 1935, enclosing Bullitt memorandum on Comintern, Box 3, R.Walton Moore Papers, FDRL; Bullitt to FDR, August 3, 1935, PSF, DC, Russia; FDR to Bullitt, August 14, 1935, PSF, DC, Russia, FDRL; Moore to Bullitt, September 3, 1935, Moore Papers, Box 3, FDRL; and George Baer, ed., *A Question of Trust, The Origins of U.S.-Soviet Relations: The Memoirs of Loy*

W. Henderson (Stanford: Hoover Institution Press, 1994), 356–365. Bullitt's advice not to break relations is in 8/21/35, 861.00/Congress Communist International VII/57. Protest note is in 8/23/35, 8/25/35, 861.00/Congress Communist International VII/72.

5. Bullitt to Hull, 4/20/1926, no. 1537, sent to Roosevelt, PSF, DC, Russia, FDRL; and Bullitt to Moore, March 30, 1936, Moore Papers, Box 3, FDRL.

6. Moore to FDR, September 22, 1936, enclosing Henderson to Hull, September 1, 1936, PSF, DC, Russia, FDRL. Henderson's dispatches on the trial are 8/18/36, 861.00/11629; 8/27/36, 861.00/11630; 9/1/36, 861.00/11636; 12/31/36, 861.00/11652; 12/31/36, 861.00/11653.

7. Moore to FDR, January 16, 1937, PSF, Departmental File, State, FDRL; enclosing Henderson to Hull, November 16, 1936, Baer, ed., *Question of Trust*, 465–468.

8. Bullitt to Wiley, 1/7/35, Box 2, John Wiley Papers, FDRL.

9. Bullitt to R.W. Moore, June 15, 1937, Box 3, Moore Papers, FDRL.

10. Bullitt to Moore, 6/15/1937, Box 3, Moore Papers, FDRL; Davies, 8/28/36 Diary, Box 3, Joseph Davies Papers, Library of Congress; Diary, with FDR, 1/2/37, Joseph Davies, *Mission to Moscow* (New York: Simon and Schuster, 1941), 6–7; and 861.00/11787, 6/6/38, Supplementary Report to Hull from Davies.

11. Charles Bohlen, *Witness to History, 1929-1969* (New York: Norton, 1973), 45, 52; George Kennan, *Memoirs 1925-1950* (Boston: Little, Brown, 1967), 82–83.

12. Arthur Bliss Lane to R.W. Moore, and Moore to FDR, 9/23/36, Box 17, Moore Papers, FDRL; Moore to Bullitt, 3/19/36, Box 3, Moore Papers; Henderson to Wiley, 6/30/36, Box 7, Wiley Papers, FDRL; Davies to Hull 2/18/37, *Mission to Moscow*, 65; and Bullitt to Hull, 7/19/37, Box 41, Cordell Hull Papers, Library of Congress.

13. Davies, 1/29/37, 861.00/11659; and 2/17/37, 861.00/11676.

14. Davies instructions to Kennan, 2/16/37, 861.00/11671; Davies critical comments, 2/18/37, 861.00/11675; and Kennan's analysis is in 2/18/37, 861.00/11675. Davies's request for Kennan's transfer is in Davies to Robert Kelley, 2/10/37, Box 3, Davies Papers, LC; Davies's letters on the terror to FDR are 2/24/37, Box 3, 7/10/37, Box 5, and 4/4/38, Box 7, Davies Papers, LC.

15. Henderson, 4/29/37, 861.00/11702; 6/10/37, 861.00/11705; 6/13/37, 861.00/11692; 6/15/37, 861.00/11694' 6/21/37, 861.00/11708; remarks of Davies are in 6/28/37, 861.00/11704.

16. Faymonville expects some guilty officers, 6/1/37, MID 2037–1780 (MID notations are to military intelligence dispatches on file at the National Archives); shocked by purges, 6/12/37, MID 2037–1833; 6/17/37, MID 2037–1833; 10/16/37, MID 2037–1833. See also, J.S. Herndon and J.O. Baylen, "Col. Philip R. Faymonville and the Red Army, 1934-1943," *Slavic Review*, 34, no. 3 (September, 1975): 483–505. Henderson, 5/13/37, 861.20/384; 6/8/37, 861.20/385; 6/11/37, 861.20/387; 6/13/37, 861.20/390; 6/23/37, 861.20/406; 9/30/37, 861.20/429; and see 6/1/37, 861.00 Communist All Union Central Executive Committee/54. Ambassador Dodd in Berlin said sources there had no knowledge of a conspiracy, and were "bewildered," see Dodd, 6/15/37, 861.20/394.

17. Davies, 7/28/37, 861.00/425; Davies, *Mission to Moscow*, 66–68, 193; and Henderson, 6/10/37, 861.00/11705.

18. Henderson, 10/2/37, 861.00/11734; 10/2/37, 861.00/11735; 12/23/37, 861.00 Party All Union Communist/193; and Davies, 11/16/37, 861.00/11739; and Davies to Marvin McIntyre, October 5, 2937, Box 6, Davies Papers, LC.

19. Henderson, 1/7/38, 861.00/11750; 1/12/38, 861.105/16; 1/25/38, 861.00/11754; 2/8/38, 861.651/17; Guenther, 7/26/38, MID 2037–1833; 10/7/38, MID 2037–1833. FDR did not view the Soviet military as an offensive threat to Europe, see Anthony Biddle to FDR, 4/18/39, "Russia not an effective strike force," cited in Donald Schewe, ed., *Franklin D. Roosevelt and Foreign Affairs* (New York: Clearwater, 1979), 14: 354–359; Bullitt to Hull, 2/13/39, purges resulted in execution of all leading Russian aircraft designers, ibid., 13: 307–313; FDR to Arthur Murray, 8/24/39 "frankly, I do not believe Russia would have given much substantial aid," ibid., 16: 284; FDR to William Leahy, 6/26/41 "I do not think we need to worry about any possibility of Russian domination," Box 3, William Leahy Papers, Library of Congress.

20. Davies, 2/28/38, 861.00/11755; 3/2/38, 861.00/11757; 3/4/38, 861.00/11760; 3/13/38, 861.00/11758 and 11761; 3/17/38, 861.00/11774 and 11775; and final report in 6/6/38, 861.00/11786. "Tired hearts" is in Davies, *Mission to Moscow*, 405.

21. Kirk, 7/20/38, 861.00/11791; 8/8/38, 861.00/11792; 8/13/38, 861.50/893; 11/13/38, 861.50/901; 11/23/38, 861.00B/689; and 4/13/39, 861.00 Party All Union Communist/221.

22. Kirk, 4/12/39, 861.01/2156; and Steinhardt, 8/14/39, 861.50/920.

23. Lane, 10/23/39, 740.0011EW/1054; 10/26/39, 740.0011EW/1055; Guenther, 1/18/40, 860C.00/802; Kirk, 8/8/40, 860C.00/863; Steinhardt, 5/13/41, 860C.48/706; Wiley, arrests in Poland, 7/12/40, 860i.00/435; FDR's concern for Beck is in FDR to Welles, 9/19/40, PSF, Departmental Correspondence, State, FDRL; Anthony Biddle, 12/10/41, 861.131/33; and J.F. Carter to FDR, 10/17/41, 11/21/41, 11/26/40, 11/30/41, PSF, Subject File, FDRL. Roosevelt was also informed of Soviet efforts to recruit Poles to spy in the United States, see Steinhardt, 11/5/40, 861.20211/67 in PSF, CF, Russia, FDRL.

24. Wiley, 6/26/40, 860P.00/283; 7/15/40, 860P.002/145; Norem, 7/15/40, 860M.00/450; 7/25/40, 860M.00/457; Gleek, 12/11/41, 860i.00/472; Johnson, 12/27/41, 860i.00/479; Steinhardt, 3/28/41, 860M.00/471; and Morris, 12/3/40, 860n.00/72.

25. Yeaton, 1/29/40, MID 2037–4552; and Michela, 4/14/41. 4/16/41, 4/18/41, MID 2037–1552; and 6/2/41, MID 2037–2324.

26. Soviet action in the Spanish Civil War is in Claude Bowers to FDR, 12/16/36; 3/31/37; 2/8/39 ("thus do the Russian hordes evaporate in the sun"), PSF, DC, Spain, FDRL; the Soviet role during the Munich crisis is in A. Kirk, 8/29/38, 760F.62, no. 614 (Russia desires that the costs should be "borne principally by others"), PSF, Confidential File, Russia, FDRL; Kirk, 9/11/38, 760F.62, no. 726; 9/16/38, no. 853; 9/22/38, no. 986, PSF, CF, Russia, FDRL; "Russia will not join England and France, preliminary discussions Nazi-Soviet Pact" see S. Grummon, 5/24/39, 741.61, no. 662 ("no anti-German coalition"), PSF, CF, Russia, FDRL; J. Kennedy, 5/8/39, 740.00, no. 1381 and 6/9/39, no. 1684, PSF, CF, Great Britain, FDRL; J. Grew, 2/27/41, 761.95, no. 1283 (USSR to promote a Japanese-American war), PSF, CF, Japan, FDRL.

27. Battleship issue is in Thomas Maddux, "United States–Soviet Naval Relations in the 1930's: The Soviet Union's Efforts to Purchase Naval Vessels," *Naval War College Review*, XXIX (Fall 1976): 28–37; military liaison is in Davies to Hull, 1/17/39, 800.51W89USSR/247, and Box 9, Davies Papers, LC; secret message is Welles to Steinhardt, 8/4/39, 741.61/824A; Welles to Bullitt, 8/4/39, 741.61/826; Steinhardt to Welles, 8/16/39, 741.61/828 1/2.

28. FDR, Memorandum for Hull and Welles, December 22, 1939, PSF, DC, Russia, FDRL. Roosevelt's official policies pertaining to the attack on Finland were restrained, see Edward Bennett, *Franklin D. Roosevelt and the Search for Security, American-Soviet Relations 1933-1939* (Wilmington, DE: Scholarly Resources, 1985), 180–187.

29. FDR's warning to Oumansky, see Hull to Steinhardt, 2/28/41, 740.0011EW, no. 8656 ("clearly indicating" attack "in the not distant future"); Thomas Maddux, *Years of Estrangement: American Relations with the Soviet Union, 1933-1941* (Tallahassee: University Presses of Florida, 1980), 139–140; analyses of dispatches and uncertainties preceding German attack (including Dr. Erwin Respondek–Sam Woods) is in Waldo Heinrichs, *Threshold of War, Franklin D. Roosevelt and American Entry into World War II* (New York: Oxford, 1988), 21–22, 89–96. State Department guidelines on the USSR are 6/13/41, 740.0011EW1939, No. 11970.

30. Japan attack on the USSR, see Steinhardt, 6/20/41, no. 12252 and 9/22/41 no. 15301 (attack unlikely unless the Soviet Union disintegrates), PSF, CF, Russia, FDRL; W. Averell Harriman and Elie Abel, *Special Envoy to Churchill and Stalin, 1941-1946* (New York: Random House, 1975), 76–105; on Lend-Lease and the USSR see Raymond Dawson, *The Decision to Aid Russia, 1941* (Chapel Hill: University of North Carolina Press, 1959), 285. Churchill to FDR, 6/14/41 urging aid to the USSR, and Churchill to FDR, 9/5/41 warning of separate peace, FDR to Churchill, 10/15/41, Japan moving north, see Heinrichs, *Threshold of War*, 171, 191.

31. FDR to Pope Pius XII, 9/3/41, PSF, DC, Vatican: Myron Taylor, FDRL; Harriman, *Special Envoy*, p. 74; and George Kennan, *American Diplomacy 1900-1950* (Chicago: University of Chicago Press, 1951), 77, 87. Joe Davies recalled Roosevelt's words concerning aid to the USSR "that threatened by Hitler's fascism, we could hold hands with the Devil himself," see Davies to McIntyre, 4/4/38, Box 7, Davies Papers, LC. An excellent study of this period (1933-1941) is John Lewis Gaddis, *Russia, the Soviet Union, and the United States: An Interpretive History*, 2nd. ed. (New York: McGraw Hill, 1990), 117–143.

6

FDR and the Baltic States

Maris A. Mantenieks

To most Americans, the name of Franklin Roosevelt conjures up an image of mythical proportions, an image of a man whose virtues encompassed the highest standards of statesmanship. On the other hand, to many of the older generation of Baltic and other East Europeans, mention of President Roosevelt evokes memories of the Yalta Conference, which is has become synonymous with what many view as betrayal during the final months of World War II.

Certainly Roosevelt remains a controversial figure. Arthur Schlesinger Jr., one of Roosevelt's ardent admirers, has listed qualities attributed to him by both his admirers and critics, in an article entitled "The Man of the Century." Schlesinger's list identifies FDR as, among other things, an isolationist, internationalist, appeaser, warmonger, impulsive decision maker, incorrigible vacillator, savior of capitalism, and closet socialist. It also characterizes him as a Machiavellian intriguer plotting to embroil his country in foreign wars, as well as a Machiavellian intriguer avoiding war in order to let other nations bear the brunt of the fighting. In addition, he is viewed as a dreamer who thought he could charm Stalin into postwar collaboration, but who ended up giving away Eastern Europe and the Baltic states. Finally, he is listed as a tightfisted creditor sending Britain toward bankruptcy, a crafty imperialist serving the interests of American capitalism, and a high-minded prophet whose vision shaped the world's future.[1] Such divergent opinions of his character illustrate the enigmatic nature of the man.

This study attempts to shed some new light on the statecraft of Franklin Roosevelt through an investigation of his attitudes and policies regarding the Baltic states, especially insofar as they played a role in the Great Power diplomacy of World War II. The subject of the Baltic states has been dealt with rather casually in most accounts of the World War II period, thus minimizing its true significance in Big Three diplomacy. Most often the Baltic states are only referred to in the context of the Nazi-Soviet Pact of 1939, which assigned the Baltic territories to the Soviet sphere of influence. Sometimes they are obscurely hidden as "Stalin's territorial demands" or the "Soviet 1941 frontiers." Few writers have attributed much historical significance to them during the World War II period. Most refer to the historic fact that for long the U.S. government, beginning with the Roosevelt administration, refused to recognize Stalin's annexation of the Baltic states into the Soviet Union in 1940. Some have gone as far as to argue that had the United States acquiesced to the Soviet demands during the Roosevelt administration, the Cold War might have been averted. Such a view is expressed by one of the well-known revisionist historians, William Appleman Williams. He argues that:

> Having reestablished its traditional authority over the Baltic States in 1939 the Soviet Union fully expected and intended to retain that control after the defeat of Hitler. In the discussions that took place during the winter of 1941-1942, however, the United States refused to return to its original position (that of 1918-1922). Stalin's blunt reaction to being blocked on this issue by Hull and Roosevelt casts an exceedingly bright light on the subsequent tension between East and West. [2]

Had the West given in to Stalin on the Baltic states, Williams claims, "certainly the postwar era would have developed in a significantly different manner."[3] This position has also been taken by others, such as Bennett[4] and Kissinger.[5] More balanced comprehensive accounts of the Baltic issue have been written by Miner and Gardner.[6]

By analyzing Roosevelt's thought and actions with regard to the Baltic states, this study attempts to demonstrate how they ironically played a significant part in changing him from a Wilsonian idealist at the beginning of the war, to a believer in realpolitik at the end of the war—to the great detriment of the Baltic states. The full story of the Baltic involvement in Big Power politics may never be written. The records of several meetings between Roosevelt and Soviet diplomats in which the Baltic question was discussed have not been found in American archives. Only the Soviet accounts are available. In contrast to the high visibility of the Baltic issue during the early war years, with the beginning of 1943 as the political realities began to change, it was relegated to an insignificant role.

Roosevelt, the Wilsonian, Refuses to Recognize Soviet Annexation of the Baltics

American interest in the Baltic states began in 1919, in an indirect manner, a year after the Baltic states had declared their independence from the USSR. As a consequence of the Bolshevik Revolution and Washington's antipathy to the Bolsheviks, American diplomats were expelled from the USSR as the Soviet government came to power, thus cutting direct channels of information accessible to the U.S. government. Washington realized the shortcomings of the situation and began to search for a place from which a reliable source could be found. The State Department established a center for the study of Soviet affairs in the Office of the Commissioner of the United States for the Baltic Provinces of the USSR in Riga, Latvia. The office began operating in Riga in 1919 and started supplying Washington with information from the Soviet Union, thus becoming an important Western "window" to the Soviet Union.[7] American officials, such as George Kennan, Loy Henderson and Charles Bohlen, whose names only later became recognized, served in the Soviet section in Riga. Despite being given a convenient observation post on the Soviet Union, the United States offered no support for Baltic independence aspirations. Wilson's famous Fourteen Points were not intended for the Baltic states. According to the Wilson administration, Russia was to remain, with several exceptions, indivisible.[8] For this reason Washington referred to the Baltic states as The Baltic Provinces of Russia. The United States finally recognized the Baltic states only in 1922 under the Hoover administration.

Almost twenty years later, in September and October of 1939, when the USSR imposed mutual assistance pacts under severe pressure with Estonia, Latvia, and Lithuania, the American administration interpreted it as directed against Berlin and accepted the infringement upon the independence of the Baltic states as a means of avoiding diplomatic protests.[9] Cordell Hull, the U.S. Secretary of State, disingeniously rationalized the government's lack of action thus: "Since nominally Estonia, Latvia and Lithuania retained their government and independence, there was no diplomatic step we felt called upon to take."[10] However, in a memo to a Finnish minister, Hull admitted that the Soviets "had assumed military domination of these two countries [Latvia and Estonia]."[11] It is during this period that the Roosevelt administration made a major diplomatic decision that would not only affect

Big Power policy in the years to come, but also leave an indelible impact on the fate of the Baltic states. Washington decided to keep its knowledge of the secret protocols of the Hitler-Stalin Pact secret until the end of the war.[12]

World opinion turned sharply against the Soviet Union after its attack on Finland. By this time Roosevelt had gained confidence and Soviet aggression was finally condemned by the President. On October 11, a memo from the President was sent to Moscow requesting "that the Soviet Union will make no demands on Finland which are inconsistent with the maintenance and development of amicable and peaceful relations between the two countries." Later, the President issued another blast at the Kremlin: "The news of the Soviet naval and military bombings within Finnish territory has come as a profound shock to the government and the people of the U.S. . . . to the great misfortune of the world, the present trend to force makes insecure the independent existence of small nations in every continent and jeopardizes the rights of mankind to self-government."[13] Especially abhorrent to the President was the Soviet bombing of civilian targets. To punish the Soviet Union, the President imposed a "moral embargo" on the Soviet Union.

On 10 February 1940, the President addressed the American Youth Congress. He proclaimed that the "Soviet Union, as everybody who has the courage to face the fact knows, is run by a dictatorship as absolute as any dictatorship in the world. It has allied itself with another dictatorship, and has invaded a neighbor so infinitesimally small that it could do no conceivable possible damage to the Soviet Union."[14] After the Nazis invaded Denmark and Norway in April of 1940, Roosevelt declared, "If civilization is to survive, the rights of smaller nations to independence, to their territorial integrity, and to the unimpeded opportunity for self-government must be respected by their more powerful neighbors."[15] Was this also a warning to Stalin?

Hull explained to Oumansky, the Soviet ambassador in Washington, that "my government will be glad, whenever the USSR sees fit, to return to a set of policies to develop more fully the relations of peace and mutual profitable cooperation in every practical way." In other words, Washington was ready to improve relations if the Soviets stopped being a bully. However, the news from the Baltic and Romania gave no indications that Stalin was about to stop carrying out his plans just to please Washington. The Red Army occupied the Baltic states in mid-June. When the Baltic diplomats in Washington requested to meet with the Secretary of State Hull, the delicate status of American-Soviet relations did not allow for such pleasantries. They were turned down. Zadeikis, Bilmanis, and Kaiv–the Lithuanian, Latvian, and Estonian ministers respectively–however, submitted strong protests to the State Department regarding the heavy-handed tactics in the Baltic.[16] In mid-July, Soviet style elections were held that were used as a justification to annex the Baltic states to the Soviet Union.

On July 15, longtime friend of the Baltic people Loy Henderson, Assistant Chief of Division of European Affairs, addressed a memo to Berle, the Assistant Secretary of State and J.C. Dunn, Advisor on Political Relations, criticizing American inaction with respect to the Baltic states:

> Recent events in the Baltic states have raised a number of rather important questions. Among these questions are the following: Is the Government of the United States to apply certain standards of judgment and conduct to aggression by Germany and Japan which it will not apply to aggression by the Soviet Union? In other words, is the Government of the United States to follow one policy with respect to, say, Czechoslovakia, Denmark, and German-occupied Poland, and another policy with respect to Latvia, Estonia, Lithuania and Finland, which before the end of the year is likely to suffer the same fate as the other three Baltic states? Is the United States to continue to refuse to recognize the fruits of aggression regardless of who the aggressor may be, or for reasons of expediency to close its eyes to the fact that certain nations are committing aggression upon their neighbors?[17]

The administration this time acted quickly. The Treasury blocked the bank accounts of the Baltic states on the July 15.[18] On July 23 the State Department issued a press release, refusing to recognize the annexations:

> During these past few days the devious processes where under the political independence and territorial integrity of the three Baltic republics–Estonia, Latvia and Lithuania–were to be deliberately annihilated by one of their more powerful neighbors, have been drawing rapidly to their conclusion. The people of the United States are opposed to predatory activities, no matter whether they are carried on by the use of force or by the threat of force. They are likewise opposed to any form of intervention on the part of one State, however powerful, in the domestic concerns of any other sovereign State, however weak.[19]

Thus, the government of the United Sates did not consider the annexation by the Soviets as legal in terms of international laws and norms. Sumner Welles, the Undersecretary of State, added that the United States "would continue to recognize the Ministers of the Baltic republics as the ministers of sovereign governments now under duress." By August 22, the U.S. chargé d'affaires in Moscow had received an official protest from Molotov attacking Washington's nonrecognition policy.[20] On August 31, Hull rejected the Soviet protest.[21]

On 15 October 1940, Roosevelt declared to a delegation of Lithuanian-Americans: "[You say] that Lithuania has lost her independence. It is a mistake to say so. Lithuania did not lose her independence–Lithuania's independence was only temporarily put aside. . . ."[22] Similar support was given by Roosevelt when President Smetona met with him on 18 April 1941.

Roosevelt's "Decision that Shaped the World"

In order to better understand the development of the Roosevelt administration's diplomatic policy, it is of importance to discuss the position the administration took with regard to the Soviet Union in August 1939 after the signing of the Hitler- Stalin Pact.

Roosevelt was a Wilsonian at heart at the beginning of the war.[23] He had formulated two tenets before the United States ever entered the war. First, he was a staunch believer in self-determination and the plebiscite. This belief manifested itself in the Atlantic Charter and the United Nations Charter. The second was that all territorial settlements should be decided at the peace conference at the end of the war. The President believed in these concepts strongly and hoped that the Allies would follow them too. The Stimson Doctrine, a corollary of the self-determination principle, remained the nation's firmest conviction. The doctrine was formulated by the Secretary of State Henry L. Stimson in January 1932, regarding territorial infractions during a conflict between Japan and China. On 11 March 1932 the League of Nations adopted a resolution, based on the Stimson Doctrine, by which the League condemned and refused to recognize any forcible seizure of territory by one state from another. The U.S. refused to recognize any Japanese territorial acquisition by force in Asia, including Manchuria. Likewise, the United States did not recognize the Italian conquest of Ethiopia, and later the Roosevelt administration rejected the Soviet annexation of the Baltic states.

There is no doubt how the first principle originated. Roosevelt was an admirer of Woodrow Wilson from an early age; he had served in his administration. The answer to the origins of the second principle regarding the territorial issue is not as clear. Most writers believe that Roosevelt's views were influenced by the flawed results of the Treaty of Versailles because of the secret territorial deals made during the war that complicated the negotiations at the peace conference. This view is given by Hull in his memoirs.[24] Some believe that Roosevelt did not want to make the same mistakes made by Wilson in announcing the Fourteen Points before gaining support for them from other Allies. However, this has been discounted by others.[25] Some maintain that Roosevelt wanted to postpone territorial settlements after the war so as not to disrupt the unity of the Allies during the war. This view was supported by Assistant Secretary of State Sumner Welles. He referred to "the decision to postpone political and territorial decisions until after the War" as one of the "Seven Decisions that Shaped History" in his book of the same name.[26] According to Welles, "the decision was based almost entirely on military factors in whose evaluation I played no part."

In reference to Eden's trip to Moscow in December 1941, Welles recounted Stalin's demand that Britain "formally commit herself to the recognition of the Soviet Union's 1941 frontiers as established by Stalin's 1939 deal with Hitler." Welles continued, "the issue was, of course, clear-cut certainly in the case of the Baltic states, it would violate the spirit as well as the letter of the Charter. From our standpoint in Washington such an agreement was unthinkable."[27] Welles thus acknowledged that the issue was also a moral one. Welles defined the "military factors" as the immediate dangers of the controversies with the USSR that might be aroused by engaging Stalin in territorial talks and having to reject his frontier demands. But the administration already had reaped the wrath of Stalin by officially not recognizing the Baltic states annexations and applying pressure to the British to do the same in 1942. Thus the "military factor" was not a military issue at all, but rather a case of arousing the ire of Stalin.

Welles himself, not considered a hard-liner against the Soviets by any means, discounted the "dangers of the controversies with the USSR" and was against the policy of postponing the political and territorial issues until after the war. Even though his influence reached the White House, he apparently never spelled out his opposition on the issue. He stated, "the more I read about the negotiations of 1919, the more I was convinced that our wisest course would be to try to work out with our allies now, before V-day, as detailed an agreement as possible. Our armed strength, our material resources, the moral authority of President Roosevelt and, even more perhaps, our allies' need of us, would give us infinitely greater leverage now

[1942] than we could have after the victory was won." He continued that "the immense influence that we possessed after Pearl Harbor was not exercised. When we did attempt to negotiate political settlements, our influence was no longer decisive."

Welles observed that from the standpoint of the United States, only Stalin's demand for the incorporation into the Soviet Union of the Baltic republics would have been "unacceptable." He argued that "On this point it is doubtful whether Stalin in the winter of 1943 would have proved altogether obdurate. . . . It is, therefore, by no means unreasonable to assume that we might have solved this one basic difficulty if we had broached the matter in the early days of the joint war effort and given him some assurance of security against a future attack by a rearmed Germany. . . . After the winter of 1943, following the victory at Stalingrad and the eventual German retreat, the Russian armies rapidly occupied the territory Stalin claimed. The moment for negotiations was gone. So it happened that at the moment most effective, it was not exerted." This proposition was in fact suggested to Roosevelt by William Bullitt[28] early in 1943 but was rejected by the President.

Welles believed that the agreements of Teheran, Yalta and Potsdam would have been far different had the President in 1942 insisted upon the creation of a United Nations Council charged with finding solutions for political and territorial problems before the end of the war. His decision not to do this was dictated by his conviction that as Commander-in-Chief his paramount mission was to win the war. Welles concluded, however, that with the advantage that hindsight gives us, it seems fair to say that this decision was "largely responsible for the division of the world today into two increasingly warring camps."[29]

A question arises as to why the two State Department officials would advance such divergent reasons for the same important issue. Hull's version is a plausible one. One might argue how similar the geopolitical-political positions were during World Wars I and II. Welles has to be commended for recognizing the importance of the territorial question, though his explanation is a clumsy one.

The difficulty encountered by Hull and Welles in explaining the origins of the territorial issue may lie in the fact that the two were writing under a constraint imposed by a policy that was decreed to be classified secret at the time.[30] In his autobiography, published in 1973, Charles Bohlen disclosed that he was receiving information directly from the German Embassy in Moscow regarding the progress of the talks between the Soviet Union and Germany in 1939. According to Bohlen's account, Washington was kept informed of Nazi-Soviet negotiations since May 16. Bohlen writes, on August 24, "[Jonny Herwath] gave me the details of the ten year pact. He said that a 'full understanding' had also been embodied in a secret protocol whereby eastern Poland, Estonia, Latvia and Bessarabia were recognized as spheres of Soviet vital interest, while Western Poland would fall under German hegemony. . . ."[31] Roosevelt knew of the secret protocols from their inception. This was the "missing link" with which Hull and Welles had to deal.

The fact that Roosevelt knew of the secret protocols from their inception raises some interesting but unanswered questions. How did the administration interpret the pact? Why did Roosevelt keep this knowledge a secret during the war? Was it only to avoid embarrassing Stalin? How did this knowledge influence Roosevelt in dealing with the Soviets? Was Washington's interference in Anglo-Soviet relations during 1942 the only time? Did Stalin know that Roosevelt was so informed? In fact, why did Hitler keep the secret, knowing full well that the information would be injurious to the Allies cause?

The British Seek to Improve Anglo-Soviet Relations with the Baltic States as Bait

Early in 1940 the English were having a difficult time deciding whether to go to war with the USSR or make friends with Moscow. Churchill and Chamberlain had been strong and vocal critics of the Soviet Union. The Hitler-Stalin Pact did not sit well with most of the British. The quick advances of German forces in the West, however, swayed the British to take the latter course. Sir Stafford Cripps was sent to Moscow on June 12 in an attempt to reach improved relations with the Soviets. Cripps met with Stalin on July 1, delivering a personal message from Churchill. Stalin was not impressed. Cripps was convinced that the British recognition of the Baltic states annexation by the Soviet Union was a definite way of establishing friendship with Stalin. In fact, as Miner points out, Cripps "became obsessed with arguing the Soviet case in the Baltic States dispute."[32]

Welles's announcement of not recognizing the Soviet annexation of the Baltic states was, however, duly noted by the British Foreign Minister Lord Halifax. He recalled that fact while recommending to the War Cabinet that such action (recognition of the annexation) by the British would be "premature."[33] On September 9, Halifax reached an agreement with the War Cabinet that "American benevolence" (Land-Lease aid) was of "far more value than the somewhat illusionary benefits of the goodwill of the USSR."[34]

On December 12, Lord Lothian, the British Ambassador in Washington, died and was replaced by Halifax. Halifax's position was filled by Anthony Eden. During the next several months, Anglo-Soviet relations remained strained.

On 10 February 1941, Hull informed Halifax that Washington was extremely interested in the course that France and Britain might make with regard to the Soviet Union.[35] No doubt this message set the British on edge. Eden reestablished Soviet discussions on 17 April 1941. The Foreign Minister asked the Soviet Ambassador in London, Maisky, what the Soviets would give "on basis of reciprocity" for concessions on the Baltic states. Maisky suggested that Eden make a list and submit it to Stalin.[36] When Washington got wind of Eden and Maisky's discussions (Eden had not volunteered the information), Hull sent Steinhardt, the American Ambassador in London, a concise American policy statement in regard to the Soviet Union and told him to inform Eden of it. The statement in part read:

> We have adopted the following: To make no approaches to the Soviet Government. . . . To reject any Soviet suggestions that we make concessions for the sake of "improving the atmosphere of American-Soviet relations. . . ."[37]

Halifax quickly assured the State Department that the British policy would be "identical" with that of the Americans.[38] There is no doubt that the "concessions" Hull is talking about refers to the Baltic states.

On 22 June 1941, Hitler broke his pact with Stalin and attacked the Soviet Union, thus scrambling the world alliances. In a day the Soviet Union became an ally of the West. The new alliance rejuvenated the spirit of Cripps in Moscow. He met with again Stalin on July 8. On July 10, Halifax inquired of Washington whether there was any opposition to a mutual assistance pact between Great Britain and the Soviet Union. Hull replied that he would not oppose such an agreement. However, he stated that it would be desirable for Halifax to be authorized to assure him specifically that no secret provisions were being included in the agreement negotiated.[39] Hull's memo clearly demonstrated that Washington had no objections to improving Anglo-Soviet relations as long as no "concessions" or no "secret agreements" were included. Eden was personally visited by Hopkins and Winant. According to Eden: "They told me that Roosevelt was most eager that we should not commit ourselves to any definite frontiers before the peace treaty. Hopkins explained that the U.S. would come into the war and did not want to find after the event that we had all kinds of engagements of which they had never been told." The intrusion of American diplomacy did not sit well with the British. Eden lamented that "the spectacle of an American President talking at large on European frontiers chilled me with Wilsonian memories."[40] An agreement between London and Moscow was signed on 12 July 1941 with no secret provisions.

The Baltic States and the Atlantic Charter

Despite British assurances that there were no secret agreements reached, Washington was skeptical. Such a concern was expressed by a Berle memo to Roosevelt:

> It is now evident that preliminary commitments for postwar settlement of Europe are being made, chiefly in London. Perhaps you are being informed. I am not clear that the State Department is being informed of all of them by the parties. Some have been told to us by the British; others we hear about. . . . I have suggested to Sumner [Welles] that we enter a general caveat, indicating that we would not be bound by any commitments to which we had not definitely assented.[41]

Persuaded by Berle, the President sent the following memo to Churchill on July 14:

> I know you will not mind my mentioning to you a matter which is not in any way serious at this time, but which might cause unpleasant repercussions over here later on. I refer to rumors which are, of course, nothing more nor less than rumors regarding trades or deals which the British Government is alleged to be making. . . . I am inclined to think that an overall statement on your part would be useful at this time, making it clear that no postwar peace commitments as to territories, populations or economics have been given. I could then back up your statement in very strong terms. . . . [42]

Gardner correctly concludes that the issue refers to Moscow's demand to recognize the annexation of the Baltic states. The British were in no hurry to respond to Roosevelt. The delay may have resulted from a meeting soon to be held between Roosevelt and Churchill to discuss "matters of common interest."

The two leaders met in secret aboard British and American naval vessels off the coast of Newfoundland on August 9. The conference had a codeword–"Arcadia." On the first day of the conference Welles's tersely reminded Sir Alex Cadogan, Welles counterpart, "that some six weeks ago the President had sent a personal message to Mr. Churchill expressing the opinion that the British government should make no secret commitments to any of its allies without the knowledge of the United States." Welles told Cadogan that as yet no reply had been received. Cadogan answered "that was one of the main matters which Mr. Churchill desired to take up with the President . . . that he would give the most specific and positive assurance that the British had entered into no agreements and had made no commitments which had to do with frontiers or territorial readjustments."[43]

A declaration was born during this conference known as the Atlantic Charter. The idea of a declaration seems to have been sprung on Churchill by Roosevelt on the opening day of the conference. The main motives of Roosevelt have been well established. He wanted a pledge from the British that they had not and would not enter into "secret treaties," and would ensure self-determination for all nations. On the last day of the conference Cadogan asked Welles if Roosevelt would still like the public disclaimer that the President had requested in a letter to Churchill. Welles replied that in view of the Eight Point Declaration "that it would be entirely superfluous and he was sure that the President would not wish for anything of the sort."[44] In mid-September the State Department replied to notes the Baltic ministers had sent to the State Department early in September. The message stated:

> That in the joint declaration agreed upon by the President of the United States and the Prime Minister of Great Britain during their historic meeting at sea, it is stated that the United States and Great Britain respect the right of all peoples to choose the form under which they desire to live and that the United States and Great Britain wish to see self-government restored to those peoples who have been forcibly deprived of it. [45]

The sequence of events and directives from the President and the State Department indicated that the eagerness of the British to recognize the annexation of the Baltic states was one of the major motivations for the Atlantic Charter's coming into being. It was also made clear that

Washington expressed no reservations that the Baltic states were covered by the Atlantic Charter.

In the fall of 1941 a bitter exchange of words took place between Churchill and Stalin. Eden was to be sent to Moscow to iron out the tense Anglo-Soviet relations. On December 4, Winant informed Washington of Eden's intended visit to Stalin. Upon the urging of Washington he requested Eden to prepare a memo regarding the purpose of the trip. Eden complied. Item number seven on Eden's' list struck an alarm bell in Washington. Hull sent a reply to Winant the next day to be read to Eden personally:

> In so far as our postwar policies are concerned, it is our belief that these have been delineated in the Atlantic Charter which today represents the attitude not only of the United States, but also of Great Britain and of the Soviet Union. In view of this fact in our considered opinion, it would be unfortunate were any of the three governments, now on common ground in the Atlantic Charter, to express willingness to enter into commitments regarding specific terms of the postwar settlement. . . . In order not to jeopardize the aims we shall all share in common looking to an enduring peace, it is evident that no commitments as to individual countries should be entered at this time. . . . Above all, there must be no secret accords. . . .[46]

The American position had now hardened. Eden agreed to the contents of the memo before he left for Moscow. By the time Eden had arrived in Moscow on December 16, the Japanese had attacked Pearl Harbor and Hitler had declared war on the United States. For all practical purposes, the United States now was in the war on two fronts. The American involvement in the war only deepened Washington's concern with regard Anglo-Soviet relations.

The content of the Eden-Stalin talks are well known, but their importance to future East-West relations has not been properly recognized. Stalin presented to Eden drafts of two treaties. In addition, Stalin proposed a secret protocol whereby the British would be required to recognize his western frontiers of 1941. Eden replied that he was not empowered to do so, besides he had promised Washington that no territorial settlements would be made. Eden also pointed out to Stalin that such an arrangement would violate the Atlantic Charter. Stalin, however, demanded that in any event Great Britain immediately recognize the Baltic states as a component of the Soviet Union. Eden again refused by stating "You would not respect me if I were to go back upon my arrangement with President Roosevelt." Eden, however, promised Stalin that he would "endeavor to obtain a favorable decision if Stalin attached so great importance to the matter."[47] On 5 January 1942 Eden sent a telegram to Churchill in Washington stating: "I am clear that this question is for Stalin the acid test of our sincerity and unless we can meet him on it his suspicion of our ourselves and the U.S. government will persist." Churchill was not at all moved by Eden's pleading. Eden later admonished the U.S. government for the difficulties they had created in the Anglo-American-Soviet relation: In his view there is bound to be difficulty in harmonizing day to day Anglo-Russian cooperation with Anglo-American cooperation. "Soviet policy is amoral; United States policy is exaggeratedly moral, at least where non-American interests are concerned."[48] London prepared to apply pressure on Washington to change its views.

The British Pressure Washington to No Avail

The extent to which Stalin's frontier demands concerned Washington can be gauged by Hull's beginning sentence in a chapter of his autobiography entitled "Stalin's Ambitions." Hull states: "One of the greatest preoccupations of the President and me during the first half of 1942 was the Soviet Union's suddenly revealed territorial aims in Europe, coupled with her determination to induce the Western Allies to guarantee them in advance."[49] On 4 February 1942, Hull prepared a long memo for the President explaining what had transpired in Moscow during the Anglo-Soviet talks. Hull once again reiterated to the President the reasons for not giving in to Stalin's demands. First of all, Hull pointed out, such an act "would break down the principle thus far observed by the Americans and the British not to make any territorial commitments prior to the peace conference. . . ."[50]

The forewarned President met with Halifax on February 17. The President's initial reaction to Stalin's secret proposal was of great shock, though he remained noncommittal. He thought "that it was largely a question of interpretation but that it would be undesirable to get into too much detail at this stage which would involve us both in a secret treaty, the difficulties of which were obvious."[51] The President suggested Halifax see Welles on the subject. Roosevelt's position on the issue was discouraging to Halifax, though he speculated that the the President was just "thinking out loud" and believed that not too much importance should be attributed to his opinion.

Halifax met with Welles the next day. He reiterated the steps that had been taken to improve Anglo-Soviet relations. He mentioned the letter that he had written to Churchill indicating that he believed that the British attitude with regard to the Baltic states in 1939 had been one of the prime reasons for the breakdown in British-Soviet negotiations, which had in large part been responsible, in his judgment, for the agreement between Germany and the Soviet Union. Halifax believed that the attitude of Great Britain with regard to the Baltic states had been the chief reason why Stalin thought that British policy was insincere.[52] Then Halifax interjected that during his meeting with the President, the President "on his own initiative, without having read the message from Eden, had suggested with regard to the Baltic states that some sort of plan such as outlined in one of the alternatives [described in Eden's memo] might be the answer to the problem." Welles assured Halifax that the President had not mentioned anything like that to him. Welles finally suggested that there was no further use in discussing the matter, because the decision of the President was the one that mattered. Halifax urged that an early reply was necessary.[53]

On February 19, Welles met with the President to discuss the issue, and the next day related the results to Halifax. The President had studied in full detail the material from Halifax, and according to Welles, had one word in reply: "Provincial." According to Welles, "After Lord Halifax had recovered, I went on to say that the President had asked me further to state that in his judgment the fundamental question, namely, a secret agreement guaranteeing the Soviet Union the re-establishment of its 1941 frontiers, was not a matter which could be discussed at this time. The President felt that this was a question which could only be settled upon the termination of the war." The President was assured that the security issues of the Soviet Union would be resolved by the disarmament of Germany, and further wanted Welles to inform the British that he himself would discuss the matter with Stalin.[54] Halifax's attempt to see the President again was denied.

Roosevelt's expressed wish to discuss the issue directly with Stalin raised a furor in London. As Eden later wrote, "Here was the first of several occasions when the President, mistakenly as I believe, moved out of step with us, influenced by his convictions that he could get better results with Stalin direct than could the three countries negotiating together. This is an illusion."[55]

Churchill felt the pressure from Stalin and Eden mounting. On March 6, Eden urged Churchill to begin high-level talks with the Soviets. Eden insisted that "for such exchanges to take place with any chance of success, it is indispensable that we should first clear this frontier question out of the way. Otherwise Stalin will neither talk or listen."[56] On the next day he wrote Roosevelt:

> The increasing gravity of the war has led me to feel that the principles of the Atlantic Charter ought not to be construed so as to deny the USSR the frontiers she occupied when Germany attacked. This was the basis on which the USSR acceded to the Charter and I expect that a severe process of liquidating hostile elements in the Baltic states was employed by the Soviets when they took these regions at the beginning of the war. I hope therefore that you will be able to give us a free hand to sign the treaty which Stalin desires as soon as possible.[57]

Eden also frantically sent a telegram to Halifax asking him to dissuade the President from discussing the frontiers issue with Soviet Ambassador Litvinov. Halifax enlisted Harry Hopkins, the President's personal envoy, to aid in changing the President's mind. In a long discussion between the two, they talked about the perceived growing danger of an impasse between the West and Stalin. Hopkins reported that Halifax is "racking his brains for some new bridge-building device that he can suggest to the President."[58]

Halifax and Hopkins met the President on March 9. The attempt failed. The President proposed to tell Stalin that, while everyone recognizes the USSR's need for security, it was too dangerous to put anything on paper now. According to Eden's account, the President implied that there was no need to worry about the Baltic states, since their future clearly depended on Soviet military progress and, if the Soviet Union reoccupied them, neither the United States, nor Britain, could or would turn her out. Eden was not happy with the President's position, because Stalin would not be satisfied and because it would "give us the worst of all worlds. We would be ungraciously conniving at the inevitable, without getting any return for it."[59]

The British Ambassador met with Welles early on March 12. According to Welles, Halifax turned right away to the Anglo-Soviet negotiations concerning the desire of the latter for an agreement concerning its postwar boundaries and handed him a message from Eden. The text in part reads as follows:

> In the light of your report of your conversation with the President we fear that the President may not fully understand the real reason for the importance which we attach to giving Stalin a satisfactory answer. We regard it of the highest importance at this stage of the

war to leave nothing undone which may enable us to get into real contact with Stalin. . . .[60]

Welles read the memorandum and stated that the President intended to see the Soviet Ambassador, despite the British protests, to discuss this question in the immediate future. Welles promised Halifax to give Eden's message to the President before his meeting with Litvinov. Welles met with the President at 10:00 A.M. The President then met with Litvinov. Later in the same day Halifax met with the President and Welles. According to Litvinov's account:

> He [Roosevelt] does not foresee any difficulties regarding our border desires after the War. But the conclusion of a secret agreement disturbs him. Public opinion in America is not prepared. The issue may cause undesirable discussions and the President may be reminded about the Atlantic Charter where it mentions self-determination . . . and he assures Stalin in a personal way that he absolutely agrees with us.

Litvinov told Roosevelt that the Baltic states had "constitutions and that Estonia already had self-determination." Litvinov finally asked the President if he had any objections to some kind of "secret agreement" between Britain and the USSR.

> Roosevelt answered that he would not be against such an agreement if it remained a secret from him. Roosevelt clearly desires that an agreement should be an oral and not formal one. I pointed out that such an agreement usually only binds the contracting individuals . . . and that Churchill and Eden are not immortal. Roosevelt understood the allusion and smiling said he hoped to stay in his place until the end of the war. He asked me to give Stalin his thoughts and proposed that he take the matter under consideration.[61]

The President and Welles met with Halifax later and told him of the meeting with Litvinov. Litvinov's account of the meeting differs from that of Halifax. According to Halifax's account, Roosevelt denied that the United States would recognize the 1941 borders, though he did say that he favored the Soviets obtaining "complete security after the war." The two accounts are not wholly contradictory, yet neither are they wholly complementary. The reaction in London to the President's meetings with Halifax and

Litvinov was one of outrage. Eden called Roosevelt's performance "a dismal tale of clumsy diplomacy."[62] The focus of the fury was that the President would be so presumptuous as to call the shots in foreign affairs for Great Britain as well as the United States. Roosevelt ruffled the feathers of the British further by sending Churchill the now famous message:

> By the time you get this you will have been advised of my talk with Litvinov, and I expect a reply from Stalin shortly. I know you will not mind my being brutally frank when I tell you that I think I can personally handle Stalin better than your Foreign Office or my State Department. Stalin hates the guts of all your top people. He thinks he likes me better and I hope he will continue to do so.[63]

The Soviets were apparently far less disappointed by Roosevelt's meeting with Litvinov than the British. According to Eden, Maisky "seemed resolved not to take a tragic view of the President's attitude." Stalin's reply to Roosevelt was equally low tempered. All it said was that the Soviet government "had taken note of the [President's] communication. When Eden met Maisky again on March 23, the Ambassador explained that the Soviet government had not solicited the American opinion, only wishing to consult with London in this matter."[64] The President had been bluntly rebuked by Stalin on the territorial issue.

Having been mocked by Maisky, Eden urged the War Cabinet to proceed with the Soviet negotiation without the consent of Roosevelt. Eden fully realized that Washington was not going to be pleased with the decision. He informed Halifax: "I fully realize that the President will not like it if we now tell Stalin that we are prepared to go ahead with our treaty negotiations on the basis of his frontier claims, and that in doing so we shall be creating trouble for him with his public opinion. Had circumstances been more favorable I should have naturally wished to spare him this embarrassment, but things being as they are I cannot take the risk of keeping Anglo-Soviet relations in a state of suspended animation any longer." Eden continued: "This country, as a European Power for whom collaboration with a victorious USSR after the war will be essential, cannot afford to neglect any opportunity of establishing intimate relations of confidence with Stalin. . . ." In an effort to smooth things with the President, Eden requested that Halifax talk to the President again, requesting him to "abstain from any overt action which would indicate that there is any divergence of opinion between us." Two days later Eden informed Maisky of British intentions to proceed without American consent.[65]

A Trade to "Take the Heat of Soviet Demands"

Roosevelt was not yet ready to concede to the British. He was no longer going to argue with Halifax or respond to memos from Eden, and had a plan to offer Churchill and Stalin. On April 3, he informed Churchill that he was sending Hopkins and Marshall to London to explain:

> What Harry and George Marshall will tell you all about has my heart and mind in it. Your people and mine demand the establishment of a front to draw off pressure on the Soviets and these people are wise enough to see that the Soviets are today killing more Germans and destroying more equipment than you and I put together. Even if full success is not attained, the big objective will be.[66]

By Roosevelt's instructions Hopkins and Marshall arrived in London on April 8. According to Hopkins's notes, he told Eden that the President did not approve of the Anglo-Soviet treaty, but that he could not prevent them from signing it. It was a decision the British must make, and no useful purpose could be served by exploring it further with the Soviets. Hopkins impressed on Eden as strongly as he could the President's belief that their mission to London should take the heat off the USSR's demands upon Britain.[67]

On April 14, an agreement was reached with the British on the American plan for a Second Front in a frontal assault called ROUNDUP to take place in northern France in 1943. In case of a Soviet front collapsing in the East, the Americans envisioned an emergency operation called SLEDGE HAMMER sometime in the autumn of 1942. Churchill labeled Roosevelt's attempts to barter the 1941 frontier issue for a Second Front a very foolish view.[68] Sherwood contends that "Roosevelt obviously saw the urgency of diverting the attention of the Soviet government from such an embarrassing postwar political consideration by emphasizing the British and American determination to establish the Second Front in the West for which the communist propaganda had been clamoring since the German invasion of the USSR."[69]

On April 23, Churchill received a reply from Stalin. The letter reads in part:

[T]he Soviet Government has decided, despite all the obstacles, to send Mr. Molotov to London, in order, by means of personal discussion, to dispose of all the matters which stand in the way of the signing of the agreements. This is all the more necessary because the question of opening a Second Front in Europe [which was raised in the last message addressed to me by the President of the United States, in which he invited Mr. Molotov to go to Washington to discuss this matter] call[s] for a preliminary exchange of views between representatives of our two Governments. [70]

Why had Stalin decided to send Molotov to London first, after the President had made an unmistakable offer of a Second Front? Stalin had to consider the Second Front as the highest priority. As Warren Kimball correctly points out, since Stalin "was well aware that the United States would not recognize those boundaries, he hoped to settle the issue before sending Molotov to Washington."[71] In other words Stalin made a last ditch effort to gain the approval of the frontier demands by the British before going to Washington. In all probability he would have achieved his goal, except he decided to play for higher stakes. Stalin added Finland and Romania to his proposed secret protocols. The British, however, had a limit on how far they would go to appease Stalin. Winant on the last day of the discussions was able to report:

Eden has spent the morning going over the draft text with Molotov which I forwarded to you last night. Molotov explained to Eden that the statements made to him by the Prime Minister, Eden and myself convinced him that there would be serious objections to the Soviet frontiers treaty in the United States. He further told him that he had recommended to his Government in Moscow that he be permitted to work out an agreement with the British on Eden's draft treaty [without the frontiers issue]. Molotov expects to get a reply by this evening or tomorrow morning.[72]

Stalin approved the changes in the treaty by the next day, and it was signed by both parties on May 26 without mentioning the territorial matters. Churchill was most grateful to Winant for his help in negotiating a treaty acceptable to Washington. This he expressed to Roosevelt. Many writers, especially British, have erroneously credited Eden with the face-saving version of the Anglo-Soviet treaty.

Molotov Outfoxes Roosevelt

When Molotov arrived in Washington as a guest of the President, the two had the following conversation at a dinner on May 29:

> Mr. Molotov then inquired whether the President was familiar with the treaty he had negotiated with the British. The President replied in the affirmative, and said he thought it was all to the good. He was glad that the frontier problem had not been mentioned. Not that it would not present itself eventually, but he thought there might be a proper time for raising this question, though the present was not the moment. Mr. Molotov remarked that he and his government had very definite convictions in the opposite direction, but that he had deferred to British preference and to what he understood to be the attitude of the President.[73]

During the discussions in Washington, Molotov claimed that if forty German divisions could be diverted from the Eastern Front by an Allied assault in the West by the autumn of 1942, the war could be settled in 1942. Molotov's insistent badgering of the President and General Marshall paid off. Inexplicably, both consented to a Second Front to be launched in the autumn of 1942. The final communiqué issued on June 11 stated, "In the course of the conversations full understanding was reached with regard to the urgent tasks of creating a Second Front in Europe in 1942."[74]

The President had made a promise to the Soviets that he could not fulfill. It was a promise Stalin and Molotov knew the Allies could not carry out. As Molotov later recalled: "From the first I didn't believe they would do it. I remained calm and realized this was a completely impossible operation for them. But our demand was politically necessary, and we had to press them for everything . . . I believe that my journey in 1942 [to London and Washington] and its results were a great victory for us." Molotov continued, "We knew they wouldn't dare mount a Second Front, but we made them agree to it in writing. . . ."[75] Molotov's and Stalin's doubts about a Second Front in 1942 did not stop them from announcing the promise to the Soviet people.

It is ironic that the President had boasted about his propensity to keep his promises. He had told Henry Morgenthau that the Soviets did not trust the English because after promising them two divisions and help in the Caucasus, they had failed to deliver. "Every promise the English have made to the Soviets, they have fallen down on. . . . The only reason we stand so well with the Soviets is that up to date we have kept our promises."[76] That date had passed.

William Standley, the American Ambassador in Moscow, was quick to point out that the Roosevelt barter deal was likely to sour. He commented from Moscow: "I feel convinced that if such a front does not materialize quickly and on a large scale, these people [the Soviets] will be so deluded in their belief in our sincerity of purpose and will for concerted action that inestimable harm will be done to the cause of the United Nations." Standley continued, "It may be reasoned further that should the Second Front not materialize they [the Soviets] would thus find themselves in a better bargaining position vis-à-vis England and the United States in any future political negotiations having to do with postwar problems and frontiers."[77] As we all know, the Second Front was not established until the summer of 1944.

Roosevelt Becomes a Realist

On 12 February 1943 Roosevelt addressed the Correspondents Association. In the talk he stressed, "It is one of our war aims, as expressed in the Atlantic Charter, that conquered populations of today be again the masters of their destiny. There must be no doubt anywhere that it is the unalterable purpose of the United Nations to restore to conquered peoples their sacred rights."[78]

In mid-March Eden arrived in Washington to discuss potential postwar problems in Europe. Eden met with Roosevelt and Hopkins on March 22. During the meeting the President again expressed his concern for the Baltic states. He told Eden that he "did not like the idea of turning the Baltic states over to the USSR and that she would lose a great deal of public opinion in this country if she insisted on this action." The President said he thought that in a plebicite the Baltic states would vote to ally themselves with the Soviet Union and that the USSR should take the trouble to go through the motions of getting that done. In the meantime there should be an agreement between Great Britain and the United States that the USSR control foreign affairs and finances of the Baltic states until the new plebiscite could be taken. Eden again told the President that he thought the USSR was going to be insistent on this.[79]

Once the promised Second Front had failed to materialize on time, the President was in the process of modifying his mind on the Baltic issue. To do it so nonchalantly and convincingly, he reverted to tactics for which he has been severely criticized. The President had insinuated that the Baltic people would join the Soviet Union of their own volition and that Stalin should only go through the "motions" of a plebiscite. Eden's recollections of the President were not flattering: "He seemed to see himself disposing of the fate of many lands, allied no less than enemy. He did all this with so much grace that it was not easy to dissent. Yet it was too like a conjurer, skillfully juggling with balls of dynamite, whose nature he failed to understand."[80] The same could be said of Eden himself.

Joseph Davies, the controversial former Ambassador to Moscow, met with the President on April 12. Davies claims that the President's impression of the postwar geopolitical picture was now "in tune" with his views, namely that Stalin ultimately could make good on his territorial claims and that Western efforts to force him to give up his border demands would be futile. At the beginning of August, Standley noted from Moscow, "The campaign for a Second Front is now in full swing." He concluded that "such attacks in the press create in the minds of the Soviet public and doubtless of many people abroad the impression that the U.S. and Great Britain are guilty of bad faith and the Soviet Union is winning the war with little assistance from the Allies. . . . [I]n such a case they will be more inclined to support a claim that the Soviet Union should have the greatest voice in determining the peace. This may be of particular importance with respect to the population of the enemy-occupied territories."[81] On August 14, the President issued the following statement:

> Today, on the second anniversary of the signing of the Atlantic Charter, I could cite particularly two of its purposes and principles on which we base our hopes for a better future for the world: First— respect for the right of all peoples to choose the form of government under which they live. When the Atlantic Charter was signed, there were those who said that this was an impossible achievement. And yet today, as the forces of liberation march on, the right of self-determination is becoming once more a living reality. . . . [82]

The stage was set for the Big Three Conference at Teheran. The Baltic issue had lost its prominence. On the last day of the conference (December 1), the President had requested to meet with Stalin by himself to talk about "internal American politics." The President told Stalin that there were a number of persons of Lithuanian, Latvian, and Estonian origin, in that order, in the United States. He said he fully realized the three Baltic republics had in history and again more recently been part of the USSR and added jokingly that when the Soviet armies reoccupied these areas, he did not intend to go to war with the Soviet Union on this point. According to Bohlen's account, the President went on to say that the big issue in the Unites States, insofar as the public opinion went, would be the question of a referendum and the right of self-determination. He said he thought that world opinion would want some expression of the will of the people, perhaps not immediately after their reoccupation by the Soviet forces, but some day, and that he was confident that the people would vote to join the Soviet Union.

Stalin replied that the Baltic republics had no autonomy under the last Czar, who had been an ally of Great Britain and the United States, but that no one had raised the question of public opinion, and he did not quite see why it was being raised now. The President replied that the truth of the matter was they should be informed and some propaganda work should be done. Stalin retorted that as to the expression of the will of the people, there would be lots of opportunities for that to be done in accordance with the Soviet constitution but that he could not agree to any form of international control. The President replied that it would be helpful for him personally if some public declaration in regard to the future elections to which Stalin had referred, could be made. Stalin repeated that there would be plenty of opportunities for such an expression of the will of the people.[83]

Thus ended the debate between Stalin and the President on the subject of the Baltic states. Charles Bohlen, the President's interpreter and subsequently a State Department official, later observed that he was "dismayed" by the President's performance in his private talks with Stalin. It was a great mistake for Roosevelt to tell Stalin in the private conference of the last day that for electoral reasons he could not take positions on a number of European countries, including the Baltics.[84]

Conclusion

Stalin had his own priorities with which he desired the Western powers to comply. These were the Second Front in France and the recognition of the frontiers already discussed. The President's Atlantic Charter and his policy of postponing frontier issues until after the war precluded the fulfillment of one of Stalin's priorities. Roosevelt promised Stalin a Second Front in 1942, which he could not deliver until 1944. As time passed, the unfulfilled promise of the Second Front and the rejection of Stalin's territorial demands grew into a major political and moral liability for Roosevelt with respect to Stalin. As the Red Army turned the tide against the Nazi forces, Stalin's position became even more recalcitrant and the President's position became more untenable. For the President's Grand Design, to win the goodwill and cooperation of Stalin after the war, to become a reality, something had to give. To mollify Stalin, FDR's idealism had to be sacrificed. To extricate himself from his predicament, the President resorted to tactics for which he has been severely criticized. He himself stated: "You know I am a juggler, and I never let my right hand know what my left hand does. . . . I may be entirely inconsistent, and furthermore, I am willing to mislead and tell untruths if it will help win the war."[85] In the process, the rights and self-determination of small nations gave way to the enforcement of international law by the "Four Policemen." The "no secret treaties" policy gave way to a secret treaty between Stalin and the West at Yalta. The shock of Soviets bombing civilians in Finland turned to acceptance of indiscriminate mass bombing of civilians and refugees in Europe and Japan. Up until the end of the war, the facade of idealism by the administration was still nurtured in public, while realism was taking hold in international Big Three diplomacy. His zeal to pacify Stalin and his misjudgment of him led the President into serious errors of judgment that failed in their purpose of earning the trust and friendship he was seeking. Yet, he continued to believe that Stalin would work with him after the war for a world of democracy and peace.[86]

Those who defend Roosevelt at Yalta claim that he did not have any other recourse, that Yalta was already predetermined by the power of the Red Army. That may be so. His supporters, however, seem to forget that the ground rules of the diplomacy guiding the war were dictated by Roosevelt himself. His vision, as articulated in the Atlantic Charter, was vague and imprecise, and it was not going to stop Stalin from taking what he wanted. Roosevelt's insistence that territorial settlements be made after the war eventually played directly into his hands. The time to pin Stalin down on specific agreements regarding the Baltic states and Eastern Europe was in 1942, when he was on the verge of defeat.

The 1939 decision to keep the secret protocols of the Hitler–Stalin pact from the public served no one. It was the first step by the Roosevelt administration to hide the true nature of Stalin. It helped to build the illusion throughout the war that "Uncle Joe" was "OK," that the "Grand Design" so carefully nurtured by Roosevelt after 1942 was the new foundation for peace and harmony after the war. It is no wonder that the American public came to a rude awakening when they saw that peace with Stalin was going to take place according to his terms. There was peace but no harmony; the Second World War ended and the Cold War began.

In all likelihood, however, even if Stalin would have settled for an equitable agreement, Eastern Europe would have been similar to the one that emerged after the war. As has been pointed out many times, Stalin had the military power to take what he wanted and he was ready to use it to protect his spoils of war despite any specific agreements reached earlier. Any real difference in the outcome of the war in Eastern Europe would have been possible only by the earlier establishment of an effective Second Front by the Western Powers, of which, ironically, Stalin was the most ardent proponent.

Over half a century has passed since the U.S. government repudiated the annexation of the Baltic states by the Soviet Union. President Roosevelt acquiesced to the annexation but, to the great consternation of Stalin, did not recognize it officially.[87] No U.S. administration afterward saw fit to do otherwise. Gorbachev's *glasnost* gave the Baltic people an opportunity to express their desire for independence. They gained their independence again in the autumn of 1991, and this served as a harbinger of the breakup of the Soviet Union. They were able to gain their independence because the Western nations, with the United States at their lead, respected the international principle that an aggressor should not be rewarded with territory acquired by force.

Notes

1. *American Heritage* (May/June 1994): 83.
2. H.W. Berger, ed. *A William Appleman Williams Reader* (Chicago: Ivan R. Dee, 1992), 141.
3. Ibid., 145.
4. E.M. Bennett, *Franklin Roosevelt and the Search for Victory* (Wilmington, DE: SR Books, 1990), 95.
5. Henry Kissinger, *Diplomacy* (New York: Simon and Schuster, 1994), 407; S.M. Miner, *Between Churchill and Stalin* (Chapel Hill: University of North Carolina Press, 1988).
6. L.C. Gardner, *Spheres of Influence* (Chicago: Ivan R. Dee, 1993).
7. Natalie Grant, "The Russian Section: A Window on the Soviet Union," *Diplomatic History* 2, 1 (1978): 107.
8. A.N. Tarulis, *American-Baltic Relations 1918-1922: The Struggle over Recognition* (Washington: Catholic University University Press, 1965).
9. Robert Dallek, *Franklin Roosevelt and American Foreign Policy 1932-1945* (New York: Oxford University Press, 1979), 208.
10. C. Hull, *The Memoirs of Cordell Hull* (New York: Macmillan, 1948), 701.
11. *Foreign Relations of the United States* (FRUS) (Washington: Government Printing Office, 1939), Vol. I, 961.
12. See, for example, G.W. Baer, ed., *A Question of Trust–The Origins of U.S-Soviet Diplomatic Relations–The Memoirs of Loy W.Henderson* (Stanford, CA: Hoover Institution Press, 1986), 568.
13. FRUS, Soviet Union, 1933-1939, 799.
14. K.S. Davis, *FDR into the Storm* (New York: Random House, 1993), 522.

15. A. Sprudzs, ed., *Res Baltica*, (Leyden: A.W. Sijhoff, 1968), 9.

16. FRUS, 1940, I, 387.

17. FRUS, 1940, I, 389.

18. FRUS, 1940, I, 391

19. FRUS, 1940, I, 401. See also William J.H. Hough III, "The Annexation of the Baltic States and Its Effect on the Development of Law Prohibiting Forcible Seizure of Territory," *New York Law School Journal of International and Comparative Law*. 6, 2 (1985).

20. FRUS, 1940, I, 428.

21. FRUS, 1940, I, 433.

22. A. Gerutis, ed., *Lithuania 700 Years* (Baltimore: Maryland Books, 1969), 389.

23. Dallek, 208.

24. Hull, 1170.

25. W.L. O'Neal, *A Democracy at Work* (New York: The Free Press), 1993, 30. O'Neal makes the comment that Warren Kimball, who has studied Roosevelt for thirty years, says that "there is no scrap of evidence to support the theory that Roosevelt was determined to avoid Wilson's mistakes–compelling though it seems," 438, n. 34

26. S. Welles, *The Seven Decisions That Shaped the World* (New York: Harper & Brothers, 1950)

27. Ibid., 129.

28. Orville Bullitt, ed., *For the President: Personal and Secret* (Boston: Houghton Mifflin, 1972), 576.

29. Welles, 145

30. The decision to keep the protocols of the Hitler-Stalin Pact hushed up had obvious repercussions in Washington. As Loy Henderson writes: "The inability of those of us in the State Department who had been given access to the series of telegrams regarding the German-Soviet political conversations and, in particular, to the telegram summarizing the contents of the secret protocol, to discuss the contents of these telegrams or even to mention their existence to persons to whom they had not circulated was a source of considerable embarrassment to us. Some of our colleagues in the department and also members of other agencies of the government regarded us as being unduly suspicious of Soviet foreign policies and intentions and particularly of Soviet insistence that it was merely playing the role of a neutral country. A number of members of the academic community and left-leaning columnists and commentators who refused to believe that the Soviet government was secretly collaborating with Nazi Germany for a time were critical of the Department of State for its apparent attitude of distrust of the Soviet Union." Baer, 568.

31. Bohlen, 83.

32. Miner, 67.

33. Gardner, 78.

34. Ibid, 71.

35. FRUS, 1941, I, 161.

36. Gardner, 88.

37. FRUS, 1941, I, 182.

38. FRUS, 1941, I, 757.

39. FRUS, 1941, I, 182.

40. Anthony Eden, *The Reckoning* (Boston: Houghton Mifflin, 1965), 316.

41. Adolf Berle, *Navigating the Rapids* (New York: Harcourt, Brace, Jovanovich, 1973), 372.

42. FRUS, 1941, I, 342.

43. FRUS, 1941, I, 351.

44. L.C. Gardner, *The Atlantic Charter* (New York: St. Martin's Press, 1994), 51.

45. FRUS, 1941, I, 642.

46. FRUS, 1941, I, 195.

47. FRUS, 1942, III, 505.

48. Eden, 370.

49. Hull, 165.

50. FRUS, 1942, III, 505–512

51. FRUS, 1942, III, 521.

52. FRUS, 1942, III, 514.

53. FRUS, 1942, III, 514.

54. FRUS, 1942, III, 521.

55. Eden, 375.

56. Miner, 211.

57. W.F. Kimball, ed., *Churchill and Roosevelt: The Complete Correspondence* (Princeton: Princeton University Press, 1984), I, 394.

58. Gardner, 130.

59. Eden, 376.

60. FRUS, 1942, III 531.

61. H. Phillips, "Mission to America: Maksim M. Litvinov in the United States," *Diplomatic History* 12, 3 (1988): 268.

62. Miner, 208.

63. Kimball, I, 421.

64. Miner, 219.

65. Miner, 220.

66. Kimball, I, 441.

67. R.W. Sherwood, *Roosevelt and Hopkins: An Intimate History* (New York: Harper & Brothers, 1948), 528.

68. Gardner 134.

69. Sherwood, 528.

70. W. Churchill, *The Hinge of Fate*, IV (New York: Houghton Mifflin, 1950), 331.

71. Kimball, I, 470.

72. FRUS, 1942, III, 564.

73. FRUS, 1942, III, 569.

74. FRUS, 1942, III, 594.

75. F. Cheuv, *Molotov Remembers* (Chicago: Ivan R. Dee, 1993), 46.

76. Dallek, 338.

77. FRUS, 1942, III, 548.

78. *Department of State Bulletin* (Aug. 1943), 43, 145.

79. FRUS, 1943, III, 35.

80. Eden, 343.

81. FRUS, 1943, III, 560.

82. *Department of State Bulletin* (Aug. 1943), 42.

83. FRUS, 1943, III, Teheran Conference, 594.

84. C.E. Bohlen, *Witness to History* (New York: W.W. Norton., 1973), 152.

85. W.F. Kimball, *The Juggler: Franklin Roosevelt as Wartime Statesman* (Princeton: Princeton University Press, 1991), 7

86. J.L. Gaddis, *The United States and the Origins of the Cold War, 1941-1947* (New York: Columbia University Press, 1972), 64.

87. After 1942 Stalin changed his tactics in his continued pursuit to gain the Western Powers' acceptance of the Baltic states annexation. Instead of asking for de jure recognition in a treaty, he requested that the occupied Baltic states be represented in world organizations at various conferences such as Dumbarton Oaks in 1944, Yalta and Moscow in 1945. All such ploys were refused by the West. In frustration Stalin exclaimed during the Moscow conference in December of 1945 that "soon the United States would have to recognize these countries [the Baltic states] and that they [the United States] would find it convenient to have consulates in Tallin, Riga, and Kaunas," FRUS 1945, II, 595.

7

FDR's Admiral Diplomats: The Diplomacy of Expediency

Calvin W. Hines

The diplomatic history of this nation abounds with examples of U.S. naval officers engaged in the implementation of American foreign policy, whether of an impromptu nature or at the specific direction of either the President or other agencies of the federal government. One need look only to any general history of the U.S. Navy to find such a ledger: there are Preble, Decatur, Bainbridge, Wickes, Perry, and others, whose efforts in furthering the interests of the nation predate the Civil War. In the post-1865 period the list is equally long and, in most respects, just as noteworthy.[1]

The value of employing senior naval officers on occasion in sensitive diplomatic circumstances is evident, and, in the case of the six admirals studied here, the motivation for their being selected either as official ambassadors or as agents plenipotentiary appears to have been the by-product of several factors: age, previous record of service, reputations as competent and capable commanders or administrators, the peculiar circumstances pertaining to the assignment for which they were chosen and, in every case initially, the confidence of Franklin Roosevelt.

Historians continue to debate the nature, methods, and objectives of Franklin Roosevelt's diplomacy during World War II. Aside from the common view that the President appeared to be singularly committed to a personal conduct of most aspects of foreign interaction from 1939 until his death, there were also areas in which he often deferred to Secretary of State Cordell Hull, Secretary of the Navy Frank Knox, and Secretary of War Henry Stimson. Such deference was never guaranteed, and more often than not they found a presidential prerogative exercised to which their assent was automatically assumed. It is more accurate to say that while the President could not keep all foreign policy matters in central focus, none were entirely outside of his field of vision. In the particular examples of Admirals William H. Standley, William D. Leahy and John W. Greenslade, Roosevelt assumed a direct role in their respective diplomatic posting. In the case of Raymond A. Spruance, Frederick J. Horne, and John H. Hoover, who performed their diplomatic services as adjuncts to their regular assignments, Roosevelt allowed the initiative to come from Hull, Knox, or Stimson.

William H. Standley: Admiral Ambassador to the USSR

Of all the choices available to Roosevelt for the American embassy in Moscow during World War II, Admiral William H. Standley appears to be the least understandable or defensible. Petulant and abrasive, frequently addressing his Soviet hosts in a "blunt, pointed and salty sailorman's fashion," Standley gives the impression of painfully lacking the traditionally essential qualities necessary in a diplomat, namely that they be knowledgeable, reserved, dignified, and skilled in the art of diplomatic finesse. Standley hardly fulfilled these criteria.

Perhaps Standley's own assessment is the best explanation. Appreciating that "the military effort was of paramount importance and diplomacy would remain in the background for the duration of the war," it seemed, at least to the admiral, that the President wished to place a representative in Moscow who would cajole the Soviets into a more cooperative war effort. He also wanted someone who could "overcome bureaucratic barriers and gain access to the real directive center of the Soviet Government," namely Joseph Stalin.[2]

Given this, Standley's task could hardly be viewed in any other way other than as Herculean. What awaited him in 1942 were such chores as accelerating the delivery of British and American aircraft, extracting intelligence from the Soviets on the German army, ascertaining the Soviet Union's Lend-Lease needs as well as their production capacities, and seeking to expand relief aid to Polish internees. Fulfilling these goals would have challenged the most accomplished diplomat, which Standley admitted he was not. Disregarding the observations of members of his staff that "advice on how to win their war is not regarded by the Soviets as a commodity of which they are in need," and habitually pounding the table with his "clenched fist" in punctuating his remarks, Standley reinforced the ingrained xenophobia the Soviet hierarchy invariably displayed. Out of such behavior only limited and occasional successes could be expected. One could almost predict that from the time of his arrival Admiral Standley's tenure would be one year or less.[3]

Still, any serious treatment of the short-lived Standley embassy must consider the fact that several alternate, and sometimes contradictory, diplomatic channels were being pursued simultaneously toward the Soviets. Chief among these was the resident head of the American supply mission, General Raymond Faymondville, whose views of the Soviet Union's relationship to and involvement in the war differed greatly from Standley's and who also enjoyed the liberty of direct communication with Washington, bypassing the Admiral altogether. Added to this internal conflict, Standley's thirteen months in the USSR found him, in his own words "an innocent bystander," and he frequently carped and chafed as several special representatives arrived, as he recalled, to "leapfrog over my top-hatted head and follow out the Rooseveltian policy" of not pressing the Soviets.[4]

Ever sensitive to criticisms of himself and his government, especially on the matter of American deliveries of Lend-Lease equipment, Standley grew more acerbic, frequently responding to affronts with accusations of his own. In one conversation with the Soviet Foreign Minister, Standley exploded:

> Since my arrival here the Embassy in practically all aspects of its work had been continually subjected to delays, interference and indifference on the part of subordinate Soviet officials and it appeared to me that almost a studied effort was being made to thwart its cooperative spirit.

He was no more restrained in his communiqués with the State Department, frequently noting that he had been "handicapped" by "not being informed of what took place or of what commitments may have been made" by Washington authorities in their meetings with Soviet representatives.[5]

Seeking almost any means of reestablishing his role, Standley offered a variety of suggestions as to how Soviet-American collaboration could improve, ranging from a showing of American-made movies to presenting American decorations to Soviet heroes to sharing our military inventions with the Soviets. Little materialized from these initiatives, and what there was proved merely cosmetic. By the spring of 1943 it was clear Roosevelt's confidence in Standley was evaporating. Direct meetings between Roosevelt and the Soviet Foreign Minister were supplemented by the President's use of W. Averell Harriman as a liaison. Failing to appreciate the historical precedent of the use of such executive agents, Standley became bitter, perhaps even paranoid.[6]

Thwarted in the limitations of his station, which he wished he could command as if it were a ship, Standley saw in Roosevelt's special emissaries a calculated strategy of both pandering to Soviet irritations at the absence of a Second Front, and the erosion of his own authority and credibility. His endurance broke in the spring of 1943 over the two issues that had plagued him from the outset—special diplomatic agents and Lend-Lease.

Roosevelt's decision to dispatch Wendell Willkie on a fact-finding tour in 1942 so aggravated Standley that, to demonstrate his pique, he asked to be recalled for instructions. In a blunt statement to the press shortly after his return to Moscow in 1943, he vented his frustration over Soviet censorship of the American Lend-Lease contributions to their recent victories. Charging that the Soviets had failed to communicate the significance of American aid to their people, Standley created a diplomatic backlash in Washington that undoubtedly accelerated his own decision to end his assignment. He "ceased to struggle" in April 1943, on learning that former Ambassador Joseph E. Davies was being sent to Moscow "with a secret message for Stalin." On 3 May 1943, Admiral Standley accepted the portents for his own future and tendered his resignation.[7]

Williams D. Leahy: Admiral Ambassador to Vichy France

Aside from their common branch of service, the closeness in their age, and the fact that they had each previously served as Chief of Naval Operations, similarities between Admirals Standley and Leahy are virtually nonexistent.

In contrast with Standley, Leahy's posting to Vichy France in 1940 was intended to keep Marshal Henri Petain's regime out of the war and to curtail its collaboration, both immediate and potential, with the Nazis. In addition, with the status of the French fleet in doubt, Leahy's interaction with the French navy's Commander-in-Chief, Admiral Francois Darlan, seemed paramount to the fulfillment of his mission.[8]

Leahy seemed well suited for this assignment. Quiet, urbane, and patient, he held none of the illusions Standley harbored. That is not to say his basic goals were less difficult to attain, or that their pursuit would be free of complications. Indeed, given the flood tide of Axis victories by the autumn of 1940, and the assumption that a German assault on Great Britain would be renewed in the coming spring, Leahy's expectations for success were minimal. He was, nevertheless, instructed to prevent Vichy from providing military and economic aid to the Axis, secure a neutralization of the French West Indies, obstruct the delivery of French shipping in Indochina to Japan, and halt the redeployment of certain French warships.

Central to achieving any of these objectives was the cultivation of a productive relationship with Admiral Darlan, who, from their earliest encounters, convinced Leahy that Roosevelt's educated guess was correct. It would be Darlan and not Marshal Petain who would decide Vichy's policy toward the war, unless and until the Nazis lost confidence and moved to install someone more reliable.[9]

Fixing the nickname "Popeye" to Darlan, Leahy confessed a curious admiration for the little Gascon. Still, he frequently cautioned Roosevelt that Darlan's anglophobia would propel him less toward closer collaboration with Germany than would his ambition for high office. This, Leahy once warned, "would land him squarely on the bandwagon as soon as he thought he could make a certain choice." Yet, despite these undisguised signals of possible intent, Darlan evidently convinced Leahy that the French fleet would never be surrendered, a pledge Leahy regarded more as a word of honor "sailor to sailor" than as an official guarantee. Darlan remarked that the latter had previously been delivered to the British only to be rewarded by their actions at Mers-el-Kebir and Dakar.[10]

The spring of 1941 provided Leahy with his ultimate challenge. As signs mounted of Darlan's tilting toward Berlin, Leahy discovered he possessed few weapons with which to intervene. Apart from reminding Vichy of the hazards for Franco-American relations if the 1940 Armistice were violated to Germany's advantage, he could only hint at a curtailment of American relief supplies or his recall if concessions were made. With the French West Indies then neutralized largely through the efforts of three of his colleagues, even an oblique threat in that direction could not be made.[11]

As it was with Standley in Moscow, so too did Leahy find he could rarely speak alone with the head of his host government, Marshal Petain. When he did manage a private conservation, he found the Marshal to be outspoken, friendly, and frank, and he believed he genuinely wished to oppose German demands. Beyond this Leahy could glean little. When Darlan was present Leahy's attempts to reach the Marshal were always blunted; Darlan "simply took over the conversation," he recalled.[12]

Under these handicaps Leahy's record at Vichy is uneven. He failed to prevent the delivery of French merchant ships to the Japanese in Indochina or the return of the French battleship *Dunkerque* to Toulon from Oran in February 1942. In two cases, however, he could claim success, though both followed the forceful delivery of presidential ultimatums. The first pertained to Darlan's planned delivery of trucks to Italy; the second concerned the brief stop of a German U-boat in Martinique to offload an injured sailor. In each case either the anticipated move was blocked or a pledge was extracted through a mixture of veiled threats and economic inducements preventing a repetition.[13]

As Roosevelt both trusted and depended on Leahy to relay his own impressions and estimates of possible Vichy reaction to Allied moves, he also acted frequently on Leahy's advice as well as his warnings. Such was the President's confidence that he allowed Leahy to initiate requests from Vichy or to clarify American policy on his own accord without having to clear such from Washington in advance.

A certain credit must also be paid to Leahy, though at Darlan's expense. The relationship he had formed with Darlan appeared to the Nazis as a major hurdle to broader collaboration. As early as August 1941, Leahy sensed in the increasing venom of the German-controlled Paris press a pressure wave looking to the demotion of Darlan and the reinstatement to power of Pierre Laval, the notorious collaborator whom Marshal Petain had previously removed. Leahy's observations proved to be remarkably accurate. By mid-March of 1942 Leahy felt secure in predicting a sea change at Vichy, a prophecy that guaranteed his inevitable recall as a calculated American response. When the German-backed reshuffle occurred in mid-April, Darlan's political leverage evaporated, though he remained as both heir apparent to Petain and retained control of Vichy's armed forces. Roosevelt could not abide a regime with Laval as Chief of Government; the sudden death of Leahy's wife only validated his decision to effect the Admiral's recall.[14]

Raymond A. Spruance, John W. Greenslade, Frederick J. Horne, and John H. Hoover: Admirals in the Diplomatic Backwater

However unique the situation in the French West Indies appeared to be at the time of France's surrender in 1940, some of the circumstances bore striking similarities, in microcosm, to those that mandated Admiral Leahy's mission to Vichy. Martinque, Guadeloupe, and French Guiana occupied, albeit to varying degrees, geographic positions with a potential for menace to the security of the Caribbean. This might occur if they either assumed hostility toward Britain after its actions against the French battle fleet in July, or, in a worst-case scenario, came under the direct control of Nazi Germany. However exaggerated such speculation might now appear, in the confused and frightening summer of 1940 such dangers had to be regarded in Washington as either immediate or potential.

Situated adjacent to one of the main avenues entering the Caribbean, Martinique commanded special attention, all the more so since in the final hours preceding the French capitulation a disparate collection of warships and merchant vessels entered on the harbor of Fort-de-France. Among these were two cruisers, one reputed to be the fastest in the world, and France's sole aircraft carrier, the *Bearn*, which carried over one hundred aircraft just delivered from American factories and intended to be used in the defense of France. Added to this impressive array of naval and air assets was a sizable quantity of gold carried on one of the French cruisers. Intended as collateral toward further purchases of American military hardware, the gold and the cruiser on which it had been loaded had been diverted to Martinique in the last hours before the Armistice.[15]

To Winston Churchill's government the transfer of these assets to the Nazis, in whole or in part, was unthinkable. Churchill much preferred that they go to the fledgling resistance movement of General Charles de Gaulle. For the United States, however, a diplomatic neutralization of the French Antilles overrode Britain's desires. This became urgent in view of the undiluted intransigence of Admiral Georges Robert, a senior French officer who had only recently assumed the post of High Commissioner of all French colonies in the Western Hemisphere, a position that conveyed the authority of Commander-in-Chief of all military and naval forces therein. That the bulk of such assets were present in Martinique, fully operational and capable of offensive action, was lost on neither Churchill nor Roosevelt. As part of a brief effort to rally outlying French outposts to continued resistance, but also as a safeguard against Admiral Robert ordering his warships to make a sudden dash toward metropolitan France, Churchill ordered two British cruisers in the vicinity to take up a blocking patrol off the harbor of Fort-de-France. Little chance then remained to enlist Robert in the Allied cause, and this disappeared completely when he learned of the Royal Navy's attacks on French flotillas at Oran and Dakar a few days later.[16]

Given the delicate nature of Anglo-American relations at this time, the presence of British warships around Martinique suggested Churchill was contemplating actions similar to those already taken elsewhere to eradicate French warships that might wind up in German hands. Considering the British had previously occupied the Dutch islands of Curacao and Aruba to safeguard the oil facilities, an early resolution of Martinique's status became vital. While Roosevelt directed a squadron of American warships to assume a patrol around the island, Cordell Hull delivered a stern warning to the British government through their ambassador in Washington. Whether it was the tough talk of the Secretary of State or an appreciation that American naval forces were sufficient to contain the French squadron, Churchill ordered his watchdogs withdrawn. This left Roosevelt unfettered by embarrassing inquiries from his critics on either the sanctity of the Monroe Doctrine or the durability of the Panama security zone, which prohibited belligerent acts within the designated waters of the Western Hemisphere.[17]

A few days prior to this confrontation, however, a policy had begun to evolve in Washington concerning the French West Indies. Between simultaneous negotiations with the "local authority" in Martinique, in this case Admiral Robert, and the newly formed defeatist regime of Marshal Petain, the doctrine adopted owes its origin in part to the hasty dispatch of Admiral Raymond A. Spruance, Commandant of the Tenth Naval District in Puerto Rico. He was charged with opening a dialogue with Admiral Robert at the time of the Armistice. Spruance was admonished to effect some form of neutralization of the islands and all military and naval forces therein until more precise arrangements could be negotiated by accredited agents. This ad hoc type of diplomacy had been accepted by the State Department despite the fact that an American Consul was in residence at Fort-de France. From this moment the role of resident diplomats in Martinique shrank. Though special diplomatic agents would occasionally appear in the periodic negotiations with Admiral Robert, the principal task of negotiation with the "goateed martinet," as one American officer described him, fell almost exclusively to the U.S. Navy.[18]

As the initial contact, Spruance's task was to ascertain Robert's intentions if, as all suspected, France surrendered. Even as he opened the dialogue, additional French warships arrived and Robert adopted a posture to which he would hold with unflinching devotion for almost three years. He was an active naval officer, would follow orders, and could not, of his own volition, obligate either himself or elements of his command without the express consent of Marshal Petain. To many this appeared little more than slavish obedience to a suspect regime that demonstrated tendencies toward collaboration. Whether or not Spruance discerned in Robert's declarations singular commitment or convenient evasion is unclear. There is no doubt, however, that he perceived Robert to be a prisoner of both geography and simple economics. Though some may have anticipated a successful trans-Atlantic assault by the Nazis against the French Antilles, neither Spruance nor any of his successors shared these anxieties. The many logistical hurdles appeared beyond the Nazis' capacity, even with surviving French warships at their disposal and the West African port of Dakar in their possession. As one later recalled, "only the total annihilation of the British navy could have allowed the Germans to even think of such." A far more likely scenario, however, was that of Robert secretly loading the gold on the cruiser *Emile Bertin* and ordering it to attempt a nighttime escape toward Dakar. Given the cruiser's speed and the chance it could enjoy several hours lead time before its absence was noted, there seemed little doubt such a bold move would succeed. Unless American warships could detect such as action in advance, the Vichy regime might regain the possible use of a valuable warship in addition to millions of francs in gold that could be used to help pay the exorbitant Nazi-imposed occupation costs.

Oddly enough, such an adventure not only ran counter to Admiral Robert's assurances against such but ignored the fact that the gold had been removed on arrival and stored in the lower chambers of one of the harbor forts in such a way that its movement could not have escaped notice. Moreover, by the limitations of fuel imposed in a subsequent protocol, oil stocks adequate only to a limited voyage existed as early as November 1940. Even so, anxiety lingered until vital parts of the cruiser's internal machinery were removed to Casablanca in 1942.[19]

An appraisal of the dealings of Admirals Greenslade, Horne, and Hoover with Admiral Robert illustrates the parallel of Roosevelt's train of thought to that which led him to post Admiral Leahy to Vichy. The President was fully aware of the chain of command that reached from Darlan to Robert, though to our naval emissaries it appeared that Robert's loyalty was less to Darlan than to Petain. Despite Robert's disclaimers that he could not act independently of Vichy, it became clear that he would do just this, providing certain limits were respected.

In early August 1940, Admiral John W. Greenslade visited Martinique. Among his instructions, on which Roosevelt and the "secret three" agreed, were several that Greenslade could modify once the negotiations began. Once particularly difficult topic involved the airplanes transported on the *Bearn*. Despite several reliable reports, both Knox and Hull believed the planes to be serviceable and Greenslade was to press for their return. His own inspection found otherwise and he declined to raise the matter further. Far more vital was reaching agreement to neutralize the islands. Warships and merchant vessels would remain, a naval observer would be admitted to residence in Fort-de-France, the gold would be open to regular inspection, and a gradual reduction of the island's garrison would commence. Robert would be allowed a set level of imports of food and fuel compatible with normal consumption levels by the island's population, drawing on frozen French credits in the United States.[20]

Once established, Roosevelt was content to allow Knox and Hull to direct subsequent adjustments in the arrangement. It may be a reflection of

Roosevelt's lack of confidence in the State Department that all further negotiations were conducted by naval officers. Also, at least until April 1942, the President found no real threat from the French Antilles; the economic noose Robert had allowed to be placed around his neck was deemed a sufficient deterrent against a unilateral abrogation of the protocol. If not, the Atlantic Fleet was judged capable of eliminating any danger that might develop.[21]

Thus, so long as the "local authorities" doctrine remained in place, the French West Indies remained in the right corner of Roosevelt's eye. But the threat that certain cabinet reassignments at Vichy could bring a change, or that the battlefield situation could develop in such a way that the Marshal would repudiate the arrangement, never vanished. Anticipating such, Roosevelt had mandated that Greenslade hint strongly that French sovereignty in the Antilles could be guaranteed only so long as the protocol was honored and Admiral Robert remained as High Commissioner.[22]

Following a meeting at Montoire between Hitler and Marshal Petain in October, however, Roosevelt and his advisers agreed that a second mission to Martinique was imperative. Once again Admiral Greenslade flew to Fort-de-France. Fearing Marshal Petain was tilting toward taking Vichy France into the war on Germany's side, Roosevelt ordered a collection of American warships and three battalions of Marines to be prepared to assault Martinique if Admiral Greenslade failed to secure an expansion of the original agreement. A few hours prior to his arrival, American destroyers took station off the entrance of the harbor, a threat hardly subtle nor intended to be so.[23]

Roosevelt and his cabinet expected much from Greenslade's talks with Robert. In the first instance he was to secure access for the naval observer to the warships and, on a more frequent schedule, to the storage rooms in the fort where the gold was stored. To guard against the possible escape of the *Emile Bertin*, the naval observer was to be granted a daily visit to check fuel oil levels. Beyond this, if possible, Greenslade was to press Robert for a thorough demilitarization of all of his warships. To each of these propositions Robert turned a deaf ear; only Greenslade's calm absorption of Robert's anger, and his soothing reassurances to the High Commissioner of continued subsistence if he accepted certain modifications in their August agreement, prevented a total rupture. While demilitarization was not achieved, Greenslade did succeed in gaining Robert's assent to the essential demands. He even persuaded Robert to allow daily aerial patrols over the harbor and extracted a promise that a two-day notice would be given before the *Emile Bertin* changed anchorage or departed for another colony under

Robert's control. Roosevelt had allowed that Greenslade would have the final word on the success of his mission. He advised acceptance and the assault force withdrew. The "Gentlemen's Agreement," briefly endangered, remained intact.[24]

In the first three days following the Japanese attack on Pearl Harbor, however, doubts resurfaced in Washington over both Vichy's reaction and Robert's intentions. The naval observer reported the *Bearn* was being readied for sea and that propellers were being reinstalled on some of the airplanes undergoing maintenance. At Roosevelt's direction, both Hull and Knox set in motion measures to advance the neutralization of the French Antilles and to secure Robert's reaffirmation of obligations under the year-old agreement. Though Greenslade would have received the assignment had he been available, his replacement, Rear Admiral Frederick J. Horne, proved equally tolerant of Robert's petulance and remarkably perceptive in discerning his capacity for mischief. As in Greenslade's case, Horne enjoyed a certain flexibility. Unlike the situation existing at the time of Greenslade's second mission, however, there was no assault force immediately available if Robert became uncooperative. Fortunately, the triangular network between Washington, Vichy, and Martinique allowed for a quick resolution of the rumored movement of the *Bearn*. A cryptic warning from Admiral Leahy through Admiral Darlan brought a prompt cancellation of the anticipated sortie along with promises that Robert would be advised not to move any of his ships. Still, Spruance's successor, Admiral John H. Hoover, received specific orders not just to intercept but to attack any French warships moving out of Fort-de-France.[25]

On his arrival, Horne immediately assessed the condition of the airplanes and warships at Robert's disposal. His findings differed considerably from Admiral Greenslade's. In the case of the airplanes, he found none serviceable, the result of a year's exposure to the tropics and a lack of effective maintenance. The same could be said of most of the shipping, plus the reductions in crews, owing to the selective repatriation program. Aside from a half-dozen French seaplanes, only the *Emile Bertin* seemed to pose a potential threat, and mainly that of escape. Though ordered to raise again the matter of demilitarization, Horne concluded the idea would either be rejected or that a protracted impasse would ensue over its technical enforcement. He did not see any chance of a mass exodus of Robert's warships; the merchant vessels were completely immobilized and both on-site and aerial observation could detect any pending movement of the *Emile Bertin* if Robert broke his word, which Horne did not anticipate. He sensed Robert intended to avoid provocation and recommended the economic lifeline with the islands remain unbroken. At year's end the French Antilles seemed poised to enjoy a somnolent and lethargic presence in the backwater of the war. Within a few weeks, however, this complacency abruptly ended.[26]

Few naval experts, least of all Admirals Horne and Hoover, anticipated the speed with which American naval units in the Caribbean would be reduced. Both the Atlantic and Pacific theaters drew ships from Hoover's command until, at one point, he had only two destroyers with which to guard the area where German U-boats were starting to appear. When one of these entered Fort-de-France to offload an injured sailor, a brief alarm sounded. Several merchant ships had been attacked in the vicinity and some suspected they were using Martinique's waters from which to prey on the sea lanes of the eastern Caribbean. A flurry of signals to Vichy quickly revealed the submarine had departed immediately after landing the wounded seaman. Robert gave a similar pledge to Hoover when it was asked of him.[27]

In April 1942, however, the elevation of Pierre Laval to Premier at Vichy forced a thorough review of the Martinique policy. Leahy's recall signaled this change, which soon led to the appointment of a new diplomatic mission led by Admiral John H. Hoover. Samuel Reber of the State Department accompanied him as further evidence of Roosevelt's determination to detach Robert from Vichy and to treat him as "the governing authority" in the Antilles "acting independently." Cordell Hull's remarks about Martinique becoming "a potential enemy force inside an American defense area" hinted at a contingency plan that extracted a dozen warships from the Atlantic fleet to assault Martinique if Robert refused the delegation's demands.[28]

Of all the missions to Martinique, Hoover's was certainly the most delicate, and carried the greatest danger of bloodshed. Acting with a thirty-six-hour window, he was to demand that Robert demilitarize and demobilize his ships, transfer communications to American control, and release all merchant shipping to allied use. Robert's acceptance would keep the economic relationship intact; his trusteeship over the islands would remain. Should he refuse, the United States, he would be informed, reserved the right of "self-defense."[29]

Hoover's assessment of Robert varied somewhat from those of his predecessors as to the degree to which Robert depended on Vichy to guide his actions. Securing an extension of time, Hoover did not mention any deadline, saying only that a "prompt and specific reply" was expected. From the beginning, he sensed Robert would comply with the essential demand concerning the warships. The three-day diplomatic minuet proved him correct; while Reber insisted on total compliance, Hoover argued the limited agreement be accepted. Though Reber remained to continue the negotiations, Hoover's recommendations were accepted in Washington. The assault force dispersed and Hoover's puny forces abandoned their surveillance, returning to anti-submarine patrol.[30]

From May to November 1942, Reber made no headway in further discussions with Robert. Even Hoover's periodic communiqués to Robert failed to influence him favorably. Nothing other than the warship demobilization had been realized at the time of the North African invasion, and few anticipated that in just a few months the entire situation would be resolved satisfactorily and primarily without the use of force.

Germany's invasion of the free zone in France, combined with the earlier break in diplomatic relations between Washington and Vichy, orphaned the French West Indies. Robert's initial request that the current economic accord be continued were evaded so long as he maintained contacts with Vichy. Despite his allegiance to a fictitious regime, the German Admiralty revoked safe conduct passes for his ships. This delayed the departure of his few merchantmen until convoys northbound from Trinidad passed nearby. Only one of his food ships was able to leave in December 1942 and the earliest it could return would be the following March. With food stocks already reduced, the potential existed for coercion that would compel Robert to rally to French resistance. To encourage this decision, Admiral Horne wrote a letter advising him to declare for the Allies, either under Admiral Darlan or, following Darlan's assassination, to General Henri Giraud. Robert's refusal in both instances brought another warning from the State Department: all existing engagements might be canceled and force was not ruled out.[31]

When French Guiana rallied to resistance in March 1943, Robert's isolation was nearly complete. Following the seizure of his only food ship in New Orleans, he was forced to invoke emergency rationing. Simultaneously the State Department suspended the "Gentlemen's Agreement," closed the consulate in Fort-de-France, and recalled all officials save for the naval observer. Martinique had been placed, said Cordell Hull, "in the hands of the Navy." Only one avenue of communications remained open to Robert, and Hull's veiled warning that time was running out required no elaboration.[32]

In this end game Hoover's relationship with Robert proved invaluable. Robert had threatened to scuttle his ships and drown the gold if force was used against him. That he had not, Hoover saw as a gesture of good faith; in several earlier exchanges he had played on Robert's sense of duty and paternalism. He now reminded Robert of his fragile situation, the plight of the people of the Antilles, and of the merits of cooperation. Certainly the spreading misery warranted capitulation; France's future sovereignty might be jeopardized as well if he refused. Hoover did not wish to see force employed and did not believe such would occur, but previous understandings would not be restored.[33]

Amid widespread suffering, frequent outbreaks of disorder, and the rally of Guadeloupe to the Allies, Robert sought the final guarantees that would allow for his retirement. Through a newspaper reporter, he revealed his preconditions: peaceful transition, continued French sovereignty, and economic support. When Hoover learned of this he privately indicated acceptance, after learning from Knox that the President approved. Robert capitulated on 14 July 1943, bringing the "local authorities" doctrine to an end. Yet while Robert surrendered his authority to the agents of the French Committee of National Liberation, he surrendered himself personally to Admiral Hoover.[34]

Conclusion

Any generalizations as to the value of posting naval officers to diplomatic assignments in the place of trained and experienced career diplomats are open to rebuttal. There are numerous examples of such individuals who served no good purpose at all. Given the situations explored in this chapter, however, in two cases—Admiral Leahy in Vichy and his fellow admirals in the Caribbean—the value of their missions is indisputable.

From 1940 to 1943, there were three distinct phases of the war: first, the period of defeat, then the holding action, and, finally, the rollback. During the first two phases the imperative of denying total victory to the Axis remained fixed. The chances of such appeared greater if the Soviet Union had been overrun in 1941 or if the Germans captured Stalingrad in 1942. That the direct involvement of Vichy France would have guaranteed a Nazi triumph appears less certain, though Roosevelt's administration shared Britain's anxieties over the incorporation of the French navy within the Axis fleets. Least likely, though never dismissed as impossible until November 1942, was the chance the French West Indies might become hostile. To counter such a possibility it was believed necessary to employ any stratagem to ensure final success.

An assessment of the individuals considered here gives the highest marks to the American admirals operating in the Caribbean. That Admirals Greenslade, Horne, and Hoover built on Spruance's nonthreatening approach is obvious. So too is the fact that Admiral Robert was isolated, exposed to a superior and potentially hostile Allied force, vulnerable to economic strangulation, and restrained by personal pledges of loyalty to Vichy. Also the American naval diplomats in the Caribbean profited from Admiral Leahy's presence at Vichy. Whether or not a career diplomat could have provided similar assistance is debatable. One could argue that Vichy would go only as far as Germany would allow, but Leahy's ability to communicate with Darlan "sailor to sailor," combined with Darlan's opportunism appears to have weighed heavily in the balance. A parallel existed between Admiral Robert and his American opposites, most of all with Admiral Hoover. Whether Darlan's defection to the Allies in Algiers or Robert's final decision to take Martinique into the resistance would have transpired without Leahy and Hoover is unanswerable. Leahy's subtle admonitions to Darlan to eschew alignment with Hitler so long as the Allies held a chance for victory may have eroded Darlan's confidence to where he not only postponed his decision but orchestrated an altogether different opportunity. Such can also be said of Robert; he refused the orders to scuttle his ships and sink the gold, delivered all intact at the time of his departure, and maintained to this own satisfaction his integrity as High Commissioner of the Antilles.

Only with Admiral Standley does one find little to applaud. Still, despite an environment hardly suited to either his background or his demeanor he may have, through his criticisms, laid the groundwork for Harriman's productive mission. Perhaps his abrasive personality did broaden the Soviet appreciation of an Allied coalition, facilitate the deliveries of Lend-Lease, and expand the American commitment to aid a fundamentally anti-democratic dictatorship.

What remains indisputable is that Roosevelt appropriated, utilized, and exploited circumstances, situations, and individuals in pursuit of his objectives. Viewed as a whole, Roosevelt's use of gold-braided diplomats appears to have served him and the country well.

Notes

1. For background, see Charles O. Paullin, *Diplomatic Negotiations of American Naval Officers, 1778-1883* (Baltimore: Johns Hopkins Press, 1912).
2. U.S. Department of State, *Foreign Relations of the United States: Diplomatic Papers: 1942*, 7 vols. (Washington, D.C.: Government Printing Office, 1960), 3:415; hereafter cited as FRUS 1942. See also William H. Standley and Arthur A. Ageton, *Admiral Ambassador to Russia* (Chicago: Henry Regnery Company, 1955), 197–199.
3. FRUS 1942, 3:555; 606.
4. Ibid., 446; 754. See also Standley, 240–249.

5. U.S. Department of State, *Foreign Relations of the United States: Diplomatic Papers: 1943*, 7 vols. (Washington, D.C.: Government Printing Office, 1964), 3:628–632. See also Standley, 240–249.

6. Robert E. Sherwood, *Roosevelt and Hopkins: An Intimate History* (New York: Harper & Brothers, 1948), 640.

7. Ibid., 705–706.

8. William L. Langer, *Our Vichy Gamble* (New York: W.W. Norton, 1947), 118–119.

9. William D. Leahy, *I Was There* (New York: Whittlesey House, 1950), 8–9.

10. William D. Leahy Diary, February 23, 1941, Library of Congress Manuscripts Division. Hereafter cited as LOCMS.

11. Ibid., March 19, 1941.

12. Leahy, 48.

13. Leahy Diary, July 16, 1941; February 24, 1942.

14. Leahy, 89–91.

15. Admiralty Records 199/367: "Collapse of France." Admiralty Records 199/897: "War Diary: America and West Indies Station." Public Record Office.

16. Sir Charles Lambe Papers, Manuscripts Division, British Museum. Frank Knox Papers, LOCMS.

17. Cordell Hull Papers, LOCMS.

18. Interview with Admiral John H. Hoover, February 20, 1968.

19. Interview with Admiral Benjamin S. Custer, June 29, 1979.

20. Knox Papers; Chief of Naval Operations to Rear Admiral John W. Greenslade, August 2, 1940, Greenslade Papers, LOCMS.

21. Hull Papers.

22. Greenslade Papers.

23. Patrick Abbazia, *Mr. Roosevelt's Navy: The Private War of the U.S. Atlantic Fleet: 1939-1942* (Annapolis, Md.: United States Naval Institute, 1979), 113–116.

24. Admiral Georges Robert, *La France aux Antilles de 1939 a 1943* (Paris: Librarie Plon, 1950), 80–84.

25. Rear Admiral Frederick J. Horne to Cordell Hull, December 19, 1941, National Archives.

26. Ibid.

27. Hoover interview; Custer interview.

28. Memorandum by Frederick J. Horne to the Joint Chiefs of Staff, April 27, 1942, Division of Naval History.

29. Hoover interview.

30. FRUS 1942, 2:611–664.

31. Memorandum by J.W. Bonbright, December 17, 1942, National Archives.

32. Hull papers.

33. Hoover interview.

34. Ibid.

8

"A Grand and Glorious Thing . . . the Team of Mackenzie and Roosevelt"

Elizabeth R.B. Elliott-Meisel

If the friendship had been as close and relaxed as President Franklin D. Roosevelt assumed, Prime Minister Mackenzie King would have been comfortable telling Roosevelt that his friends called him "Rex."[1] If the friendship had been as intimate as Mackenzie King wished for, he would not have admitted to his diary, much less to Roosevelt himself, that he had a hard time calling the president "Franklin." But as implied in the chapter title–a phrase taken from a November 1941 letter from FDR to Mackenzie King–these two wartime leaders rightly believed they had a strong, unique, and unpretentious relationship that benefited not only Canada and the United States, but the entire Allied cause.

Analysis of Roosevelt and King underscores how this personal relationship developed and laid the foundation for the bilateral cooperation of the subsequent sixty years. It was the intersection of two powerful leaders at a time necessitating international cooperation that maximized the talents and responsibilities of Roosevelt and King. World War II necessitated a change and redefinition of the relationship between Canada and the United States. While the resultant association has had its ebbs and flows, its synergy has never really waned since the foundation was laid by Roosevelt and King.

But if this relationship was as novel and important as both men believed, why do scholars, much less the public, know so little about it?[2] How many Americans know, for instance, that during World War II, the U.S. Army working in the Canadian North answered the phone "Army of Occupation"? Or that the Americans and Canadians cooperated in building two different air routes through Canada (the Northwest Staging Route and the Crimson

Project) to facilitate Lend-Lease deliveries to Great Britain and the Soviet Union? Or that the two nations built the Alaska Highway? Or that both nations built important meteorological and communication stations that supplied vital weather information for Allied shipping and military planning? Or that the crucial Atlantic convoy system was a model of onsite inter-navy cooperation when diplomatic channels were at times tense over the division of authority? Or, for one last example, that the Canadian and American forces formed the unique First Special Service Force that truly mixed men of all ranks from both nations and saw action in the Aleutians, Italy, and southern France?

The reason these efforts are overlooked might lie in the fact that the Canadian North constituted a very small theater in a much larger war, and as no continental invasion took place, preventative efforts, never put to the test, are easily forgotten. Canadian historian Shelagh Grant offers another theory; she contends that Canadians might not want to publicize foreigners' work on Canadian soil and, with no invasion in the North, there is no need to put it in the spotlight.[3] In the same vein, the Cold War left neither the Americans nor the Soviets wanting to thank the Canadians for getting the Lend-Lease planes to the USSR. (Unfortunately, neither do Canadians enjoy much recognition of their role in the Atlantic Convoy that delivered Lend-Lease materiel to the United States' greatest ally, Great Britain.) Perhaps the collaboration is overlooked because weather and communication stations, vital as they are, are not as large or impressive as bases. Consequently, their contribution to the war effort is easily shunted aside. And finally, perhaps neither the United States nor Canada wants to admit too loudly that the enemy did, in fact, reach North America: the Germans sunk ships in the St. Lawrence Seaway and established an unmanned (and, for forty years, undetected) weather station in Newfoundland, and the Japanese launched nuisance raids and balloon-dropped bombs along the Pacific coast.

There is another theory, however, for the general ignorance of the Canadian-American cooperative efforts. In 1945, Canadian-American historian John Bartlet Brebner wrote the final volume in a collection of works on U.S.–Canada relations, sponsored by the Carnegie Endowment for International Peace. In his book *The North Atlantic Triangle*, Brebner confessed that he gave more space to Canada than to the United States or Great Britain, not because it was more important, but because Americans and Britons were so uninformed about the third leg of this important triangle. This lack of awareness was mainly the result of the fact that both nations "have usually been able to take [Canada] for granted without serious consequences to themselves."[4] This observation is especially relevant in looking at the U.S.-Canada relationship during World War II. Therefore, any analysis of the cooperative wartime efforts must illuminate and emphasize the contributions of King and his nation.

There is a tendency to view Canadian-American relations as essentially a history of peaceful coexistence, if not constant cooperation. In reality coexistence has evolved from outright invasion of Canada by the United States to a "close association amounting to actual alliance."[5] Pre–World War II Canadian foreign policy was closely tied to Great Britain, but there was also a belief that the Old World had something to learn from the New World's "undefended border and shared institutions, where statesmen talked their problems through."[6] Both North American nations shared a desire to avoid being drawn into European conflicts, their historical and emotional attachment to Britain notwithstanding.[7]

The transition years from hostility to alliance were not without growing pains and separation anxiety, but it was the leadership of Mackenzie King and FDR that helped soften the blows and blunt the edges of this novel relationship.[8] Again, "compatibility" of leadership was important in the Canadian-American relationship because "it set the tone for discussions at every level of the bureaucratic hierarchy."[9] Despite the disparate size and power between the United States and Canada, Canada's role in continental defense during World War II elevated its importance and status in the world arena, and it also helped define Canadian foreign policy in these years. Mackenzie King, acting as his own Secretary of State for External Affairs, was the major Canadian player in that formulation, especially with regards to the United States, and his role was inextricably linked to the presidency of Franklin Roosevelt. Like FDR, Mackenzie King has been the subject of extensive historical debate. In fact, one historian has argued that "King promises to become the FDR of Canadian historiography."[10]

The two leaders' careers overlap from 1935, when King became prime minister, until FDR's death in April 1945. During that time the men met eighteen times, twelve times after Canada entered World War II on 10 September 1939.[11] In addition, there were countless phone calls and written letters, many recorded in FDR's personal papers and Mackenzie King's diaries. Early on, FDR urged King to circumvent official channels and use the phone at any time.[12]

Letters were equally revealing. FDR's private letters to heads of state and men of position, such as Prime Minister Ramsay Macdonald, King George V, and the Canadian Governor General began with "My dear ____," noting their titles, rarely their names. Letters usually closed with "Faithfully yours." But to Mackenzie King, in 1936, FDR wrote "My dear Mackenzie King;" by 1937 it was "My dear Mackenzie," and finally his least formal salutation of "Dear Mackenzie." He usually closed with "As ever yours."[13] King, for his part, signed his letters to FDR "Mackenzie," and closed with such phrases as "With affectionate good wishes" and "Your good neighbor."[14]

Initially in public and on the phone the men addressed each other as "Mr. President" and "Mr. Prime Minister," but that quickly passed and it became "Mackenzie" and "Franklin," although King still used "Mr. President" often, and as late as the end of 1942 admitted to Roosevelt that he found it difficult to use "Franklin."[15] But the men found it easy to be in each other's company, to speak frankly, to share ideas, to hammer out agreements, and to get their staffs to work smoothly together.[16] FDR placed great importance on the informality, frequency, and easy access of the relationship, especially in the days before Pearl Harbor,[17] often arranging meetings outside official Washington at such places as Warm Springs and Hyde Park.

FDR was arguably "the first . . . [and] only American president to take more than a passing interest in Canada."[18] There is much speculation as to the reason. John H. Thompson speculates that this could have been due to personal sentimental feelings; Roosevelt's summer home was on Campobello Island in New Brunswick. It could have been because Canada represented a politically safe haven to circumvent isolationist sentiment in the United States, as Canada appeared to be a partner in a "seemingly innocuous bilateral relationship."[19] To this could be added FDR's real concern with continental security against Hitler, whom he completely opposed. Or this friendliness could have reflected an extension of the new American attitude toward the Western Hemisphere–that of the Good Neighbor–as opposed to previous Big Stick and Dollar Diplomacy attitudes.[20] Reflecting this interest in Canada, FDR placed an early importance on the appointment of American ministers to Canada. In 1933 he made his cousin, Warren Delano Robbins, Minister to Canada, and in 1939, when he asked Daniel C. Roper to serve, he called the Ottawa posting "among the top two or three of our Diplomatic posts, even though the Empire's relationship prevents it from being called an Embassy."[21]

To King's chagrin, he was less popular in Canada than FDR.[22] Although eight years FDR's senior, King was not elevated to the heights of FDR or Churchill.[23] Canadian historian Jack Granatstein notes that "to the

[Canadian] electorate [King] was only a pudgy little man, inscrutable, cautious, undynamic, a poor Canadian substitute for a Roosevelt or a Churchill."[24] And many historians have not been much kinder, characterizing the relationship as that of teacher and student, the younger instructing the elder,[25] and selectively utilizing physical attributes to reflect their lesser opinion of the Canadian. For example, as historian Blair Neatby notes, FDR was crippled and often in a wheelchair, but this factor was usually overlooked, as historians sought "to convey his exuberant vitality." Despite his size/girth, Winston Churchill was called "cherubic." But descriptions of King as "short, squat, stock, pudgy [omitted] his stamina, . . . endurance, [and] remarkable powers of concentration."[26]

The 1935 signing of the bilateral Trade Agreement was not the first time King and Roosevelt met. They had met years before at Harvard. FDR liked to emphasize the longevity of their friendship, at one point stating that he had "been close to Mackenzie King almost since we were boys."[27] But in truth the friendship did not develop until both men were their nation's leaders. For instance, prior to King's return as prime minister in 1935, while he was leader of the Opposition and FDR was president, the Canadian was not without reservations about Roosevelt. King endorsed FDR's liberalism and shared some of FDR's goals and principles, but he clearly did not agree with their method of implementation. King believed the New Deal was "dangerous in the extreme"[28] and "not in Canada's best interest."[29] King opposed economic nationalism and an extended role of the federal government in the economy.

As the friendship between the two leaders developed, however, Mackenzie King "found it exceedingly easy to talk with the President, and those around him tell me that he feels it the same with me."[30] King was sure that FDR liked him; those close to Roosevelt concurred, as did other leaders, such as Winston Churchill.[31] King also sought assurance of his place in Roosevelt's life by way of the spiritual world. A practicing spiritualist, King was told of Roosevelt's affection during séances.

FDR was the only non-Canadian or non-Briton whom King spoke with from the spirit world. In a 1938 séance, prior to the North American visit of King George V and Queen Elizabeth, Sir Wilfrid Laurier, a supporter of Canadian-American and Anglo-American trade agreements, told King, "The President is very fond of you. He will treat you like a Prince."[32] British Prime Minister Churchill reiterated this sentiment during a séance in 1941.[33] Although King did not participate in many séances during the war years, he continued to encounter Roosevelt in the spirit world even after the president's death."[34]

For all their personal closeness, however, King was never without a healthy skepticism toward the United States and its designs on Canada.[35] This wariness even extended to Roosevelt. When O.D. Skelton, Undersecretary of State for External Affairs, stated before the war that Canadian security depended on the United States, King noted in his diary: "I do not like to be dependent on the US; change of leaders there might lead to a vassalage so far as our Dominion was concerned. There was more real freedom in the British Commonwealth of Nations, and a rich inheritance."[36] He feared American "efforts that would . . . bring Canada out of the orbit of [Great Britain] and into their own orbit." His desire was to see Canada develop into "the greatest of nations of the British Commonwealth."[37] Yet despite these reservations, King was convinced that the way to prevent absorption was not through confrontation, retaliatory actions, or fostering anti-American sentiment in Canada, but by closer U.S.–Canada relations.[38]

King was not an isolationist, a neutralist, or a colonialist. Most historians, whether they support Mackenzie King's foreign policy or not, argue that he was an "autonomist,"[39] a term used for those wanting greater Canadian autonomy. "Autonomy" to King was a Canada free from manipulation and/or control by either Britain or the United States. He did not like the term "independence" because it reminded him of those seeking to leave the British sphere, and it sounded too American.[40] He fostered good Canadian-American relations as a way to help Anglo-American relations. King was convinced that a harmonious Anglo-American relationship was an asset to Canada, which had ties to both nations. Positive Canadian-American relations were not to be at the expense of Anglo-Canadian ties, which King, in the position of Prime Minister and Secretary of State for External Affairs, could protect.[41]

The idea of Canada acting as a link between the United States and Britain was not new, but it was personalized and applied to King in the late 1930s.[42] King was sure of his ability to facilitate Anglo-American relations, yet he was also aware that such a role would necessitate "tact and understanding."[43] Never comfortable being completely open with either Roosevelt or Churchill,[44] King "could not be an intermediary in the grandiose way he might have liked, but he realized that he could be [in King's words] 'a medium of communication'" between the two great leaders.[45] FDR also nurtured the Canadian role and applauded the Canadian-American relationship as a feather in the cap of both King and himself. In

1941 he wrote to King, "Probably both nations could get along without us but I think we may be pardoned for our thoughts, especially in view of the fact that our association so far has brought some proven benefits to both nations."[46]

While FDR seemed to appreciate the differences between Canada and the United States, he also stressed the close feelings between King and himself, the shared experiences of Canada and the United States, and the common attributes of both nations. Noting at the end of 1942 that King was "a very old friend" with whom he would be spending an informal weekend, Roosevelt also mentioned that he expected to discuss with King "some of the deeper problems of humanity—human life in the days to come after the war; remembering always that the people of Canada and the people of the United States essentially have the same problems."[47] The groundwork for a new Canadian-American association was laid by Roosevelt and King prior to the outbreak of World War II. The exigencies of war transformed a personal relationship into a comprehensive bilateral defense arrangement that forever changed U.S.-Canadian relations.[48] In terms of continental defense, FDR's attention to Canada was ahead of his military advisors in recognizing the benefits of collaboration with Canada and creating an atmosphere of cooperation before the outbreak of hostilities.

Both Roosevelt and King had to be careful in public, as too close a show of friendship would work against each domestically. In Canada King had to be vigilant in protecting Canadian military, political, and economic interests.[49] He also had to assure the Canadian public that by fostering closer Canadian-American relations, he was aiding Britain and the Commonwealth, and not abandoning Canada's commitment to the mother country. In the United States, FDR had to avoid being seen as developing international ties with a belligerent when isolationist sentiment was so pervasive. Roosevelt and King sought consensus within their respective nations for most of their policies,[50] but, of course, that only applied to those policies they revealed to the public. Both men told the public as little as possible when controversial situations arose. For Canada this included the number and extent of Americans and projects on Canadian soil; for the United States it was the amount and form of aid America contributed to the Allies prior to Pearl Harbor. Both leaders believed their course of action was in the best interest of their respective nations[51] and they were convinced that, when necessary, it was their role to persuade the public of their visionary, and potentially unpopular, course of action.

The 1937 Sino-Japanese War led to increased concern by FDR about American and Canadian Pacific coastal defenses, and increased attention to Atlantic defenses quickly followed. On 18 August 1938, at Queen's University in Kingston, Ontario, FDR delivered the well-known and often cited speech that pledged U.S. protection of Canada if the latter was attacked. But this was not the first time FDR had linked American and Canadian defense. On 14 August 1936, in a speech at Chataugua, New York, he stated, "Our closest neighbors are good neighbors. If there are remoter nations that wish us not good but ill, they know that we are strong; they know that we can and we will defend ourselves and defend our neighborhood."[52] But it seems that neither the Canadians nor the Americans grasped the implications of this speech at the time, that military cooperation lay just around the corner.[53]

Military commitments in Canada had historically been linked to Great Britain. The American pledge to Canadian defense was new, and the Canadians were not completely comfortable with it. "A narrow interpretation [of Roosevelt's Kingston speech] . . . is that it extended the Monroe Doctrine to Canada."[54] "[A] broad interpretation . . . is that it created a link between the collective security system of Pan America and Great Britain."[55] FDR himself later explained his view of the Kingston speech. The original interpretation of the Monroe Doctrine, according to FDR, included a definite thought that no European power should reestablish sovereignty over any territory that had gained its independence, and that this also applied to the changing of European sovereignty over those portions of the Americas that had not revolted and established their independence. So one might say, Roosevelt suggested, that the speech he had made in Canada, about Canada, was not anything new but only a restatement of the original intent of the Monroe Doctrine.[56]

Mackenzie King followed the Kingston speech with a statement of his own two days later in Woodbridge, Ontario. King did not disagree with Roosevelt, but he wanted to assure the United States that Canada was committed to its own defense, and that Canada felt it would be safe if it cooperated with the United States and the British Empire. In reality, Canada was ill-prepared to back up this rhetoric, as Canadian defenses were sorely lacking. The Canadian military, for its part, wanted to cooperate with the Americans because it realized that continental defense needed American participation.

The Munich Pact of September 1938 was welcomed by both FDR and Mackenzie King. Although both were very anti-Hitler and, as FDR wrote to

King, not convinced the agreement would end Hitler's territorial appetite, they wanted to avert war.[57] In March, King publicly stated his trepidation at the prospect of Canada being drawn into another European conflict. Despite his personal commitment to the British, he was trying "to balance bellicosity with caution; the requirements of the domestic scene demanded this."[58] This need to address isolationist sentiment was true for FDR too, as his public rhetoric against American involvement in war was at odds with the conversations he had privately with King.[59]

When the war broke out in Europe, there was no doubt that Mackenzie King and Canada were committed to actively supporting Britain, but delaying a declaration of war for a week benefited both the Canadians and the British. In the week between British and Canadian declarations of war, American aircraft could be shipped over the border, as Canada was not yet a belligerent. Some in the Roosevelt administration questioned the legality of this, as Canada was part of the Commonwealth, but FDR insisted the shipments take place.[60] Asked at a press conference on September 5 if his government still viewed Canada as a nonbelligerent, FDR evaded a direct answer by noting that the Canadian Parliament would vote on the matter later in the week.[61] At this point, Canada was technically neutral. Consequently, the United States could technically continue to trade with Canada.[62]

Joint defense discussions after Canada entered the war, when the United States was still neutral, had to proceed carefully lest anyone accuse Canada of trying "to influence the policies or to interfere in the domestic affairs of a neutral country." King continued, "had there not been, between the president and myself, complete confidence in each other's purpose and motives, I question if the situation could have been met without occasioning genuine embarrassment to one side or the other, if not indeed to both."[63] The reason the two leaders pursued conversations was their shared concern with continental defense. The root of this motivation, however, was different: for the Americans it was defense of the United States; for the Canadians it was the defense of Canada and the defense of the British Commonwealth at large.[64]

Although Canada was loyal to Great Britain, reality and geography dictated that the United States was the nation that Canada would have to deal with militarily and economically. But as the Ogdensburg Agreement of 17 August 1940 reflects, the dynamics of the North Atlantic Triangle were neither static nor inflexible. The question is still unresolved as to who initiated the meeting that eventually led to the Ogdensburg visit,[65] but the

Declaration and the resultant Permanent Joint Board on Defense broke new ground in Canadian-American defense cooperation and heralded a change in both American and Canadian attitudes. Prior to this, some in Canada feared that closer U.S.–Canada relations could weaken the Anglo-Canadian connection. Now, however, good U.S.–Canada relations were seen as the way to facilitate better Anglo-American relations, which would, in turn, be to Canada's benefit.[66] For the United States, Ogdensburg was a step toward a form of collective security with a belligerent nation. By narrowly focusing on "mutual defense," both Roosevelt and King were able to avoid strong domestic opposition. In Canada, King defused charges that the United States would exact concessions contrary to Canadian interests and Anglo-Canadian relations. In the United States, Roosevelt was able to avert charges that this would drag the nation into war.[67]

The meeting was "strictly the Franklin-Mackenzie axis at work,"[68] as no military personnel or advisors were present. The subsequent Declaration was "a masterpiece of political timing" for which both men were known.[69] Roosevelt noted that the creation of the Permanent Joint Board on Defense (PJBD) was "another proof of the solidarity existing among the American Republics" made closer by the war.[70] Military historian Charles Stacey contends that there is considerable difficulty in military cooperation between two greatly disparate nations unequal in population and power. But he insists that the more informal the setting and the more participants strive for "mutual understanding,"[71] the better the chances of successful cooperation. This was true of the PJBD, and it reflected the personal relationship of the heads of state. Subordinates followed the lead set by FDR and King, and successful compromises and accommodations were found when negotiating cooperative agreements.

The board's mandate was to "consider in the broad sense the defense of the north half of the Western Hemisphere" and submit "studies relating to sea, land and air problems including personnel and material."[72] Established by no more than an executive order and an order-in-council, the PJBD succeeded as a forum where two nations of disproportionate size functioned as equals. During the war, it made thirty-three war recommendations, all unanimously approved by a board that worked on consensus, not majority rules. All but two recommendations were completely accepted by both governments. The board served as "an early instance of effective inter-Allied military co-operation which was encouraging as an example and valuable as a model."[73] The PJBD's success exceeded the expectations of either FDR or

King. FDR was convinced that other nations should look to the U.S.–Canada mechanism as a model to try to adopt.[74]

The Hyde Park Agreement of April 1941 was initiated by Mackenzie King and endorsed by Roosevelt. "The economic corollary of the Ogdensburg Declaration,"[75] it was born out of necessity. The United States was the "international bank" with whom Canada needed to deal, and something had to be done to alleviate Canada's dollar crisis. In the past, Canada had balanced its dollar deficit with the United States by its sterling surplus with Britain. But during the war, Britain could not pay Canada, and the United States offered incentives for British purchases from America, further hurting sales by Canada to Britain. Thus an arrangement was needed to reestablish a balance. The Hyde Park Agreement "symbolized the convergence of the Canadian interest with the American search for hemispheric self-sufficiency and with FDR's personal commitment to the British."[76]

Precedent-setting in its approach to the Canadian-American financial arrangement, the Hyde Park Agreement established a plan by which Canadian and American defense production would concentrate on those war materials each produced most efficiently.[77] Canadian production of goods contracted by Britain, under the Anglo-American Lend-Lease agreement, were also included in the agreement. Consequently, Canada was able to redress its dollar deficit and, at the same time, continue to aid the British.[78]

The familiarity and concern of both Roosevelt and King with the state of each other's nation helped produce the quick agreement, and no great concessions were made by Canada. Of course, politically and economically, Hyde Park was not of great importance to the United States; Canada was a cash buyer and the United States was still getting what it needed in the way of Canadian war materials. In addition, with heavy American investment in Canada, any Canadian difficulties could spell problems for these investments and possible retaliation against branch plants.[79]

While the Canadian-American and Anglo-Canadian legs of the North Atlantic Triangle were strengthened, the Anglo-American leg was just taking shape. The August 1941 Atlantic Meeting off the coast of Newfoundland provided an opportunity for Roosevelt and Churchill to meet face to face and begin to develop their personal rapport. It was at this exclusively Anglo-American meeting that the Atlantic Charter was issued. Mackenzie King was not invited, much to his chagrin. FDR explained that he had not even visited King prior to the meeting because to do so would not look good, as it would magnify the fact that King was not to attend the meeting. Although FDR had a strong personal relationship with King, Roosevelt was adamant that King could not be the only Dominion leader present.[80] FDR feared that other Dominion leaders would seek a presence at the meeting. And later, as FDR and Churchill quickly got to know each other, there was no need or desire for an intermediary, even one as hospitable as Mackenzie King.

While neither Roosevelt nor Churchill could overlook the Canadians or ignore Mackenzie King, King found that he was more informed than consulted about Allied arrangements, even those that directly affected Canada. At the same time, FDR was not without appreciation for King. It was at this point, in the pre–Pearl Harbor days, with the United States far from a disinterested neutral, but still technically a nonbelligerent, that FDR took time for self-congratulatory praise and praise for Mackenzie King. "Sometimes I indulge in the thoroughly sanctimonious and pharisaical thought, which I hope that you are also occasionally guilty of, that it is a grand and glorious thing for Canada and the United States to have the team of Mackenzie and Roosevelt at the helm in days like these!"[81]

The realities of war brought the issues of sovereignty and security to the forefront for King and his government, as they strove to balance continental security, commitments to the Allies abroad, and maintenance of sovereignty at home. American interest in the North was initiated by FDR in the mid-1930s, and preceded interest by the American military, which as late as 1937, advised against fortifying Alaska. Eventually, the joint military wartime projects in northern Canada included communication and meteorological stations, the Alaska Highway, the Northwest Staging Route (which supplied materiel to the USSR), the Northeast Staging Route/Crimson Route (which supplied materiel to Europe), the Mackenzie River air route, a joint military operation in the Aleutian Islands, blanket arrangements for USN transits in Canadian waters (particularly the Inland Passage), and the construction of military bases on Canadian soil.[82] Most of these projects were discussed and recommended by the PJBD, usually before commencement of the operation, although there were times that the Board rubberstamped projects already in progress.

By 1943 there were 33,000 Americans, military and civilian, in the Canadian North. They reputedly answered the phone "Army of Occupation,"[83] and it was true that their numbers were greater than the Canadians' until 1944, when American men and equipment were transferred to other theaters of the war. It is important to realize that Mackenzie King did not acquiesce to all Roosevelt's plans. King never wanted "an American

Canada"[84] and he suspected American motives, even those of FDR.[85] While Canada was willing to permit the American military to have a large number of forces and big bases on Canadian soil, using Canadian facilities or building on Canadian sites, King would not lease the bases or sell the land to the Americans as Britain was willing to do in Newfoundland. The Canadian land was to stay Canadian.[86] Tensions certainly arose between Ottawa and Washington over the joint ventures in the Canadian North, and diplomatic papers reveal the extent to which attempts were made to smooth ruffled feathers on the one hand and to expedite bilateral projects on the other.

After Pearl Harbor, FDR had less time and interest in Canadian complaints, despite his friendship with Mackenzie King. The personal relationship "won no special concessions," for leading America in the war left the president precious little time to worry about relations with Canada.[87] Canadian diplomat and civil servant Norman Robertson described the unmistaken shift in American attitudes. "The United States is, not unnaturally, inclined to take Canadian concurrence and support entirely for granted. . . . [However] the transition has been rather abrupt and not too tactfully handled."[88] Robertson further noted that the United States tended "to regard Canada as an internal domestic relationship rather than an international one."[89] King, for his part, accepted the diminished attention Canada found in Washington and, wanting to protect the relationship as much as possible, did not rock the boat. He made every effort to at least appear involved at Anglo-American conferences, even if there was no substance to his presence.[90]

Roosevelt and Churchill knew King loved to be in Washington when Churchill was there too, making the "Big Two meetings into Big Three or even to Big Two and One-Half ones."[91] King was very aware that he was dwarfed by FDR and Churchill, and this fed his insecurities. It disturbed King that Canadians viewed and spoke of FDR and Churchill as "our leaders."[92] To compensate, King ingratiated himself to both leaders and made concerted efforts to be seen with them. Both Churchill and FDR were very polite to King and played on his egoism, according to Lester Pearson.[93] Canadian historian D.C. Creighton maintains that "King never hoped or expected to be given a real voice in the management of [Allied] affairs[;] all he wanted was a semblance so outwardly convincing that to the uninstructed Canadians it would look like the real thing."[94]

Throughout the war, King was convinced that it was easier to get what Canada wanted from the United States than from Great Britain, but in reality, the opposite was true. It was the United States that was afraid of giving Canada too much of a voice because of the precedent it would set. FDR feared that other lesser powers would want a say in Allied strategy and operations. Part of the reason for King's misconception was "that FDR, with his informal *bonhomie*, knew the way to King's heart much better than" Churchill.[95] Of course, FDR's public praise of King and their relationship had helped elicit bilateral cooperation, but there is no reason to doubt Roosevelt's genuine appreciation of the relationship. Just a month before he died, FDR stated at a press conference, "Of course, Mr. King and I are very, very old friends—personal friends, as you know. But since he has been Prime Minister, we have developed that friendship into a practical way of handling common problems . . . and it was an outstanding example of what you can do by common consultation and laying one's own problems before the other fellow."[96] Conversely, King's depth of feeling for FDR and his ability to be especially sensitive to others was recalled by Eleanor Roosevelt in her memoirs. At the time of FDR's death she noted that she "was deeply touched by the number of our friends who had left their homes very early to drive to Hyde Park for the funeral, and especially by the kind thoughtfulness of Prime Minister Mackenzie King. My niece (Mrs. Edward P. Elliott) was living in Ottawa at the time and he had invited her to go to Hyde Park on his special train."[97]

Perhaps it was not quite "a grand and glorious thing," but the relationship between Franklin Roosevelt and Mackenzie King certainly was that of a team. It was not a team of two equally powerful partners. In many ways, it mirrored the disparate size and power of the two nations that the men served. But there is no denying that the closeness was a departure from the past, and it set a new course for both nations. The personal stamp of Roosevelt and King on the nascent relationship carried through to the military cooperative efforts of World War II and laid the foundation for the next sixty years. From the onset, the U.S.-Canada partnership reflected Canadian apprehension over sovereignty and American concern with continental security. But it was the pragmatism, sensitivity, and healthy skepticism evidenced in the personal relationship between Roosevelt and King that laid the groundwork for the synergetic U.S.-Canadian association that has developed and endured.

Notes

1. King's friends (and even Vincent Massey, whom King did not particularly like) called him "Rex," while only FDR and Winston Churchill called him "Mackenzie." Canadian

historian C.P. Stacey believes this reflected the fact that the relationship was never "particularly intimate." Charles P. Stacey, *Canada in the Age of Conflict* (Toronto: University of Toronto Press, 1981), 2:230; hereafter referred to as *Conflict*.

2. A look at books on FDR for this paper was revealing: of ten books dealing with FDR and specifically World War II, neither Mackenzie King nor Canada was mentioned more than 14 times, and this was in Dallek's *Franklin D. Roosevelt and American Foreign Policy 1932-45* (New York: Oxford University Press, 1979). All of the other books mentioned either the Prime Minister or the nation fewer than eight times, and most often between zero and three times. Few entries were more than a passing reference, such as the fact Mackenzie King hosted a conference or was at a state dinner. Often his name only appeared in the caption of a picture where the other leaders were present. It was not unusual to misspell his name. Mention of Canadian participation in continental defense and contributions to atomic energy and bomb research was usually omitted. Some exceptions existed but they were a rarity. William D. Hassett, a newspaperman and an aide to FDR, kept an "uncensored record on Roosevelt on most of the important days when he was off the record." (Introduction by Jonathan Daniels in William Hassett, *Off the Record with FDR, 1942-1945* [New Brunswick: Rutgers University Press, 1958], ix; hereafter referred to as *Record*.) In his book he mentions Mackenzie King only twice: he called FDR and King "very old friends" (ibid., 322) dating back to the mens' Harvard days, and he noted King's poor news media reputation by recording a song about King among the correspondents: "'William Lyon Mackenzie King/Never tells us a goddam thing'" (Ibid., 323).

3. Shelagh Grant, "Weather Stations, Airfields, and Research in the High Arctic, 1941-1959: An American Perspective" (Vancouver, BC: Canadian Historical Association Annual Meeting, 27 May 1990), 3; hereafter referred to as "Weather Stations."

4. John Bartlet Brebner, *North Atlantic Triangle* (New York: Columbia University Press, 1945), xii; hereafter referred to as *Triangle*.

5. Charles P. Stacey, "The Canadian-American Permanent Joint Board on Defense," *International Journal* 9:2 (Spring 1954): 107; hereafter referred to as "PJBD."

6. Norman Hillmer, *Partners Nevertheless: Canadian-American Relations in the Twentieth Century* (Toronto: Copp Clark Pitman, 1989), 2; hereafter referred to as *Partners*.

7. Ibid., 34.

8. John Thompson and Stephen Randall, *Canada and the United States: Ambivalent Allies* (Athens: University of Georgia Press, 1994), 146; hereafter referred to as *Canada and the United States*.

9. Charles Doran and J.H. Sigler, eds., *Canada and the U.S.: Enduring Friendship, Persistent Stress* (Englewood Cliffs, NJ: Prentice-Hall, 1985), 233.

10. Robin Winks, Review of *William Lyon Mackenzie King, Volume II, 1924-1932: The Lonely Heights*. In *Political Science Quarterly* 80:2 (1965): 316.

11. Thompson and Randall, *Canada and the United States*, 165.

12. FDR to King, 21 December 1937. Elliott Roosevelt, ed., *FDR: His Personal Letters*. (New York: Duell, Sloan & Pearce, 1950), 1:735; hereafter referred to as *Letters*; see also Stacey, *Conflict*, 2:174.

13. FDR, *Letters*, I:347, 370–371, 556–557, 578, 735; II:850.

14. C.P. Stacey, *Arms, Men and Governments* (Ottawa: Queen's Printer for Canada, 1970), 150; hereafter referred to as *Arms*.

15. Pickersgill, *Record*, 1:436.
16. Malcolm MacDonald goes so far as to assert that FDR had "evident respect for [King's] statesmanlike gifts. He regarded King not simply as a pleasant friend but also a wise counsellor to whom he occasionally appealed when he wanted experienced, prudent advice.... [Their] conversations were extraordinarily intimate and uninhibited on the president's part by any official restraints or diplomatic respect for other personages." Malcolm MacDonald, "The View from London," in English and Stubbs, *Mackenzie King: Widening the Debate* (Toronto: Macmillan of Canada, 1978), 48; hereafter referred to as *Debate*.
17. FDR to King, 16 April 1936, *Letters*, I:578–579.
18. Thompson and Randall, *Canada and the United States*, 143.
19. Ibid., 144.
20. Ibid., 143.
21. FDR to Daniel C. Roper, 10 July 1939, *Letters*, 2:906.
22. FDR was arguably the most popular American president in Canada to date. In the war era, those who did not admire Roosevelt were usually those who feared that close Canadian-American ties would adversely affect Anglo-Canadian ties. For example, historian Donald Creighton called FDR "that outspoken critic and covert enemy of the British Empire." D.G. Creighton, *The Forked Road* (Toronto: McClelland & Stewart, 1976), 163. Creighton felt the destroyers-for-bases deal took unfair advantage of Britain's weakened state during the war; FDR wanted "absolute and irresponsible military power" and Mackenzie King acted "as Roosevelt's stooge" with the deal (ibid., 42). Creighton also condemns FDR for making decisions that, to too large a degree, were in response to domestic considerations and politics. But what politician does not operate with such issues in mind? Mackenzie King certainly did too . . . and earned Creighton's contempt. He called the two leaders "the two veteran manipulators of public opinion" (ibid., 82).
23. "In his life, few admired Mackenzie King, fewer still loved him. Yet 'sustained and soothed by an unfaltering trust,' he went on and won through. . . . What an extraordinary jumble of courage and timidity, of percipience and insensitiveness, of party loyalty and deep patriotism, of Christian and Machiavellian attitudes, of humility and childish egotism; what a piece of work was King. How well he deserves of his country!" Lower, Review of *The Mackenzie King Record*, vol. 2 in *Queen's Quarterly*, 349. Lester Pearson described him as "[an] enigmatic and contradictory personality, with that combination of charming friendliness and self-centered calculation, of kindness and ruthlessness, of political vision and personal pettiness which so many who worked for him found disconcerting." Lester Pearson, *Mike* (Toronto: University of Toronto, 1972), 1:197.

An example of the British Prime Minister's and the American President's popularity in Canada was the proposed postage stamp of February 1941, which would have placed Mackenzie King in the middle, with Churchill and FDR on either side. The stamp was never issued, however, as only dead people (except royalty) appear on Canadian stamps.
24. J.L. Granatstein, "King and Country," review of *The Mackenzie King Record*, vol. 2, in *International Journal* 24: 374. Granatstein's assessment noted, however, that King was also a "shrewd" judge of character, "wise in his assessment of the forces that played upon men and governments." Granatstein, "The Mackenzie Kingdom," review of *The Mackenzie King Record*, vols. 3–4, in *Canadian Forum* 50 (1970): 273.
25. D.G. Creighton, *Forked Road*, 64; J.L.Granatstein, *Canada's War*, 116.

26. Blair Neatby, "Mackenzie King and the Historians," in English and Stubbs, *Debate*, 5.

27. FDR to Australian Prime Minister John Curtin, 3 January 1944, *Letters*, II:1477.

28. William S. McAndrew, "Mackenzie King, Roosevelt, and the New Deal: The Ambivalence of Reform," in English and Stubbs, *Debate*, 130.

29. Ibid., 135.

30. Pickersgill, *Record* (1940), 1:111.

31. In December 1942, Harry Hopkins told King this was the case and encouraged King to keep in frequent and close touch with FDR (Pickersgill, *Record*, 1:435) and in August 1941, Churchill "'spoke of the President's great affection for me. Said in the presence of his colleagues, there was no one who knew the president as well as I did'" (Pickersgill, *Record*, 1:242).

32. Laurier quoted in C.P. Stacey, *A Very Double Life* (Toronto: Macmillan of Canada, 1976), 189; hereafter referred to as *Double Life*.

33. Ibid., 196. It needs to be pointed out that Mackenzie King did not let the spirit world dictate his policy-making.

34. Ibid., 210.

35. Ibid., 30.

36. King quoted in J.L. Granatstein and Robert Bothwell, "A 'Self-Evident National Duty': Canadian Foreign Policy 1935-39," *Journal of Imperial and Commonwealth History* 3, 2 (1975): 224–225; hereafter referred to as "Duty."

37. Pickersgill, *Record*, 1:436.

38. Jack Pickersgill, "Mackenzie King's Political Attitudes and Public Policies: A Personal Impression," in English and Stubbs, *Debate*, 18.

39. John H. Thompson and Allen Seager, *Canada, 1922-1939; Decades of Discord* (Toronto: McClelland and Stewart, 1985), 41. Historians D.G. Creighton and W.L. Morton loathed the autonomous path taken by Canada under King, while A. Lower, J.L. Granatstein, and Blair Neatby viewed it in a more favorable light. C.P. Stacey, however, insists that King was not an autonomist, as his values were British, he sought British ways, and wanted British approval. Undoubtedly King was committed to Britain and the Commonwealth, but he opposed ties that bound Canada to British foreign policy and decreased Canadian autonomy; and, he had no intention of letting Washington replace London.

40. Pickersgill, "Attitudes," in English and Stubbs, *Debate*, 18.

41. Granatstein and Bothwell "Duty," 212. See also Pickersgill, "Attitudes," 18.

42. In 1930, Churchill, writing in the *Saturday Evening Post*, proposed that "Canada . . . is a magnet exercising a double attraction drawing both Great Britain and the United States toward herself and thus drawing them closer to each other. She is the only surviving bond which stretches from Europe across the Atlantic Ocean. In fact, no state, no country, no band of men can more truly be described as the linch-pin of peace and world progress." (Churchill quoted in *Saturday Evening Post*, 15 February 1930 in Pickersgill, *Record*, 1:106.)

43. Pickersgill, *Record*, 1:30.

44. Stacey, *Arms*, 332.

45. Granatstein, *Canada's War*, 119.

46. FDR letter to King, November 1941, quoted in Pickersgill, *Record*, 1:279.

47. FDR, *Complete Presidential Press Conferences*, vols. 9–25. (New York: Da Capo Press, 1972), 20:279; hereafter referred to as *Press Conferences*.

48. This marked a change from the old relationship, "a real *rapprochement* to the point where I could think in terms not only of friendship but of alliance" (Stacey, *Arms*, 95).

49. W.A.B. Douglas and Brereton Greenhous, *Out of the Shadows* (Toronto: Oxford University Press, 1977), 45.

50. Pickersgill, "Attitudes," 25.

51. "Like most successful political leaders, [King] felt the heavy hand of destiny upon him–a fact that is not surprising in a man so lacking in self-confidence." Ramsay Cook, review of *The Mackenzie King Record* vol. 1, in *Canadian Historical Review*, 350. FDR was a man who believed "He was on the side of right." Ted Morgan, *F.D.R: A Biography* (New York: Simon and Schuster, 1985), 553.

52. S.W. Dziuban, *Military Relations between the United States and Canada, 1939-1945* (Washington, DC: Department of the Army, 1959), 3; hereafter *Relations*.

53. Ibid., 3. See also Stacey, *Arms*, 96, and Soward, *Canada in World Affairs 1941*, 107.

54. Basil Rauch, *Roosevelt: From Munich to Pearl Harbor* (New York: Creative Age Press, 1950), 68.

55. Ibid., 69.

56. FDR, *Press Conferences*, 12 Sept 1939, 14:162–164.

57. FDR to King, 11 October 1938, *Letters*, 2:816–817.

58. Granatstein and Bothwell, "Duty", 227.

59. Thus, King should have been less surprised, and disdainful, of FDR's public statement that the United States would not be drawn into the war once it had begun. Stacey, *Arms*, 327.

60. In July Roosevelt sought "repeal of the arms embargo as a deterrent to Hitler." When he was unsuccessful, he went so far as to ask the Attorney General "how far do you think I can go in ignoring the existing act–even though I did sign it?" (Memo from FDR to Attorney General Frank Murphy, 1 July 1939, *Letters*, 1:899–900.)

61. FDR, *Press Conferences*, 14:141–142; see also Pickersgill, *Record*, 1:30–31.

62. Pickersgill, *Record*, 1:30–31.

63. King to Parliament, House of Commons *Debates* 12 November 1940 (Ottawa), 58.

64. King to Parliament, House of Commons *Debates* 12 November 1940. There were certainly differences in perspective regarding the war: Canada went to war one week after Britain, while the United States stayed out until the end of 1941; Canada saw the first line of defense in Europe, therefore military ties to Latin America were of secondary importance, partly because they threatened Canada's ability to help Europe. The United State's first line of defense was North American waters and coast, so it needed to work with Latin America. Issues within the Western Hemisphere, such as the Free French occupation of the French islands of Miquelon and St. Pierre, and the occupation of Greenland, were viewed differently. To the United States, they were judged on their impact on American neutrality; to Canada they were judged in terms of Canada as a belligerent and as part of the Commonwealth. Dziuban, *Relations*, p. 161.

65. Those who credit FDR: Dana Wilgress and David Beatty; those crediting King: S.W. Dziuban, Hugh Keenleyside; C.P. Stacey maintains that the evidence is inconclusive.

66. J. Pierre Moffatt to Sumner Welles, 14 August 1940, *Foreign Relations of the United States Diplomatic Paper, 1940*, 144.

67. Dziuban, *Relations*, 25.

68. Stacey, *Conflict*, 312.
69. Stacey, *Arms*, 340.
70. FDR, *The Public Papers and Addresses of Franklin D. Roosevelt, 1940* (New York: Harper & Brothers, 1950), Item 80, 331.
71. Stacey, "PJBD," 122.
72. Dziuban, *Relations*, 46.
73. Stacey, "PJBD", 121.
74. Willard Range, *Franklin D. Roosevelt's World Order* (Athens: University of Georgia Press, 1959), 73.
75. Creighton, *Forked Road*, 54.
76. R.D. Cuff and J.L. Granatstein, *American Dollars–Canadian Prosperity* (Toronto: Samuel-Stevens, 1978), 7; hereafter referred to as *Dollars*.
77. Ibid., 8.
78. Mackenzie King saw Hyde Park as "more than an extension of the Ogdensburg agreement for hemispheric defence. It is also a joint agreement between Canada and the United States for aid to Britain." House of Commons *Debates*, 28 April 1941, 286–289.
79. J.L. Granatstein and R.D. Cuff, "The Hyde Park Declaration 1941: Origins and Significance," *Canadian Historical Review* 55, 1 (1974): 77.
80. Stacey, *Arms*, 150.
81. FDR to King, 5 November 1941, *Letters*, 2:1232.
82. The bases were seen, from the American point of view, as the primary achievement of bilateral cooperation, as they facilitated military efforts against the enemy. S. Conn and B. Fairchild, *The Framework of Hemisphere Defense.* (Washington, D.C.: Department of Army, 1960), 409.
83. J.L. Granatstein and Norman Hillmer, *For Better or for Worse: Canada and the United States to the 1990s* (Toronto: Copp Clark Pitman, 1991), 155.
84. Hillmer, *Partners*, 4.
85. Pickersgill, *Record*, 1:436.
86. Stacey, *Conflict*, 361.
87. Thompson and Randall, *Canada and the United States*, 165.
88. "Memorandum from Under-Secretary of State for External Relations to Prime Minister, [Ottawa] 22 December 1941," in *Documents on External Relations* vol. 9 by John Hilliker, ed., 1126.
89. Norman Robertson quoted in *Sovereignty or Security* by Shelagh Grant (Vancouver: University of British Columbia Press, 1988), 71.
90. Hillmer, *Partners*, 49; see also Stacey, *Conflict*, 307–317.
91. Pearson, *Mike*, 1:230.
92. Cook, review of *Mackenzie King Record, Canadian Historical Review*, 349; see also C.P. Stacey, *Mackenzie King and the Atlantic Triangle*, 54. This was true of a Canadian church's brochure on war bonds, which did not refer to King at all.
93. Lester Pearson cited in C.P. Stacey, *Mackenzie King and the Atlantic Triangle* (Toronto: Macmillan of Canada, 1976), 55.
94. Creighton, *Forked Road*, 66.
95. Cook, review of *The Mackenzie King Record*, 348.
96. FDR, *Press Conferences*, 13 March 1945, 25: 91, 92.
97. Eleanor Roosevelt, *This I Remember* (New York: Harper & Brothers, 1949), 346.

9

Franklin D. Roosevelt, the Caribbean, and the Postcolonial World

Thomas C. Howard

The long and often unhappy history of U.S. involvement in the Caribbean region is well known. Far less familiar is the frequency with which the Caribbean has served as a model for the formulation of American foreign policy elsewhere around the globe. This occurred during the Second World War when the United States engaged in postwar planning for the colonial world—those regions of the globe that later came imprecisely to be included in the "Third World." During these years the U.S. President, Franklin Roosevelt, believed that European colonialism represented one of the greatest threats to the creation of a democratic, prosperous, and peaceful global order. His administration moved forcefully to put into place plans aimed at political independence and economic development for the colonial worlds. That the United States did not act on these plans and promises after the war led to disappointment and disillusionment. This analysis attempts to illustrate, through a case study of the influence of the Caribbean on the postwar planning of the Roosevelt administration, how American leadership in the emerging postcolonial world began to be sacrificed even before the end of the war.

Effective nationalist movements developed late in the Caribbean region, and independence from colonial rule came even later. Despite sporadic outbursts of anti-colonial sentiment earlier in the century, it was not until the depression conditions of the 1930s had so magnified existing inequities that tensions erupted in a succession of riots and strikes throughout the area, especially within the British West Indies. During these years, British colonial authorities became increasingly conscious of the indirect influence of the United States on this growing climate of discontent. According to the report of the 1938 Royal Commission that investigated the causes of the unrest, a significant stimulus behind the popular demand for better conditions were the reports of West Indians who worked abroad, particularly in the United States of America.[1]

Direct intrusion by the United States in the affairs of the British islands, however, did not come about until the war years, the same years that witnessed the emergence of a mature West Indian nationalism. The convergence was by no means coincidental, because the dramatically heightened American presence in the region after 1941 created a unique arena for the playing out of the opposing forces of British colonialism, indigenous nationalism, and American anti-colonialism. The last of these was pivotal. It reflected one of the most important dimensions of the worldview of Franklin D. Roosevelt, the most internationally minded American president since Woodrow Wilson. The policies formulated by Roosevelt and his advisors during the war provided an unprecedented official sanction for nationalist voices. These voices often served American interests, weakened British authority, and contributed to the emergence of the more militant nationalism of the postwar era. To grasp better the complex history of these years, it is necessary to understand the roles played by a few key individuals. Franklin Roosevelt was the most influential player of all.

Although Roosevelt has often been characterized as a Wilsonian internationalist who concealed his views for political reasons following the triumph of populist isolationism in the interwar years, only to reveal them again once the United States entered the Second World War, study of the evolution of his thought and decision making during the war suggests the need for a far more complete explanation.[2] Certainly Roosevelt was a Wilsonian internationalist, but with pragmatic differences which his experiences during the war accentuated and expanded. While he shared many of Wilson's goals, especially the creation of a new international system to ensure global order and prosperity, his schemes for bringing this about led him to the use of Wilsonian rhetoric to advocate concepts beyond and, at times, seemingly contrary to those promoted by Wilson. This was most evident concerning two crucial issues: his strong advocacy of self-determination and eventual independence for colonial peoples, and his attempt to square his desire for a new international order with the creation of regional security arrangements.

Roosevelt's position on these two interrelated issues evolved dramatically between 1941 and 1945 as a result of many developments and influences. It seems, however, to owe far more than has been recognized to the advice of one individual and the example of one region of the globe. The individual was Charles W. Taussig, and the region was the Caribbean. Both served to intensify Roosevelt's anti-colonialist views, especially against Britain, and to nurture his instinct for the pragmatic pursuit of idealistic goals. Both directed Roosevelt along a path that led to resurrection of the Wilsonian principle of self-determination recast for the postwar world.

In September 1940 the Destroyer-Bases Deal transfered fifty aging destroyers to Britain in return for U.S. rights to ninety-nine-year leases on bases in Bermuda, the Bahamas, Jamaica, Antigua, St. Lucia, Trinidad, and British Guiana. This represented not only a significant step by the United States in its undeclared resistance toward Germany, but began a chapter of intensified collaboration with Britain.[3] Certainly the relationship that emerged from the destroyers and bases deal was unique. In the Caribbean suddenly there were what amounted to colonies within colonies—American bases, air strips, and service facilities constructed on British colonial soil, all with vast potential for discord and the spread of American influence. What better place to cite examples of colonial neglect to feed the flames of rekindled American anti-colonialism than right here in the United States' "own backyard"? What better place for Britain to attempt to spruce up its colonial image through economic development schemes? In short, Britain during the war years felt the impact of a revived American anti-colonialism in the Caribbean before it became a factor in Asia, Africa, the Middle East, and elsewhere during and after the war.

Two months after the destroyers and bases deal was announced, Roosevelt appointed a commission to study social and economic conditions in the region. His decision to do so was the outgrowth of a memorandum from Taussig, then chair of the President's Advisory Committee of the National Youth Administration. Taussig's memo concluded that because Britain and the United States had such an important stake in the Caribbean, it would be advisable that a joint study be made "with a view to improving the economic and social conditions in the islands."[4]

Between the winter of 1940 and the spring of 1942 global events transformed the Anglo-American relationship from one, in Roosevelt's homely image, of a neighbor "lending his fire extinguisher to help put out the fire in the house next door" to that of a full-fledged wartime partnership.[5] Reflecting international developments during this period, the Caribbean moved both tangibly and symbolically to occupy a larger place in the relationship between the two allies. The recommendations of the 1940 commission led by the fall of 1941 to the creation of a new Caribbean office in the State Department, which, after close consultation with Taussig, was instrumental in the creation of the Anglo-American Caribbean Commission of March 1942.[6]

The new commission, with its origins in an exclusively American initiative, and with Taussig as its American co-chairman, now received enthusiastic American promotion. It quickly launched an ambitious program focusing on emergency food supplies and transportation, research plans, health issues, and the creation of a regional broadcast service.[7] It was mainly an American agenda. From the start the stature of the American permanent members reflected the greater importance accorded the commission by the United States. In addition to Taussig, they included former Assistant Secretary of State Rexford Tugwell, then Governor of Puerto Rico, and Coert du Bois, the chief of the new Caribbean Office of the State Department.[8] Taussig and Tugwell enjoyed direct access to the President, a comparable advantage never enjoyed by their British counterparts.

The relatively high status and enthusiasm of the American delegation clearly alarmed the British commission members. It is important to note that 1942, the year of the formation of the commission, coincided with a period of strident American criticism of British colonialism. In January 1942 Winston Churchill sent a memorandum to Roosevelt reminding him of his promise to make some statement that "there is to be no question of the transfer to the United States of the British West Indies Colonies either under the Bases Agreement or otherwise." He added that this was an action he considered especially important in light of the anxiety "likely to be revived by the proposed communiqué about the Anglo-American Caribbean Commission."[9]

Although Roosevelt agreed to give the assurances Churchill requested, tensions between the two allied powers over the future of the region did not subside. Had they been aware of the tenor of a number of the communications between the President and Taussig, British officials would have been all the more alarmed. One revealing example is Taussig's long personal report (the commission later submitted a formal one) to Roosevelt in June 1942 after his return from a fact-finding trip to sites where bases were under construction. After listing various concerns, especially regarding political unrest and nationalist aspirations, Taussig proceeded to make a number of specific recommendations, including changes of policy in the American administration of Puerto Rico, such as the popular election of a

Puerto Rican as governor as a good example for the European colonial powers in the region. He then speculated about the region as a whole:

> I received the impression that the people of the Caribbean are looking toward the United States for progressive leadership and that colonial governments, while not looking for such leadership, will accept it if only for the reason that they realize their physical safety is entirely in the hands of the United States. The Caribbean perhaps is the only area of the world where it is possible during the war to give a preview of what the post-war world may look like. Within this area is represented independent republics, colonies of three European powers, and the possessions of the United States. Major problems of regional, hemispheric and world trade are involved. Political aspirations of subject peoples are being pressed. Racial problems exist in an aggravated form. . . . Obviously the Caribbean represents opportunities for constructive statesmanship.[10]

What sort of statesmanship should this be, and why was it needed then? Taussig elaborates:

> It seems to me the time is at hand when by using our possessions in the Caribbean as the spring board you could pave the way for a "charter" granting more political freedom to all colonial people. Just as our changed policy toward Cuba and the abrogation of the Platt Amendment in 1933 became the keystone of the "Good Neighbor Policy" so could a Second Caribbean Emancipation bring hope to all subject peoples of the United Nations.[11]

Taussig's strong advocacy of some sort of colonial charter places him squarely in the midst of the debate then taking place in the State Department over the desirability of issuing a statement of principles applicable to all dependent areas. The Atlantic Charter of August 1941 had implicitly included colonial peoples, despite British disclaimers that it applied only to Axis occupied territories. By the spring and summer of 1942 momentum was building in the State Department for a statement that would make clear the American position on the wider applicability of the Charter. In May 1942 the Far Eastern Division of the Department, guided by the wishes of Secretary of State Cordell Hull, drafted a proposal for a "World Charter" that would broaden the scope of the Atlantic Charter to include the concept of international 'trusteeship' for subject peoples.[12] As a member of the

Department Areas Committee of the State Department, and in private discussions with Hull and others, Taussig contributed to these deliberations.[13]

Throughout the remainder of the war, Britain was uncomfortable with this concept of trusteeship as it seemed to be applied by the Americans. Most significantly, Roosevelt tended to view trusteeship through an international organization as the best means of promoting self-determination and ensuring ultimate independence for colonial territories. The British tended to view this "internationalized" trusteeship as little more than a vehicle for the spread of informal American political influence and a mask for American commercial covetousness.

Of the two major State Department wartime initiatives dealing with the colonial world, namely trusteeship and the creation of regional commissions, only the second held any appeal for the British. It was a Hobson's choice, but regional commissions at least held out the chance of assuaging American skepticism through close cooperation on colonial questions. Practical experience could temper American hostility. They might at least rein in their rhetoric as they became exposed to the difficulties of the colonial situation at ground level. This was the positive side of the regional commission concept. At first reluctant and defensive, the British became determined to make the best of the Anglo-American Caribbean Commission. They might even turn the tables a bit on the Americans by themselves promoting the commission as a model for other regional cooperative ventures.

Taussig was often the recipient of such British overtures and proposals, for they recognized the influence he wielded and hoped to sway his opinions wherever possible. Much to the dismay of the British, however, Taussig increasingly chose to use his influence to rattle skeletons in colonial closets and generally to keep British officials off balance. Numerous examples of this could be cited, though two should serve well enough to illustrate the point. Both involve the appointment of blacks, one American and one West Indian, to positions with the commission.

The American, Judge William H. Hastie, civilian aide to the Secretary of War, was appointed as an advisor to the commission in the early stages of its work. Hastie was not controversial aside from his color, though this was sufficient to heighten the differences between the American and the British delegations. Taussig attributed in reports to the President the excellent local reactions when the commission went on tour to the fact that a nonwhite had been included, if even in an advisory capacity. He speculated that because of this the British might seriously consider the appointment of a "colored West Indian" to the commission.[14] As it turned out such a person did receive an appointment through the commission, although it was made against strenuous British objections. Taussig happily, one might even say gleefully, supported the appointment of Eric Williams to a position with the commission.

Eric Williams later became one of the most famous Caribbean nationalist leaders, and ultimately the first Prime Minister of independent Trinidad and Tobago. He was far from being completely unknown in 1942. An Oxford graduate, Williams had been teaching at Howard University in Washington since 1939. In 1942 he published the book that established his reputation in many quarters as the foremost West Indian scholar on Caribbean issues. The book, *The Negro in the Caribbean*, was among other things a frontal attack on colonialism in the Caribbean. Although it earned much applause for Williams in West Indian and American black communities, the book acquired quite the opposite reaction toward Williams in British colonial circles. It was just because of this that Taussig pressed for his inclusion in some capacity with the commission. As Williams later described it, he had applied unsuccessfully for a job with the commission through Sir John Huggins, Taussig's British counterpart, before he met Taussig, who was, in his words, the "live wire" of the commission. Taussig was "a man of great personality, and withal a very pleasant and likable person," wrote Williams. He added that Taussig, "who knew all about *The Negro in the Caribbean*, decided that I was to be associated with the Anglo-American Caribbean Commission. And then the fun began."[15] It did indeed.

Following his appointment Williams used the commission, and the American delegation used Williams. In the course of his years of association both with the wartime commission and its postwar successor, Williams was able to travel, lecture, and write, most all of it aimed at undermining the colonial establishment in the British Caribbean. In general Taussig and the other Americans supported Williams's work, and laughed with him at some of the more foolish manifestations of British intransigence. But the time came, as Williams put it, when the Americans didn't laugh.[16] They were not amused when he wrote of racial problems in Puerto Rico, or criticized aspects of the naval bases agreement, including the racial tensions created in the vicinity of the bases. As Williams put it, the Americans "just did not want to acknowledge that there was a race problem in their possessions. They could see the mote in other people's eyes, but would not see the beam in theirs."[17]

The criticism was not altogether just, for Taussig and other Americans concerned with the region were aware of racial problems in Puerto Rico and elsewhere where Americans lived and worked. They were convinced, however, they were far more qualified to deal with the problem than were the British. Puerto Rico was especially held up as a model of enlightened administration, and the Americans did move cautiously in the direction of greater self-government and indigenization of highly visible posts in government, education, and other areas. Taussig showed photographs of Puerto Rican slums to Roosevelt, who reacted with dismay and urged that reforms be undertaken. Roosevelt was especially sensitive of such criticisms, for they were strikingly similar to ones he was accustomed to leveling at Churchill about conditions in the British colonies.

Much of the information that came to Roosevelt concerning colonial issues came from Charles Taussig, including questions far removed from those directly affecting the Caribbean. For this reason Caribbean issues assumed global dimensions, especially insofar as they influenced the formulation of American policies concerning the entire colonial world and plans for the postwar era. With colonialism, as with so many other areas, the Roosevelt administration was attempting to devise plans for a new era of peace and progress. Of course it was assumed that the United States would play the most critical role in the new world to come, but for Roosevelt, at least, this did not mean American political dominance. It did mean the internationalization of all questions that might threaten the stability of the new order, and European colonialism was high on Roosevelt's list of such potential threats. As the war moved toward its conclusion, planning for the future became more critical. During this period, especially in the months proceeding and immediately following the death of the President on 12 April 1945, a succession of decisions were made that would permanently shape the contours of the postwar settlement. They reflect a working-out of the themes stressed here—colonial rigidity, nationalist pressures, and American anti-colonialism. The new ingredient added to the mix was superpower rivalry and the formative stages of the Cold War. In all of this, Charles Taussig played a key, though ultimately losing, role.

By 1945 Britain had successfully ridden out the worst of American anti-colonialism. They accomplished this in part by indicating their agreement to the creation of a number of regional commissions on the Caribbean model.[18] This allowed the Americans to become associated with colonial development schemes at a time when more funds than ever were being allocated for such purposes by the British Treasury.[19] There nevertheless remained serious Anglo-American differences when Sir Oliver Stanley, the Secretary of State for the Colonies, visited President Roosevelt at the President's request and at Taussig's urging in January 1945 to discuss the future of the Caribbean Commission and, by extension, other colonial issues.

In consultation with Taussig the State Department prepared a long briefing memorandum for the President outlining the main differences between the United States and Britain on colonial policy.[20] One key section dealt with differentiating between trust territories and colonies. As the memorandum phrased it, "in our usage, 'trusteeship' has an international significance whereas the British apply it in a national sense, with themselves as trustees."[21] The memo also emphasized the American position on the need for requiring some sort of "international accountability" for the administration of all dependent territories and the desirability of declaring that independence, rather than self-government, was the ultimate goal for all dependent peoples.[22] Actual conversations between Roosevelt and Stanley skirted many of these issues, leaving Stanley with the impression that the American position on the matter of international supervision of dependent areas was flexible and open to negotiation. The Yalta Conference the next month suggested otherwise.

By the time of the Yalta meeting Roosevelt had at least for the present modified his position on trusteeship in response to the objections of the Joint Chiefs of Staff—especially the Navy. Their concern over the need for continued U.S. control over captured Japanese Pacific islands and other strategic considerations led to a new working definition of trusteeship. Under the projected United Nations organization, it would formally apply only to existing League of Nations mandates and captured Axis territory. Roosevelt was willing to allow this concession, for it was compatible with his emerging conception of the postwar world, a conception that combined idealistic goals such as independence for the colonial world with recognition of the necessity of spheres of influence for the United States and the Soviet Union. But he did not want this to be carried too far; he hoped still for greater internationalization of global problems.

When Roosevelt met with Stalin and Churchill at Yalta in February he successfully pressed his trusteeship formula, deftly deflecting Churchill's fears that it endangered the British colonial empire.[23] But of course in the long run it did. It laid the foundation for the Trusteeship Council of the United Nations, which over time would find the basis for applying both official and public pressure on Britain regarding her colonial policies as well as providing an expanded model for the internationalization of colonial questions. The final fate of Roosevelt's ideas and hopes concerning trusteeship, colonialism, and self-determination was not determined until the weeks following his death on 12 April, shortly before he was to travel to San Francisco to address the organizational meeting of the United Nations. When he met for the last time with Taussig on 15 March, he reaffirmed his desire for a broader concept of international trusteeship at San Francisco, despite the necessity of certain concessions in the name of military security in the Pacific. At the same meeting he agreed to include Taussig in the San Francisco delegation as an advisor because he felt Taussig would be "extremely useful on matters pertaining to negotiations on colonial matters."[24]

Taussig lived up to the trust Roosevelt placed in him, despite the fact that what were widely perceived as American security needs now combined with increasing tensions with the Soviet Union to provoke a retreat from Roosevelt's view of trusteeship as a vehicle for preparing dependent peoples for independence. In the debates over the establishment of the United Nations trusteeship system may be observed early signs of subsequent bitter disputes over the decolonization of the European empires. After a number of compromises on the structure of the Trusteeship Council, the critical issue was a determination of the true purpose of trusteeship. Should it clearly and explicitly aim toward independence? The American delegation was divided. One delegate, Harold Stassen, took the position that the word "independence" was provocative, and that "self-government" would be sufficient. "If one goes beyond that phrase," declared Stassen, "there was danger that we would be interpreted as butting in on colonial affairs."[25] Taussig was the chief advocate of the opposite view. He maintained that to repudiate it would be nothing less than a repudiation of the ideals of Franklin Roosevelt. On May 18 he circulated a memorandum stating several reasons for supporting the goal of independence for all colonial peoples. It included these points:

> 1. Independence as a goal for all peoples who aspire to and are capable of it has been the traditional and sacred policy of this Government. It has been exemplified in our policy in the Philippines, and it has been reiterated on numerous occasions by President Roosevelt and former Secretary of State Cordell Hull.
> 2. An excellent opportunity is afforded to make a profitable gesture on behalf of the peoples of the Orient as well as those in Africa and the Caribbean.
> 3. The Soviets especially and the Chinese will be able to capitalize on their stand for "independence" against the opposition of the non-Asiatic peoples of the West unless we take a strong position.[26]

It was a powerful statement, but the battle was lost. Taussig considered it a betrayal not only of him but of Roosevelt's memory.

It is clearly possible only to speculate on how different the postwar world might have been had Roosevelt lived and his hopes fulfilled. Most probably Roosevelt would have been forced to alter further his anti-colonial doctrines in view of strategic considerations and the speed with which the colonial world was subjected to nationalist explosions and the demand for immediate independence in one territory after another. Still, it is tempting to argue that Roosevelt would have remained as basically committed as ever to the principles he had long espoused, especially to his belief in the right of all peoples to choose their own form of government. Roosevelt had learned much about the colonial question around the globe through the prism of the Caribbean during the war, and he almost certainly would have tried to place the United States more forcefully on the side of nationalist movements demanding independence. We know what did happen. We know that as the tensions of the Cold War increased in the months and years following San Francisco, the United States was increasingly stigmatized by both the Soviet bloc and the new developing nations as another colonial power, determined to maintain the status quo wherever possible. The fears and paranoia of the postwar world led the United States into the contradictory policy of avowing support for colonial independence while simultaneously propping up the old colonial powers. And the Caribbean, which had served so well as a model for much postwar planning during the war, was transformed into but another area for Cold War rivalry and confrontation. In the process, U.S. plans for the promotion of independence, human rights, and the creation of liberal democratic institutions in the region were largely forgotten by those who either lacked or did not share the vision of the Roosevelt years.

Notes

1. Lord Moyne *West India: Royal Commission Report* (London: HMSO, 1945).
2. For a fine account of Roosevelt's "style" of conducting foreign policy, see Robert Dallek, *Franklin Roosevelt and American Foreign Policy, 1932-1945* (New York: Oxford University Press, 1979).
3. Philip Goodhart, *Fifty Ships That Saved the World: The Foundations of the Anglo-American Alliance* (New York: Doubleday, 1965).
4. Memorandum concerning the Caribbean from Charles W. Taussig. No date, but with handwritten notation "Memo Sent to the President, Sept., 1940–also Sec. Hull," Taussig Papers, Box 35, Roosevelt Library, Hyde Park, New York. Taussig, who was president of the American Molasses Company, was associated with the original "brain trusters" around Roosevelt. He also served as a member of the president's Advisory Council for the Virgin Islands.
5. Leon Martel, *Lend-Lease, Loans, and the Coming of the War* (Boulder, CO:Westview Press, 1979), 2.

6. Draft letter from Sumner Welles, Assistant Secretary of State, to Roosevelt, 24 October 1941, FW844.00/7-1244, Decimal Files of the State Department, National Archives, Washington, D.C. (Hereafter cited as USSD). The commission was formally created on 9 March 1942 and the American members named on 14 March.

7. Recommendation of Anglo-American Caribbean Commission, First Meeting, 26–31 March 1942 (typescript), Taussig Papers, Box 33. Also see file on "Radio" in Box 34.

8. Draft Letter, Welles to Roosevelt, 24 October 1941.

9. Copy of Memorandum left by the Prime Minister with the President on 14 January 1942, 844.00/26, USSD.

10. Letter from Taussig to Roosevelt, undated but marginally noted 22 June 1942, Taussig Papers, Box 34.

11. Ibid.

12. Cordell Hull, *The Memoirs of Cordell Hull* (New York: Macmillan, 1948), 1234–37.

13. For example, see Memorandum of conversation with Cordell Hull, 30 November 1942, Taussig Papers, Box 46.

14. Letter from Taussig to Roosevelt, 22 June 1942, Taussig Papers, Box 46.

15. Eric Williams, *Inward Hungar: The Education of a Prime Minister* (Chicago: University of Chicago Press, 1971), 81.

16. Ibid., 84.

17. Ibid.

18. David Reynolds, "Roosevelt, Churchill, and the Wartime Anglo-American Alliance, 1939-1945: Toward a New Synthesis," in William Roger Louis and Hedley Bull, eds., *The "Special Relationship"* (Oxford: Clarendon Press, 1986), 28–29.

19. Ibid.

20. Memorandum for the President: The Forthcoming Conversations with Colonel Stanley, British Secretary of State for the Colonies, 13 January 1945, FW844.00/1-134, USSD.

21. Ibid.

22. Ibid.

23. William Roger Louis, *Imperialism at Bay* (New York: Oxford University Press, 1977), 458.

24. Ibid., 486.

25. Ibid., 535.

26. Ibid., 537.

10

Soldiers on the Homefront: Protecting the Four Freedoms through the Office of Civilian Defense

Julia M. Siebel

> The four freedoms–freedom of speech and expression, freedom of every person to worship God in his own way, freedom from want, freedom from fear. They are the ultimate stake. They might not be immediately attainable throughout the world, but humanity does move toward those glorious ideals through democratic processes.
>
> And, if we fail–if democracy is superseded by slavery–then those four freedoms or even the mention of them will become forbidden things.[1]
>
> –Franklin D. Roosevelt

When President Franklin D. Roosevelt spoke of the Four Freedoms, some Americans argued that he was abandoning many who had not yet recovered from the depression. Rather, he was concerned that the expanding war in Europe would threaten these inalienable rights on the homefront. While freedom of speech may be guaranteed by the Constitution, FDR saw that wartime censorship and misguided patriotism could lead to grave infringements of this First Amendment right. In much the same manner, suspicion and racism threatened to limit American freedom to worship. Roosevelt's references to freedom from want were directly related to the decade of social, economic, and cultural deprivation. Freedom from fear was

FDR's pledge to his constituents that the United States would remain free of the devastation that was rampant in Europe.

Roosevelt recognized that someone would need to accept specific responsibility for protecting these Four Freedoms for Americans. However, he also understood that popular opinion and his own personal limitations would not allow him to accept that responsibility. He found a solution to this dilemma by creating yet another special wartime agency designed to maintain the cultural, social, and economic security of the United States so that he would be free to pursue the challenges of World War II. The agency FDR envisioned found a home within the Office of Civilian Defense (OCD). Titled the Civilian War Services Division (CWS), it partially alleviated the conflict between FDR's concern for his constituency and his broader focus on world politics.[2] The CWS also represented a fundamental attempt to keep the idealism of the Roosevelt administration directed at the homefront as well as at the war front. A careful reassessment of the CWS's records shows that the mission of the New Deal was transplanted into the new agency, and reconfigured to meet a new set of challenges and problems.

Mentioning civilian defense in the United States during World War II generally elicits visions of air raid wardens wearing tin hats, blackout curtains, bomb shelters, and a strong military presence on the homefront. As it turned out, these preparations proved unnecessary. Physical attacks were limited to random and harmless shelling along the California coast, balloons carrying incendiary devices that started a few wildfires in the Northwest, and a bungled "invasion" attempt by German agents on the east coast. Yet prewar public concern for civilian safety was great enough that on 20 May 1941 Franklin Roosevelt created the Office of Civilian Defense as part of the Office of Emergency Management by Executive Order 8757.

The construction of this executive order represents FDR's personal concern that the threat to the United States was twofold. While he worried over the possibility of an enemy attack from the air or sea, he was more concerned with the possibility of a subtle failure to protect the sanctity of the United States. Continued years of deprivation could prove equally as damaging as a bomb attack. To prepare the United States for this bilateral threat, FDR envisioned two divisions within the OCD. He wanted a division of civilian protection and a division of community welfare to act in tandem and reduce the trauma of war on the civilian population. He clearly saw protection and community welfare as a single issue and separated them in the executive order for administrative purposes only.[3]

The OCD was given three specific jobs in the war effort:

1. The coordination of federal, state and local civilian defense relationships.
2. Planning and implementing programs designed to protect civilian life and property in the event of an emergency.
3. Promoting activities designed to sustain the national morale and creating opportunities for constructive civilian participation in the defense program.[4]

The first of these jobs reflects a national concern for a smooth and efficient defense buildup. From experiences during the initial stages of the defense emergency, federal bureaucrats predicted that state and local officials would need assistance across jurisdictions. The second job was in direct response to the perceived threat to the physical safety of the homefront. The Division of Civilian Protection was modeled closely on British protection efforts during the Battle of Britain. The third job grew directly from FDR's concerns for the homefront. The CWS was developed to protect the Four Freedoms on the homefront and create a healthy nation that was strong enough to withstand any threat from within.

Previous examinations of the OCD have focused primarily on the Division of Civilian Protection, with little attention to the broader mission of the agency.[5] The protection side of the OCD played on fears of a new approach to warfare. Respected educators, military commanders, elected officials, and community leaders warned of the new type of warfare that had little respect for nonbelligerent citizens. U.S. Army Colonel Augustin M. Prentiss urged Americans to avoid complacency and warned that "civilians in this country must be prepared to defend themselves and their homes" in a manner recently discovered by so many victims of aggression on Europe and Asia.[6] The OCD was even more specific by defining this new approach to warfare as "total war." Agency rhetoric warned that Germany had "employed terror to compel surrender and insure success."[7] Ultimately, events in the Pacific on 7 December 1941 brought the fears of total war to a very personal level. It destroyed Americans' sense of isolation and feeling of comparative safety caused by a two-ocean barrier. It also served as a catalyst for the national unity and belief in the need for a strong civilian defense force.

The Protection Division offered many communities an emotionally comforting way to contribute to the war effort and counteract this perceived threat. With New York's Mayor Fiorello LaGuardia as its Director, the OCD gained a valuable proponent for extravagant displays of preparation and aggressive shows of national power. LaGuardia was committed to the protection side of the agency and saw the OCD as his path to national political power. He lobbied hard to make his position a cabinet-level appointment and regularly exploited the extensive national exposure that came with his responsibilities. In addition, the high public relations value and concrete opportunities for accountability helped the protection side of the OCD find approval in Congress. With friends in Congress, the Protection Division never lacked for funding or support. Unlike other aspects of the OCD, the Protection Division offered simple and concise examples of Americans and their elected representatives doing something for the war effort. As a result, the Protection Division emerged as the most recognized element of the OCD's efforts.

There is far more to the OCD than just Civilian Protection, however. Underneath the cheerleading efforts of Director Fiorello LaGuardia there is another story, one that was neither as visual nor as popular with the press and elected officials. Yet it was a priority for the Roosevelts and one that connects the OCD to the local communities and their welfare. Under analysis, the OCD emerges as an agency that worked to encompass social welfare, community service, and national morale in the name of the war effort. The CWS side of the OCD attempted to revitalize many New Deal programs and preserve the Four Freedoms for Americans on the homefront. The goal of the CWS was to consider the whole impact of the war upon a community and formulate plans to counteract it. The CWS worked as a "flexible instrument designed to ensure full participation in the war effort."[8] Unfortunately, LaGuardia barely tolerated the CWS efforts in "his" organization. He felt that they belonged in a separate agency. He often remarked privately that the whole concept was made of "sissy stuff."[9] Though the concept had been an integral part of the Executive Order forming the OCD, LaGuardia expended minimal initiative and almost no money to develop that side of the agency.

As LaGuardia's recalcitrance became clear, FDR appointed his wife Eleanor to the post of Assistant Director of the OCD and put her in charge of the CWS division. The objective of her efforts within the OCD was to "leave every community stronger before the emergency is over."[10] She envisioned the CWS as a human organization dealing with human problems. It would help Americans confront their daily problems, and work toward a goal of alleviating the social, cultural, and economic dislocations caused by the war.

Defense industry boomtowns, displaced families in search of work, and those who were following soldiers introduced both a new migration pattern and a new set of challenges into the local communities. These served to exacerbate national morale and welfare, which were already severely strained. Local communities weakened by the depression lacked sufficient medical care, adequate housing, appropriate nutritional resources, sufficient school buildings and teachers, functional public utilities, reliable community recreation facilities, and positive morale. Fearing that these deficiencies could produce greater long-term devastation than any attack by the Axis powers, the volunteers of the CWS considered themselves soldiers on the homefront. By helping to support and rebuild these devastated communities, they worked internally to defend the integrity of local communities. Defending these communities from external acts of overt aggression was left to the Protection side of the OCD.

ER's personal style emerged quickly as the formation of the CWS division occurred. Rather than create yet another layer of bureaucracy, ER turned to the federal, state, local, and private agencies and organizations already in place. With the CWS serving as an information clearinghouse and coordination center, she felt that the local communities would be best able to define and solve their own problems. Thus, she called on the existing network of women's volunteer organizations for help. Specifically, she challenged representatives from seventy-three of the most prominent women's organizations to identify morale and welfare problems within their communities, find and mobilize internal resources to meet those problems, or search for creative new solutions where existing ones were unavailable.[11] At an early organizational meeting, Archibald MacLeish explained that the OCD was ultimately about the right of individual human beings to organize themselves in order to fulfill an obligation to their communities. Eleanor Roosevelt defined that obligation later in the meeting as the preservation of the Four Freedoms on the homefront.[12]

By the summer of 1940, many of these women's volunteer organizations had already begun working privately to ease the strain caused by the defense mobilization. All too often, these varied efforts led to multiple groups working in similar directions. This overlap caused unnecessary competition for the extremely limited resources of volunteers and money. As the nation's "number one volunteer," ER argued that with effective community organization, the elements for a successful program already existed.[13] Under her guidance, the CWS found an existing vehicle for coordinated community service in forty-four Volunteer Bureaus that had emerged around the country. These bureaus were also interested in eliminating duplication and focusing efforts in the community welfare arena. The Volunteer Bureau concept was first developed by the Association of Junior Leagues of America (AJLA) during the depression to help communities overcome welfare problems. These bureaus drew organizations, agencies, and religious groups into partnership and provided an opportunity to bring concerned individuals in as well. They developed, implemented, and directed community welfare efforts by forming coalitions among agencies, channeling resources efficiently, and imposing order on chaos with a centralized distribution system. Each bureau documented the services available and the services needed within the community. Bureau staff then worked to match those in need with those who wanted to help. In every solution, the goal was to establish and maintain clear lines of communication to ensure effective action within the community.

As depression problems began to recede in the face of the growing defense buildup, the AJLA Board of Directors offered suggestions on how to convert existing bureaus to meet the new challenges. The goal for these new bureaus was to "coordinate and organize volunteer service so that the essential social and health services in a city may be maintained in time of emergency and that additional services necessitated by preparedness and defense programs shall be effectively carried on." Bureaus were to recruit and organize community members who wanted to become involved in the war effort on the homefront. Then bureau volunteers were to go out and survey the community and its problem areas. Finally, bureau volunteers were to place interested community members in positions where they would have the most impact. Wherever possible, bureaus were encouraged to use or modify existing programs. In some cases however, bureaus had to create new programs to meet a need, or assist other agencies in developing a program to meet an identified need.[14]

On 17 January 1941, the AJLA contacted fellow Junior Leaguer Eleanor Roosevelt with a proposal for a national network of Volunteer Bureaus. In addition to the forty-four already existing bureaus, there were also wartime bureaus functioning in the six Canadian cities that had Junior League chapters.[15] These bureaus formed the core of a network that eventually coordinated the wide variety of emerging programs and widened the pool of volunteers available. They envisioned a system that could recruit volunteers for all facets of home defense, but most importantly those related to community welfare.

In an initial telegram, Executive Director Katharine Van Slyck briefly outlined their proposal and stated "We are interested by newspaper reports of government's plans for volunteer service and are anxious to put our experience at the disposal of the government." In a letter following the telegram, Van Slyck offered additional details for the motivation behind their offer of help:

> I imagine we are all agreed that the serious social and health problems facing the country today demand the attention and active participation of more women, if the homefront is to be maintained. It seems important to us that many more women be brought into the existing community agencies, both public and private, as volunteers and that the creation of new organizations be avoided. . . .
>
> We can assure you the cooperation of local Junior Leagues in any local effort looking toward a coordinated plan for recruiting, placing and training of volunteers. Because of League members' familiarity with social programs and their long experience in volunteer service . . . we believe that our members can be useful in helping to develop volunteer service programs.[16]

This letter was probably not the first ER had heard of the Junior League plans for wartime community organization. Undoubtedly, she was fully aware of the Junior League's activities as an interested past member. Many friends from her League days remained regular visitors at the White House and participated in an informal network of those dedicated to social welfare.[17] Because of the timely nature of Van Slyck's letter, as well as its highly detailed presentation and firm offer of support, it seems likely that ER sent word through this network to alert League leaders of her need for assistance with the program of coordinating volunteers for the homefront. As expected, she invited Junior League leaders to take an active role in the development of a coordination system for welfare services in wartime.

During the summer of 1941, the Junior League loaned its Executive Director and another staff member to the CWS to help write a manual on community volunteer participation.[18] This manual is almost identical to the internal document circulated by the AJLA in 1940. With the manual nearly completed, a memo dated 20 August 1941 offers additional clues about a more permanent role for the AJLA in the development of the CWS. In this memo to the Junior League Board of Directors, Van Slyck introduced federal plans for training volunteers on health, medical aid, and welfare for defense; discussed the development of local civilian defense centers; and reviewed plans for community field visits by a staff of CWS personnel.[19] As with the first Civilian Defense Volunteer Bureau manual, the staff set-up, field visit schedule, and goals of the CWS closely mirrored AJLA suggestions. Not surprisingly, Van Slyck remained on the OCD staff as an advisor and was listed as an employee "without compensation." Her salary continued to be paid by the AJLA. The second Junior League staff member, Wilmer Shields, was loaned to the OCD for the duration of the war as the head of Community Volunteer Participation. She received an annual salary of $5,600 and reported directly to ER.[20] Together with many of the local AJLA chapters around the country, Van Slyck, Shields, and ER worked to implement their plans for coordinated and efficient community welfare programs.[21]

The joint CWS and AJLA leadership developed a network of Volunteer Bureaus across the country. In order to do this, they began by identifying possible leaders in each community. The initial contact began through the local Junior League chapter where they existed. When no local chapter could be utilized, the leadership team worked through the informal network of volunteer women's organizations. Leadership for each bureau was drawn from trained volunteers representing a wide variety of groups and interests. Under ER's direction, the League strongly recommended that this board of directors represent religious and ethnic diversity as well as union organizations. In addition to managing the bureau, this board of directors was responsible for going out into the community and recruiting volunteers on a wide basis. They were expected to draw on their own contacts as well as utilize press and other options to generate interest in the bureau. Ultimately, the CWS developed a master list of over 400 organizations that provided 103,979,209 members for possible volunteer service. These were categorized by type of organization: youth, women, veterans, patriotic, fraternal, church and religious, church youth, churchwomen, farm and agriculture, professional and educational, business and industry.[22]

When a local bureau was set up, it became the "official arm of the OCD" in that city. Cities formed into county defense councils. These in turn reported to the state defense council. The states were grouped into nine defense regions that were modeled after the army's defense regions.[23] At each level, the defense councils and bureaucracy were staffed by volunteers, with the assistance of an occasional paid Executive Director. The first order of business for a recently established bureau was to survey the community and identify both problem areas and solutions. In order to assess the adequacy of a community's welfare and war mobilization, the CWS encouraged bureau volunteers to ask the following questions:

> Does your community have the organization necessary to recruit, classify, train and use the needed volunteers quickly and efficiently? Has your community a program to recruit, train and use most proficiently all available labor (men, women, youth, all races, nationalities, creeds)? Have the people been adequately informed of significant war and defense issues, programs and activities, through press, radio, speakers bureau, posters, town meetings? Is a program of American unity and citizenship, including send-offs for soldiers, parades, minority-group relations, forums, in operation? Are adequate housing facilities to meet the problems brought about by war industry or military concentrations being provided? Have adequate day nurseries to care for children of war works been established where needed? Are family war relief problems, such as unemployment due to industrial dislocation, broken homes resulting from war work, military service, and casualties being handled, where needed? Are health, accident, and sanitation problems arising out of war effort, such as venereal disease, garbage and sewage disposal, water supply, adequate medical personnel, clinics, hospitals, being cared for? Are food production, preservation, distribution, and storage problems being met? Is a nutrition program involving proper food service in war factories, hot school lunches, cooperative kitchens and canning centers, nutrition education, and emergency canteens underway? Is a consumer service program, including price control, fair rent, rationing, wise buying, budgeting, repair of home equipment, and conserving consumer goods in operation? Are the recreational needs of soldiers on leave and the families of war workers being met? Is the wisest possible use of all community transportation facilities, through staggered hours and group riding plans being made? Have successful salvage campaigns been waged? Has the sale of War Bonds and Stamps met minimum quotas?[24]

Not every community Volunteer Bureau attempted to resolve each of the problems highlighted in the questions above. While the CWS defined them all as threats to the Four Freedoms for American citizens, each community shaped its program according to the specific needs of the region.

Volunteer Bureaus maintained extensive files on the areas of need as defined in the initial survey. In general, Bureaus coordinated day care centers, provided housing lists for migrant war workers, worked to ease the strain of overcrowding on a variety of community services such as schools, public transportation and utilities, assisted in setting up social activities for soldiers and teenagers, and placed volunteers in hospitals. In short, they worked to "fill the gaps" and create stronger communities in spite of the war. Specifically, the CWS encouraged them to explore a wide variety of volunteer opportunities including:

> Programs for unity–town hall meetings, essay and poster contests, library exhibitions, multinational events, classes in American History and Government, and safeguarding civil liberties. Recreation services for soldiers and defense industry workers– information centers, restaurant listing, lodging coordinators and room registries, guides to community facilities, athletic contests, chaperoned dances and gatherings complete with local women to serve as hostesses, and transportation. Consumer protection programs–coordination centers to assist with ration booklets, study clubs to look for greater efficiency, provide home economists for consultation on healthy meals during rationing, and education against purchase of black market goods. Programs in the health field –assisting in every department of the hospital, providing training for assistants, running clinics to supplement overcrowded hospitals, developing community awareness programming, and visiting shut- ins. Educational programming–fill in any vacancies in a public school including class room aide and clerical assistance, conduct a clean-up campaign for the schools, supply school lunches, and work closely with emotionally or physically impaired children. Recreation and informal education programs–provide leadership and assistance for existing programs with city recreation departments, libraries, national youth groups, help implement activities where no programs currently exist, and develop awareness campaigns. Family security and day care programs–develop and staff day nurseries and nursery schools, assist casework agencies, support travel's aid societies, and provide mentoring service for teenagers who are in need. Red Cross chapters and other war relief organizations–train for emergency medical services, roll bandages,

and meet other defined needs for the theaters of war and the war refugees.[25]

It is clear from the scope of proposed programs that the CWS was working hard to organize communities in keeping with FDR's statement in the introduction of the first Volunteer Bureau manual that "when we join together to defend our local community we add strength not only to our local community but to our national community as well." It is also apparent that ER's soldiers on the homefront had an enormous mission to complete.

In January 1941, there were forty-four Volunteer Bureaus started by local Junior League chapter. One year later, there were 235 Volunteer Bureaus dedicated to civilian defense. The number continued to climb rapidly throughout the first two years of the war so that by the end of 1943, there were 4,300 active Civilian Defense Volunteer Bureaus registered with the OCD.[26] The OCD's Office of Facts and Figures reported a total of 9,538,634 volunteers registered for homefront war service in October 1942. This number represents approximately 10 percent of the "eligible" citizens.[27] Figures from October 1942 show that registration was fairly consistent across the nine defense regions in the United States.

Reflecting FDR's own fear that the threat to the United States was twofold, many volunteers accepted positions with both the Protective Division and the CWS. It is estimated that at least 4,836,000 volunteers participated in the CWS programs. In order to accommodate the flood of volunteers reporting for service, the CWS encouraged the Bureaus to form committees that addressed the various problems in the communities. These committees accepted scores of volunteers and directed their efforts within the specified issue area.[28] In addition to the information on the committees formed over the first two years of United States involvement in World War II, the Office of Facts and Figures provided estimates of the number of volunteers working in many of the issue areas by 1943.

When the CWS was fully operational, it served as a clearinghouse for information and a source to coordinate efforts between the various regions. After one bureau developed a successful program, the CWS worked to share it with other bureaus. It offered suggestions, guidance, and solutions for the various Civilian Defense Volunteer Bureaus around the country. Though the system was developed and implemented by ER and her AJLA leadership team, it was structured to function independently. This supposition was tested when ER left her position as Assistant Director of the OCD in February 1942. Though her departure was precipitated by substantial negative publicity, ER left feeling that she had accomplished her mission. In final correspondence, she assured one colleague that she was leaving the agency to "good people to carry it on and that it will perform a vital and important service to the people of the country."[29] Even without ER at the head of their division, the CWS did survive. It helped implement a variety of unique and unusual programs, as well as the more expected ones. School lunch programs and classes on quality nutrition during rationing, dances for soldiers and war industry workers, Victory Gardens, first aid classes, and salvage drives were all key parts of almost every bureau. Visiting field workers encouraged the bureaus to think more creatively as well. They believed that the unusual times called for unusual solutions.

One of the most nontraditional programs emerging from the bureaus was the "Men Hospital Volunteers." Ohio, Wisconsin, California, Massachusetts, Rhode Island, New York, Connecticut, Pennsylvania, Michigan, and Virginia developed a cadre of nursing aides who were male. Though this position was traditionally considered a strictly female domain, the exigencies of war led gender boundaries to loosen as the men assumed full responsibilities as nursing aides. From the training courses and work assignments, it appears that these male volunteers were utilized in exactly the same manner as their female counterparts. Volunteers of both genders were expected to handle admissions and discharges; transfer patients; bathe, dress, and weigh them; clean and prepare the ward; take rectal temperatures; and measure output of urine or evacuations, among their other duties. Publicity for this program claimed that the volunteers included professors, clergy, a governor, plumbers, and a variety of other occupations.[30]

The agricultural recruitment campaign of 1943 also introduced new variables into traditional boundaries between race, class, and gender under the sponsorship of the CWS. The Department of Agriculture called for 3.5 million volunteers to assist with the 1943 harvest. This group was needed to meet the increased needs for food and fiber, as well as supplement the labor force that had been depleted by military service and war jobs. Volunteers were needed for seasonal and emergency harvest help, as well as year-round support. The bureaus used their recruiting campaigns and block leaders to help fill this unusual request. They were most successful recruiting for the seasonal and emergency harvest jobs. Ultimately, the labor pool for the harvest was made up of high school and college students, merchants and other professional, off-duty members from labor unions, and urban women.[31]

Childcare became another major issue. The CWS's concept of childcare was much more encompassing than simply babysitting. The Bureau committees addressed issues such as medical and dental care, nutrition, counseling for the working mother, protection against juvenile delinquency, and positive morale activities to counteract the emotional strain of the wartime environment. Worried that the war production zones and the emergency zones would "cause neglect, exploitation, and undue strain on children," the CWS leadership reminded their volunteers that "children are the strength of the Nation. In war as in peace, their welfare is of primary importance to the Nation, to States, to local communities, and above all, to parents."[32]

In order to facilitate this broadly defined vision of childcare, the CWS worked with the Works Progress Administration (WPA) to continue their programs that had been started during the depression. Bureaus either absorbed existing WPA programs, assisted with their expansion by providing funding and additional volunteers, or drew on their expertise to begin new ones. In response to a variety of childcare standards, the CWS defined four types of childcare needed. In addition to the more traditional group activities connected with a school or church, the CWS urged bureaus to explore daily foster families, in-home care, and recreation programs such as weekend day camps and organized play sessions for the after-school hours. These programs helped provide childcare for women who were active in a variety of war service jobs. Efforts were also made to provide childcare for women who returned to nursing, teaching, and public service for the duration of the war.

There were many other programs that emerged from the CWS Bureaus as well. Along with providing programs that addressed specific community needs, the CWS worked closely with other government wartime programs that met a national need. The OPA received help from the Boy Scouts in the spring of 1942, when it needed to distribute a booklet entitled "What You Should Know About Wartime Price Control." The OPA also asked the bureaus to provide volunteers for ration boards, price control compliance, conservation efforts, and car sharing programs. The Office of Defense Health and Welfare Services utilized volunteers in their education, family security and welfare efforts. The Department of National Housing relied heavily on bureau surveys to identify locations for housing lists and on volunteers who would act as rent control monitors. The War Manpower Commission gained assistance from the CWS for its publicity campaigns and enrollment of women in war work. Sales of war bonds and stamps for the Treasury Department were regularly organized through the bureaus. While the Office of War Information operated as an independent agency, many of its distribution programs, public speaking campaigns and town meetings would never have happened without the organizational support of the bureaus.[33]

Field staff visited the regions regularly to oversee the bureaus and work to ensure that the standards outlined by ER and the AJLA leadership team were being upheld. What the CWS could not do, however, was actively manage the bureaus. In response to public concern over the growing reach of the federal government, Executive Order 8757 clearly limited the powers of the OCD. Though the war emergency was a national problem, FDR let the states maintain their sovereignty by not enforcing a single solution to the crisis. With these restrictions, the CWS was unable to do more than advise developing bureaus about ER's vision for a broadly based, community motivated welfare system. Because the CWS was also unable to dictate how bureaus functioned and which programs they pursued, some regions were far more successful than others. Primarily, Region I along the eastern coast and Region IX in the west were the bureaus that most closely followed the recommendations of the CWS. The southern regions were plagued by racial tensions, while those in the midwest were highly individualistic.

As the war in Europe was winding down and the threat of invasion of the United States mainland was recognized as negligible, many previous opponents saw that the CWS was providing a viable wartime service. Even those who were not supportive of a coordinated community welfare system recognized the value of national involvement, continued patriotism, and civic commitment. The CWS provided programs that were keeping people involved in, and committed to, the war effort. With the CWS gaining status among Washington insiders, the volunteer network began exploring options to keep their system functional in the postwar world. OCD *Bulletin* 61 on 29 April 1944 asserted that "for the first time, many communities have coordinated the activities of childcare, recreation, nutrition, health, [and] medical care . . . through one over-all planning group–the War Services Division."[34]

The acting CWS Director, Thomas Devine, sent a proposal to the White House on the need for "community planning and action based on the principles and leadership developed during the war" during the transition from war to peace. He argued that the CWS would be needed to offer a clearinghouse and liaison service for the returning servicemen and their families, as well as for the many families who participated in the war effort at home and who would be attempting to return to a "normal" life.[35] Efforts were also under way to preserve the agency within the private sector. The

AJLA, the Council of Social Agencies, the National Social Welfare Assembly, the Family Welfare Association, the Community Chests and Councils (CC&C), and many other private national organizations were lobbying for a new federal agency that would continue the efforts of the CWS in a peacetime environment. In an effort to clearly define the perceived need for this new agency, the CC&C and the CWS sponsored a special committee to study the effect of coordinated volunteer work in community welfare.[36] Committee members included leading political and community figures who met the CWS criteria of a representative sample from a variety of cultural, social, and economic backgrounds. The study drew a great deal of attention from the media, Congress, and other wartime agencies, and promised to make a substantial impact on the whole issue of coordinated community welfare when it was completed.

Ultimately, the CWS was an experiment in a federally sponsored, community based welfare system. Wartime patriotism and the rhetoric of the Four Freedoms did little to protect the CWS from those who continually challenged the Roosevelts' vision of equal opportunities for all Americans. This distrust of federally mandated welfare systems, together with confusing bureaucracy, lack of firm direction from the national headquarters, and adverse publicity caused the experiment to fail. Devine's proposal was turned down by the Bureau of the Budget on the grounds that the wartime patriotism and community spirit that drove the CWS would rapidly disappear with the end of the war. The analysis also held that "The OCD does not offer a solid foundation for a long-range program to improve Federal-State-local relations, since it has not been uniformly effective in dealing with States and cities, nor with Federal agencies."[37] The study commissioned by the CC&C and the OCD was not completed until 1947. Though it offered firm support, as well as a number of specific examples of how a network of Volunteer Bureaus could help strengthen a community, it was eighteen months too late.

Although the CWS was disbanded with the OCD on 30 June 1945, its legacy remained. Throughout the preface to the papers housed at the National Archives, and other postmortem studies, OCD volunteers conveyed the assumption that their work had only been stopped temporarily.[38] Early Cold War tensions caused some Washington insiders to question the advisability of closing the OCD so quickly. Because of this, the OCD papers were stored for others to use "should the need arise" for future civilian protection against aggression aimed at the United States.[39] The CWS leadership moved to the private sector, where they continued working to regain their nationally recognized status. Though the fighting was over and the United States was experiencing levels of prosperity unseen since the mid-1920s, members of the volunteer network felt their work was incomplete. They wanted to develop a system that would be in place prior to the next national emergency. Many of the OCD staff and volunteers believed that the conservative politics of the era would pass and the need for a nationally coordinated defense and welfare system would again be recognized. Their attitude is best revealed in a poem written for the farewell party at the CWS headquarters:

> The Federal Role in the Community Organizing Movement, or
> Another War Wasted
>
> A plan to help the nation
> To achieve coordination
> And to make up for integration
> Was drawn up in OCD
>
> Federal-State Cooperation
> Gave the Plan wide circulation
> Sending it for consummation
> To the Bureau of the B.
>
> After some investigation
> With definite coloration
> Of Public Administration
> Came the answer "No Siree."
>
> With a proper combination
> Of brass and trepidation
> Not accepting this frustration
> T.D. went to Franklin D.
>
> For awhile there was elation
> But the final culmination
> Was simply termination
> Of our gang at OCD.
>
> It's a sorry situation

But by way of consolation
Community organization
Might come out of World War III.[40]

Notes

1. "Aid to the Democracies: Our Country is Going to Play its Part," Speech by Franklin D. Roosevelt, Washington, D.C., March 15, 1941. In *Vital Speeches of the Day*, VII, 12 (1 April 1941).

2. The CWS division changed names at least four times during the course of the war. In order to avoid confusion, I will be using only the name CWS throughout this analysis. Though the names changed, the essential purpose of the division did not change.

3. Memo from J.C. Russell to Corrington Gill, OCD Papers, RG 171, Historical File, Box 2, National Archives and Records Administration (NARA), Washington National Record Center (WNRC).

4. OCD Papers, RG 171, Entry 99, Box 301, NARA, Regional Archives, San Bruno, California.

5. The most comprehensive assessment of the OCD to date can be found in Robert Ernest Miller's *The War That Never Came: Civilian Defense, and Morale During WWII* (University of Cincinnati: Doctoral Dissertation, 1991). Miller argues that the policies of the OCD form a "window through which we can view the homefront during the World War II" (p. 12). He employs a race, class, and gender paradigm to assess the extent of total community involvement in the homefront war effort. His conclusions are mixed, but support the general assessment that women, minorities, and others benefited temporarily by the war effort, though suffered in the long run. Unfortunately, an examination of the OCD is overwhelmed in this dissertation by Miller's concern to document the role of race, class, and gender in the community. Joseph Lasch also offers a brief, but reliable, review of the Roosevelts' involvement in the OCD in *Eleanor and Franklin* (New York: Norton, 1971). Doris Kearns Goodwin provides a brief glimpse into ER's activities with the OCD in *No Ordinary Time* (New York: Simon and Schuster, 1994).

6. Louis L. Snyder, *Handbook of Civilian Protection for the College of the City of New York* (New York, no date), introductory pages. Historical Documents Collection, Honald Library, Claremont California.

7. OCD Papers, RG 171, Entry 232, I-1, NARA, WNRC.

8. OCD Papers, RG 171, Entry 232, Section IX-8, NARA, WNRC.

9. A.E. Bourneuf, *History of the OCD*, (unpublished manuscript, 1943) p. 41. OCD Papers, RG 171, Historical File Box #2, NARA, WNRC.

10. *Defense*, 2, 45 (1941), Honald Library, Claremont, California.

11. Archibald MacLeish to the Women's Organizations Meeting, November 8, 1941, Washington, D.C. OCD Papers, RG 171, Entry 16, Box 70, NARA, WNRC. For a partial list of those considered as "leading women's organizations," see Appendix A.

12. OCD Administrative Order #22, 5 February 1942, OCD Papers, RG 171, Entry 10, Box 99, NARA, WNRC.

13. OCD Papers, RG 171, Entry 232, Section VII-11, NARA, WNRC.

14. *Suggestions for a Local Central Volunteer Bureau*, notes from the Association of the Junior Leagues of America, Eleanor Roosevelt Papers, Record Group 71, Entry 2603, Roosevelt Library, Hyde Park, New York.

15. The six Canadian cities were: Montreal, Quebec; Toronto, Ontario; Winnipeg, Manitoba; Vancouver, B.C.; Hamilton, Ontario; Halifax, N.S. Janet Gordon and Diana Reische, *The Volunteer Powerhouse* (New York: Rutledge Press, 1982).

16. Correspondence between ER and Katharine Van Slyck, 17 January 1941. Eleanor Roosevelt Papers, Record Group 71, Entry 2603, Roosevelt Library, Hyde Park, New York.

17. Susan Ware first proposed that an informal network existed among Eleanor Roosevelt's acquaintances in her *Beyond Suffrage: Women and the New Deal* (Cambridge: Harvard 1981). Since then, the existence of a network surrounding ER has become an accepted analytical framework. As William Chafe argues in his *The Paradox of Change: American Women in the 20th Century* (New York: Oxford, 1991), 37: "By virtue of her distinctive background and personal situation, Eleanor Roosevelt became the critical link for a network of social workers to social welfare with a new readiness to act politically as well."

18. The loan of these two professional staff members also represents the commitment of the AJLA volunteer membership to this project. In the early years of the AJLA there was no clear distinction between paid staff and members. In the case of these two women, they were members first and professional staff second. Unlike many volunteer organizations today where there is a gap between the desires of the professional staff and the activities of the volunteers, the AJLA members and staff were in full agreement over the level of their organization's involvement in the war effort.

19. OCD Papers, RG 171, Historical File Box #8, NARA, WNRC.

20. Eleanor Roosevelt Papers, Record Group 71, Entry 951, Roosevelt Library, Hyde Park, New York.

21. The OCD papers were inventoried and stored with "the long range objective of aiding future administrations, historians and interested groups as a guide to the experience of the United States Government in the staggering task of providing for the defense of its civilian population during WWII"(Preface to the Index, p. 13). Unfortunately, many papers that were deemed unnecessary in this goal where destroyed. Among them were the personnel files documenting specific volunteer leaders who contributed their time, "without compensation," to the CWS. Luckily, notes in the Index to Record Group 171 at the NARA, WNRC, are surprisingly detailed and thorough. While individual personnel files, volunteer organization, and many other records relating to the volunteer aspects of the OCD were destroyed, others are available by searching through files that were cross-referenced to the original documents. The most revealing link between the OCD and the Junior League is the stationery used by the local Volunteer Bureaus and Defense Councils. Through 1942, more than half of all the letters to the OCD were sent on local Junior League stationery. Generally, the name of the Junior League was crossed out and the name of the Bureau or Council was added. The address remained the same, suggesting that the Junior Leagues provided office space as well as money and staffing.

22. OCD Papers, RG 171, Entry 33, Box 58; and RG 171, Entry 10, Box 83, NARA,WNRC. For a complete listing of organizations, see Appendix B.

23. Regional Offices were located in major cities or industrial centers for each sector:

Region I: (North-East) – Boston, Massachusetts;
Region II: (New York) – New York, New York;
Region III: (Mid-Atlantic) – Baltimore, Maryland;
Region IV: (South East) – Atlanta, Georgia;
Region V: (Eastern, Mid-West) – Cleveland, Ohio;
Region VI: (Northern, Mid-West) – Chicago, Illinois;
Region VII: (Southern, Mid-West) – Omaha, Nebraska;
Region VIII: (South-West) – Dallas, Texas;
Region IX: (West) – San Francisco, California.

24. June 1942 Mobilization Reports, OCD Papers, RG 171, Entry 31B, NARA, WNRC.

25. *Civilian Defense Volunteer Office Manual*, September 1941, OCD Papers, RG 171, Entry 129, File #34, NARA, WNRC.

26. OCD Papers, RG 171, Entry 231, Section XIII-15, NARA, WNRC.

27. OCD Papers, RG 171, Entry 38B, Statistics File, NARA, WNRC. "Eligible" citizens were those 15-69 years old, who were able to participate in any way. This included physically disabled as well as members of various ethnic and religious groups.

28. OCD Papers, RG 171, Entry 38B, Statistics File, NARA, WNRC. The Office of Facts and Figures within the OCD was responsible for regularly compiling various pieces of statistical information about Defense activities throughout the country. The 1942 figures were taken from the 10/31/42 report and the 1943 figures from the 12/31/43 report. By 1943, the statistical reports were far more detailed and were broken down into three categories: community population under 5,000, 5,000-25,000, and over 25,000.

29. Letter to Mrs. Gifford (Leila) Pinchot, 19 February 1942, Eleanor Roosevelt papers, Entry 100, File 1656, Roosevelt Library, Hyde Park, New York.

30. Training Kit, OCD Papers, RG 171, Entry 38A, NARA, WNRC.

31. Ibid.

32. Ibid.

33. Ibid.

34. OCD Papers, RG 171, Entry 32B, NARA, WNRC.

35. Memo to FDR from Tom Devine, 14 November 1944, FDR Official File, Entry 4422, File 2, Roosevelt Library, Hyde Park, New York.

36. National Social Welfare Assembly Papers, RG 4.2, Entry 21, Publications file, Social Welfare History Archives, University of Minnesota, East Bank Campus.

37. Memo to FDR from the Director of the Bureau of the Budget, January 4, 1945, FDR Official File, Entry 4422, File 2, Roosevelt Library, Hyde Park, New York.

38. Preface to the Papers, Volume I, National Office, 1941-194, OCD Papers, RG 171, NARA, WNRC.

39. Ibid.

40. OCD Papers, RG 171, Historical File (1), NARA, WNRC.

11

The American Jewish Community, the Roosevelt Administration, and the Holocaust

Carol Silverman

The Holocaust formed a watershed of brutality and inhumanity in twentieth-century life. Between June 1941 and May 1945, 5 to 6 million Jews were systematically exterminated by the Nazis and their collaborators. Hitler's effort to wipe out an entire people was unprecedented.

Jews have a long history that accentuates community responsibility. American Jews have long felt an obligation to help those in less fortunate situations around the word. In this tradition, American Jews felt it necessary to take action as the situation in Germany deteriorated in the 1930s, but they were able to accomplish relatively little. Why?

Why was the American Jewish leadership unable to have more influence over government policy, and why did their activities fail to achieve any real results? How was it that American Jewry was unable appreciably to move the Roosevelt administration to attempt to rescue the Jews of Europe? This failure is all the more striking in view of the fact that American Jewry held an important position in the liberal-urban-ethnic coalition that served the New Deal so effectively, and that many Jews had access to the innermost circles of the administration. Jews also headed three major congressional committees—Sol Bloom, House Foreign Affairs Committee; Samuel Dickstein, House Committee on Immigration and Naturalization; and Emanuel Cellar, House Judiciary Committee.[1]

Certainly no action taken by the United States could have saved all European Jews. But a substantial commitment by the United States could have saved perhaps several hundred thousand of them without compromising the war effort.[2] Yet the United States never seized the initiative for such action, and when action was taken, it was too little too late. Why did the Roosevelt administration respond with such indifference at this critical a juncture? Why did Roosevelt let down his most overwhelmingly loyal constituency? What was the role of the American Jewish community during this period? These questions will be explored by analyzing the historical context of the period and by examining the American Jewish community as an interest group. The role of the Roosevelt administration and of Roosevelt himself will then be considered.

Challenges in the Political Environment

The greatest challenge for the Jewish community in the late 1930s and early 1940s lay in the restrictions on immigration into the United States. Every ethnic group was involved, but the Jews were most affected because of the persecution in Germany. America in the thirties was under the shadow of the Great Depression, and out of this experience developed the widely accepted concept of immigration restriction. Restrictionists believed that refugees who immigrated to the United States took jobs that would otherwise have gone to unemployed American workers.[3] In addition to this economic argument, opinion was marked by strong feelings of xenophobia, expressed through the idea of keeping "America for Americans." This attitude gave rise to the immigration quota system in the 1920s, the first significant restriction of immigration of the century. Xenophobic sentiments intensified during the thirties and World War II years. Despite wartime prosperity, the economic argument against immigration remained. There was a widespread fear that the depression would return at the end of the war, and that demobilization of the armed forces would bring, at the very least, a return of large-scale unemployment.[4]

The strength of this attitude was reflected in the substantial political power of the anti-immigration forces. A large number of congressmen were staunchly restrictionist, reflecting their personal views as well as the popular views of their home districts. The mood of the country was restrictionist, and it took great effort by refugee and social-service organizations to avoid even greater limitations on immigration. Yet these organizations were not powerful enough to effect any change in the existing quota systems.[5]

A second factor that acted as a barrier to significant political action during this period was widespread anti-Semitism in the United States. While there were many who opposed immigration in general, much restrictionist sentiment was tinged with strong anti-Semitic feelings as well. In the thirties, more than one hundred anti-Semitic organizations were active throughout the country.[6] Hostile stereotypes were fundamental to this outlook; in 1940, for example, 63 percent of the respondents in a national survey said that Jews as a group had "objectionable traits."[7] Almost half the respondents polled in 1938 and 1939 described Jewish businessmen as less honest than others. Even more damaging was the opinion reflected in a poll taken in 1944, with the war still raging: 24 percent of the respondents regarded the Jews as a "menace to America," while only 6 percent considered Germans to be a menace and 9 percent the Japanese. These surveys were conducted during a period when Hitler's treatment of the Jews was public knowledge. Earlier, in March 1938, polls revealed that a majority of Americans believed that the persecution of German Jews was either wholly or partly their own fault.[8]

However ugly the overtly anti-Semitic acts may have been—the street gangs, the snide leaflets, the hate letters sent to government officials—these examples were merely the superficial manifestation of a more pervasive anti-Semitism in America. As Herbert Stember states, "Negative attitudes toward Jews penetrated all sectors of wartime America. Many millions were not anti-Semitic in any overt sense of the term. They would not personally have mistreated a Jew. Beneath the surface, however, were uncrystallized but negative feelings about Jews."[9] These amorphous feelings are revealed in the polls taken between 1938 and 1946. David Wyman notes, "In ordinary times, this passive anti-Semitism would have worked little damage. But in the Holocaust crisis it meant that a large body of decent and normally considerate people was predisposed to not care about European Jews or to care whether the government did anything to help save them."[10]

Challenges within the Government

Consideration must also be given to the prevailing political atmosphere in the State Department, the part of the government most involved in the refugee issue. No one argued, either before 1942, when the news of the massive extermination of Jews was publicly acknowledged, or afterward, that the immigration laws needed to be changed; the sentiment of public opinion was too strongly aligned against such a move. Moreover, State Department officials opposed any liberal interpretation of the law so that even existing quotas were not filled.[11] Because of such policies, only 21,000 refugees, most of them Jewish, were allowed to enter the United States during the war years—only 10 percent of the number that could have been legally admitted under the immigration quotas of the time. More significantly, according to Wyman, the State Department and the British Foreign Office "had no intention of rescuing large numbers of European Jews. On the contrary, they continually feared that Germany . . . might release tens of thousands of Jews into Allied hands." [12]

There was a real fear of a German fifth column during this period. This fear, common among the general public, was reflected by numerous magazine and newspaper articles of the time and was also evident in State Department policy. Although there were undoubtedly German attempts to create a sympathetic climate in America (and also to plant spies), there was no evidence that refugees were involved. Nevertheless, the suspicion spread that such spies were secreted within refugee circles. The charges attracted enhanced coverage in the press as 1940 progressed, and the State Department utilized this hysteria to turn the flow of refugees into a mere trickle by the late fall of 1941.[13] Roosevelt was generally content to let the State Department handle the refugee matter, remaining aloof from the battle except for an occasional inquiry or suggestion. He had followed this policy in other troublesome areas in order to deflect pressure that otherwise would be directed at the White House. In the case of American Jewry, this policy proved extremely successful. Jews continued to believe in Roosevelt's support, and his reputation with American Jews remained strong throughout the war.[14]

Unfortunately, Breckinridge Long was one of those who believed most firmly that aliens and Jews were potential fifth columnists, and he had the power to do something about it. Long served as an Assistant Secretary of State and supervised twenty-three of the forty-two divisions in the State Department, including those governing overseas relief, transport, civilian internees, prisoners of war, and the vitally important visa section.[15] Entries from Long's diary show that he linked communism and Jewish internationalism, positions that eventually developed into feelings of conspiracy and paranoia.[16]

In September 1941, Long wrote in his diary about meeting with Rabbi Wise and others on the Refugee Committee:

> Wise always assumes such a sanctimonious air and pleads for the "intellectuals and brave spirits, refugees from the tortures of the dictators." . . . Of course only an infinitesimal fraction of the immigrants are of that category and some are certainly German agents and other sympathizers. . . . Each one of these men hates me

[referring to those active on the Refugee Committee]. I am to them the embodiment of a nemesis.[17]

In September of 1942 Long wrote, "I took [a departmental order] to the Secretary, told him I had decided I had won all the battles and the war in the immigration fight."[18] It was true. Long was completely successful in keeping the number of immigrants below the allowed quotas during the most crucial years of the rescue effort. His leadership over second-echelon officials created snarls and miles of red tape, forming the "paper walls" that David Wyman describes.[19] The State Department tightened immigration procedures and closed the United States as a place of asylum. Long also stymied attempts by others in the executive department, such as Treasury Secretary Morgenthau, to apply pressure for looser immigration policies. Not only were 62,000 fewer refugees admitted between 1938 and 1941 than were allowed by the Immigration Act of 1924, but many thousands more were kept out through the denial of temporary visas, or the failure to issue rulings exempting children from the quota system, or the killing of possible projects such as "temporary havens" or "fire ports," which did not fall under the Immigration Act but would have allowed for admittance of additional refugees.[20] As a defender of America's shores against immigration until the end of his influence early in 1944, Long was tragically successful.

The Organized Jewish Community

Because Jews were such a small percentage of the American population, it is important to look at the degree of cohesion and unity that existed in the Jewish community during the late 1930s and 1940s. Although Jews were viewed from the outside as a fairly homogeneous group (and by anti-Semitics as a unified, powerful conspiracy), the fact is that the Jewish community in America was, and continues to be, characterized much more by diversity than by unity. Besides the more obvious divisions among the reform, conservative, and orthodox movements, the greatest divider of Jews in the first half of the twentieth century in America was "uptown" and "downtown."[21] "Uptown" refers to the assimilated, financially successful descendants of German Jewish immigrants of the 1800s. Their method was to avoid overt controversy by having wealthy, powerful, and intellectual members of the community quietly approach their gentile counterparts in business, government, or the media to work out possible solutions. The term "downtown" referred to the wave of less assimilated, less affluent, post-1881 immigrants from Eastern Europe. This group had a strong contingent of the more traditional orthodox Jews, less eager to lose their characteristic expressions of Jewish culture. Represented by many groups, these downtown Jews provided the primary impetus of the Zionist movement of the 1930s, represented by the Zionist Organization of America and other groups.[22]

The crisis in Germany in the thirties deepened the divisions within the American Jewish community. As Feingold states, "No unified plan of action emerged; instead, half-forgotten conflicts were given a new lease on life."[23] As the situation worsened, the schisms within the community deepened and disagreement grew on both the degree of danger and what could or should be done about it. Roosevelt was well aware of the split in the Jewish community and the political weakness such a split indicated.[24] At this time there were over 300 national Jewish organizations, with thousands of local branches, which never were able to act in unison. Bitter personal and interorganizational factionalism was the rule.

The situation grew even more desperate in 1942, as rumors of the concentration camps were confirmed by facts and the Jewish leaders realized the scope of the disaster they faced. There was bitter fractional conflict between the Zionist groups such as the Zionist Organization of America, who believed that the path for rescue lay in fighting the impact of the British White Paper limiting immigration to Palestine, thereby opening Palestine to European Jews, and non-Zionist organizations such as the American Jewish Committee, Jewish Labor Committee, B'nai B'rith, and the ultra-Orthodox groups, who believed in applying further pressure for rescue efforts. The split over Zionism became irreconcilable.[25] In January of 1944, Breckinridge Long writes in his diary, "The Jewish organizations are all divided and in controversies of their own. . . . There is no adhesion nor any sympathetic collaboration–rather rivalry, jealousy and antagonism."[26]

The problem was not a lack of activity. The Zionist groups had many resources, such as an active membership, strong organizational skills, a few prestigious leaders, and valuable contacts in government. The American Jewish Committee had wealth, experience, and influence in high places. The Jewish Labor Committee was backed by a sizable constituency. B'nai B'rith had the allegiance of a broad cross-section of American Jews. The Bergsonite Emergency Committee offered energy, publicity skills, and the capacity to win friends in Congress and elsewhere in Washington.[27] The effectiveness of the numerous activities of each of these groups was limited by their failure to create a united Jewish movement that would speak with one voice and concentrate sustained action on a particular goal over time.

Perhaps the task was too great, the opposing forces too overwhelming, the chance for success of any of the differing strategies too slight, for the prospective leaders of the Jewish community to be effective in bringing about a unified effort. The resources of the Jewish community, even if completely mobilized in a unified effort, were inadequate to the task. Confusion, disarray, frustration with unresponsive world leaders, the overwhelming apathy of world opinion, and a sense of hopelessness in the face of a tragedy of inexplicable proportions pervaded this period.

This impotence was all the more frustrating because of the active Jewish involvement in national politics, especially presidential. Though comprising only about 3 percent of the national electorate, Jews played a major role in the New Deal Democratic coalition fashioned by Franklin Roosevelt. In a few major urban states that controlled large blocs of electoral votes—especially in New York and California—the Jewish population was concentrated enough to be a significant factor in determining electoral outcomes.[28]

Jews had moved clearly into the Democratic camp with the election of 1928, but the vote for Roosevelt increased dramatically in both 1932 (82 percent) and 1936 (nearly 90 percent). During the depression, it was natural for urban immigrant Jews to support a party and candidate with more liberal economic and ethnic policies.[29] In addition, Jews as a group persisted in their attachment to Roosevelt long after the support of large numbers of other minority populations had waned. Roosevelt's strength for other hyphenated groups reached its zenith in 1936, but for America's Jewish population it did not peak until 1940 and 1944, even though by this time the Jewish economic and occupational situation had improved significantly.[30]

Yet this loyalty may have backfired. So strong was the attachment of the Jewish voter to Roosevelt that Jewish leaders were denied the ability to use withdrawal of the vote as a threat when meeting with the president. Because of the strength of the support from Jewish voters, there was little political incentive for Roosevelt to pursue an active rescue policy, which could cause the loss of votes from those opposed to the policy. Unable to gain leverage by threatening a voter realignment, Jewish leaders were denied one of the most effective tools in the political arena and were forced to accept less satisfactory rewards for political loyalty.[31]

What kind of access did the Jewish establishment have in the Roosevelt government, and what use did they make of this access? It is clear that individual Jews and certain Jewish leaders such as Rabbi Stephen S. Wise did have entree to Roosevelt personally. What is less clear is whether or not such access was utilized to address immigration and, later, rescue issues. The list of well-positioned Jews in the Roosevelt administration was so impressive that the pejorative term "Jew Deal" was in common usage by 1936.[32] Prominent Jews in Roosevelt's administration included Samuel Rosenman, the president's speech writer and special counsel; Benjamin Cohen, personal advisor; Ambassador Laurence Steinhardt; Bernard Baruch, economic advisor; Isador Lubin, head of the Bureau of Labor Statistics; and David Niles, presidential assistant.

Yet one of the most fascinating paradoxes of the period was that so little political use was made of Jewish access to the president. Various explanations have been offered, but little research has been done in this area and none of the explanations are backed by more than supposition.[33] It is not even clear if there were efforts by Jewish organizations to activate these individuals in an attempt to influence Roosevelt. The outstanding exception, of course, was Treasury Secretary Henry Morgenthau.

American Jewish organizations were responsible for several truly important achievements. Intense efforts by various Jewish groups brought about some results in Congress. The House Committee on Foreign Affairs called Breckinridge Long to defend the government's refugee policy, which led to his eventual removal and to a major shift of responsibility of rescue efforts to the Treasury Department. This initiative also provoked the congressional pressure that eventually led to Roosevelt's establishment of the War Refugee Board. In addition, American Jewish organizations carried out large-scale rescue and relief work overseas. During the war, the American Jewish Joint Distribution Committee provided more aid to European Jews than the combined aid of all the world's governments. They paid for nearly 85 percent of the work of the War Refuge Board, and American Jewish groups and their overseas affiliates were central to most of the War Refugee Board's direct action projects.[34]

Actions of the Roosevelt Administration

The Roosevelt administration's involvement in the rescue process can be divided into two phases that reflected the intensification of Jewish persecution. First were the years leading up the Holocaust (1938-1941), and the years of the Holocaust itself. Conditions had been growing steadily worse during the 1930s for the Jews of Germany. The situation grew more desperate after Krystallnacht, the "Night of the Broken Glass," a "spontaneous" orgy of arson and looting against the Jews throughout the country on 10 November 1938. Following this dramatic incidence of government-sanctioned violence, most German Jews understood for the first time the hopelessness of their situation. Even the most assimilated Jew was now forced to think in terms of emigration. During this period, initially Jews were allowed to leave Germany if they could find any country to take them in. Yet, as Saul Friedman states, "there was a tragic element of truth in the statement circulated among Europe's Jews in 1938 that the world was made up of two types of countries: the kind where Jews could not live and the kind where Jews could not enter."[35] During the later years, leaving Germany became increasingly difficult.

The second phase began in January 1942 with Hitler's decision to liquidate the Jews, the actual beginning of the Holocaust. Jews were no longer allowed to leave Germany or the other countries under its control. Hitler had made his decision on how to solve the Jewish question, and emigration was no longer an option.

The First Phase

The first specific act of the Roosevelt administration concerning the rescue process was an invitation in March 1938 to thirty-two nations to meet at Evian-les-Bains to try to supply some order to the chaotic refugee situation brought on by Berlin's policies of expulsion. The Evian Initiative was rather astonishing since Roosevelt, bound by a highly restrictive immigration law, was virtually powerless to act. The preface of the agenda for the conference stated that the United States could not change its immigration laws and expected no other country to do so.[36] Thus the U.S. delegation had no bargaining power at all. In light of American promises that participating countries would not be committed to changing their immigration laws, the eventual failure of the conference was almost a foregone conclusion. The hope was that Latin America would provide the havens that the United States could not. Instead the Latin American republics chose to emulate the United States' policy of closed doors.[37] The failure of any suitable mass resettlement havens became the cause of the lack of success of this first phase of the rescue effort.[38] The only concrete accomplishment to come out of the Evian conference was the establishment of the Intergovernmental Committee on Refugees (IGC), which was the main American contribution to a possible solution of the crisis, and which was to be a voluntary organization, totally dependent on private donations. The organization's primary purpose was to reach some agreement with Berlin and to impose order on the confused and burgeoning refugee situation. In 1938 it was still believed that a solution to the refugee problem could be reached through negotiations. The German government did agree to negotiate, and in 1939, much to everyone's surprise, George Rublee, IGC director, reached a "Statement of Agreement" with Berlin.[39]

The Statement of Agreement was an informal arrangement and constituted, in essence, a ransom offer. In return for a forced sale of German goods by an outside agency representing "international Jewry" and the establishment of a trust fund from confiscated German-Jewish capital, Berlin would allow an orderly, phased emigration of the Jewish community. It would even give some guarantee that overt persecution would be eliminated. Before the details of the agreement could be completed, however, Hitler dismissed the main negotiator, Nazi financial wizard Hjalmar Schacht. The question arises whether there was ever any real chance of success for such negotiations. Feingold argues that the volatile internal political conditions in Germany during this period, when the government was concentrating on the invasion of Czechoslovakia, were simply too unstable to guarantee the future of anything, much less such a complex and difficult plan.[40]

Roosevelt was personally interested in finding possible areas in which to resettle Jews. Shortly after Krystallnacht, Henry Morgenthau had contacted the president about the possible settlement of refugees in Central and South America. Cordell Hull, the secretary of state, cabled American missions to explore such possibilities, with no positive responses. Hull sent Roosevelt a comprehensive report on potential havens around the world, favoring sparsely populated areas of Africa such as Angola, Rhodesia, Madagascar, and New Caldonia.[41] No plan actually passed the proposal stage, for the truth was that no one wanted the Jewish refugees. But all of these possibilities became moot once the decision to liquidate the Jews was made in January 1942, when Hitler gave up on the idea that a solution by resettlement was possible.[42] The failure of emigration proposals convinced the Nazis that Europe could never be made free of Jews by emigration, and therefore a more drastic solution, the Final Solution, was the chosen alternative.[43]

The period of the "phony war," September 1939 to April 1940, highlighted a special problem–the rescue of Europe's cultural elite. Many prominent figures in Washington were asked to act as conduits for visa requests for such people. Soon dozens of special committees sprang up. The committees' often-successful requests for special treatment, which bypassed the normal visa procedures, proved extremely troublesome to the State Department. During this period the Orthodox Agudat Israel and the Socialist Jewish Labor Committee, with the help of friends in high places, extracted several hundred emergency visas for Jewish political and religious leaders then living in Poland.[44] In his diaries, Breckinridge Long complained bitterly of the constant barrage of requests for special visas by Rabbi Wise and others.[45] In June and July of 1941, a new series of State Department regulations issued by Long, in addition to restrictions on visitors or transit visas, stemmed the tide of these entreaties.[46]

The Second Phase

The date of 24 November 1942 marked the beginning of the second period in the history of the Holocaust. This is the date when Rabbi Wise publicly confirmed to the world Hitler's plan for the systematic extermination of Europe's Jews. News of the existence of the plan had actually reached the United States in August 1942, but because of skeptical reaction in the State Department, Wise was asked not to publicize the information until the government could provide confirmation. It was not until November that the news, along with corroborating evidence, was released to the press.[47]

Following the announcement in November 1942, Wise called an emergency meeting of national Jewish organizations. A torrent of activity followed. Jewish organizations issued proclamations and held memorial services in synagogues and churches around the country. In New York City, half-a-million workers stopped work for ten minutes.[48] On 8 December 1942 a delegation led by Wise consisting of representatives of six organizations visited the president. They delivered a memorandum pleading with Roosevelt to appoint a commission to collect and examine the evidence of Nazi barbarities against civilian populations. The President talked to the delegation for about a half hour, assuring them of his sympathy. Nine days after the meeting, the Allies issued their first warning on war crimes. It mentioned nothing about the "Final Solution"; it did not state that the Nazis would be held accountable for crimes against Jews.[49]

By the early months of 1943 public pressure was mounting as the American Jewish community's efforts to rescue the European Jews intensified into a massive effort. On March 1, a huge rally was held at Madison Square Garden, co-sponsored by the Church Peace Union, the AFL, and the CIO. The rally was addressed by Governor Thomas E. Dewey, New York Mayor Fiorello La Guardia, and other prominent personalities.

Press estimates of attendance ranged as high as 50,000 and the event received extensive coverage. Similar rallies were held in a number of other cities. Dramatic full-page ads were taken out by Jewish organizations in major newspapers. On March 9, a pageant entitled "We Will Never Die" premiered. Produced by Billy Rose and directed by Moss Hart, with music composed by Kurt Weil, the pageant eventually played to over 100,000 Americans.[50]

The combination of these pressures with the even more forceful public reaction and cries for action in England resulted in British Foreign Secretary Anthony Eden's suggestion, while visiting Washington in March, that a new refugee conference be called.[51] The purpose of the resulting Bermuda Conference, which was held in April, was to respond to the growing agitation over rescue policy. The agenda was prepared by Breckinridge Long. It was decided that it would be a closed-door meeting and that no Jewish delegation would be permitted to attend. The excluded Jewish leaders besieged conference participants with memorandums. A meeting in Washington on March 27 was arranged between Rabbi Wise and Joseph Proskauer, president of the American Jewish Committee, and Anthony Eden, who found the proposals they presented "fantastically impossible."[52] The Bermuda Conference produced no significant action. American Jewish leaders and organizations reacted with outrage, tinged by a deeper current of despondency. The Conference had provided no help for the Jews. Developing real solutions to the crisis was not the purpose at Bermuda. As Lucy Dawidowicz points out, "Its purpose was to dampen the growing pressures for rescue."[53] In 1943, in response to growing pressure from Jewish activists, various resolutions were introduced in Congress to remove the rescue operation from the State Department and to create a new agency for that purpose. When hearings on the resolutions were held in November, Breckinridge Long asked to be allowed to testify in executive session. During his testimony, he presented the Committee with vastly exaggerated figures of the number of refugees admitted, a distortion of the facts concerning lack of shipping to transport refugees, and insisted that the Inter-Governmental Committee on Refugees had plenary power to negotiate with the enemy through an intermediary. When his testimony was made public on December 10, its blatant inaccuracies provoked a burst of criticism. The controversy reverberated in Congress, where Samuel Dickstein assailed Long for creating the false impression of action, and Emanuel Celler asserted he was not fit to supervise refugee policy.[54] The furor over Long's testimony helped end his control of refugee policy. State

Department reshuffling took the refugee and visa responsibilities away from Long and assigned them elsewhere.

The War Refugee Board

A major change came on 16 January 1944 when Henry Morgenthau, then Secretary of the Treasury, met with Roosevelt to deliver what he called "my personal report" to the President. According to Morgenthau, "The report pulled no punches."[55] He urged the president to create a rescue committee. Roosevelt was under greatest pressure however, because the Rescue Resolution in Congress had a strong possibility of passage, and hearings on the issue would precipitate a debate in which the State Department's record and Long's testimony could be closely scrutinized, to great embarrassment. Roosevelt's quick acquiescence to Morgenthau showed that he recognized the pressures in Congress and knew he could no longer avoid the rescue issue.[56]

The establishment of the War Refugee Board was thus the result of two sets of developments. The first was the persistent call for action by Morgenthau and the Treasury Department. The second was the culmination of the campaign for a rescue agency led by the Emergency Committee to Save the Jewish People of Europe. This campaign had been supported by several other Jewish groups that had worked over the months to publicize the extermination news and had created a limited, but vitally important, degree of public awareness and political support in Congress for rescue.[57]

On 22 January 1944 the President announced the establishment of the War Refugee Board. The State Department's responsibility for refugees was transferred to the members of the Board, which included the secretaries of State, Treasury, and War. But the actual responsibilities of the Board were in the hands of the Treasury Department.

Of all of the actions of the Roosevelt administration concerning rescue issues, the establishment of the War Refugee Board was the first substantial government effort. It was set up to have a certain degree of real power; but the actual operations of the Board developed on a diminished level of effectiveness. Although the Executive Order establishing the Board required the full cooperation of the State and War departments, they offered almost as much opposition as help. The Soviets did not participate in any of the Board's rescue activities and the British were obstructive to any such actions. Roosevelt took little interest in the Board after its establishment, and the funding situation caused it to operate at a disadvantage from the start. As

Wyman points out, the Board "turned into a valuable, but limited, collaboration between the government and the private agencies . . . [which] carried most of the load."[58] The private agencies referred to were Jewish funding agencies such as the American Joint Distribution Committee, which supplied nearly 85 percent of the funds of the WRB.[59] A viable rescue effort was in place and functioning. What was the Board able to accomplish? Morgenthau wrote, concerning the Board, that

> It was instrumental in getting thousands of Jews out through the Balkans in 1944 and 1945. Its agents had powerboats running across the Baltic ferrying refugees to asylum in Sweden. It negotiated through intermediaries with Heinrich Himmler, chief of the Nazi secret police, to get several trainloads of refugees out of Germany. It sent funds to France to assist refugees who had long been in hiding. It helped get South American passports for refugees in Switzerland.[60]

The War Refugee Board did play a crucial role in saving approximately 200,000 Jews: 120,000 Jews survived in Budapest; 48,000 Jews were moved to safe areas of Romania; at least 10,000 were protected within Axis Europe by underground activities financed by the War Refugee Board; and about 15,000 refugees were evacuated from Axis territory.[61] Perhaps the greatest weakness of the War Refugee Board was that it was established so late. Morgenthau concluded, "It did a magnificent job. But think what it might have done had it begun work a year earlier! As a result in part of the delays in beginning a serious rescue program, only one out of seven European Jews is alive today."[62]

Public Opinion

Public opinion was critical to the task the American Jewish community faced. As David Truman notes, "Being almost inevitably minorities in the total population, organized interest groups must find some means of allying themselves with other groups and of mobilizing their "'fellow-travelers.'"[63] The Jewish community was never able to accomplish this task.

Although the leaders of the Jewish community tried to get their message out to the American people, they failed. The events taking place in the concentration camps never reached the consciousness of the general public, even after the facts were publicly confirmed and published in the major newspapers. By January 1943, it had already been reported that 2 million Jews had been killed or deported since the beginning of the war, yet less than half the population believed that this was true: the rest thought it was "just a rumor," or had no opinion. The results of a poll conducted in December 1944 showed that over three-quarters of the public believed that the Germans had murdered many people in concentration camps. Yet the survey did not refer to Jews specifically, and when asked to estimate how many people had been killed, most respondents named a figure of 100,000 or less. As Stember describes it:

> The public almost certainly was not aware at first how large a proportion of the victims had been Jews. Even by the end of the war, when Hitler's policy of systematic murder probably was generally known in this country, the public did not seem to have realized the extent to which Jews were special targets of his wrath.[64]

It is difficult to understand why the American populace registered so little knowledge of the plight of the Jews in Europe when the facts were available and had been reported, albeit on the back pages, in the newspapers. One reason often given is that people found the idea of mass extermination, using modern techniques, simply impossible to imagine. How do you believe the unbelievable? There were many editorials after the camps had been opened, and this question was the main theme of editorial after editorial. The *New York Times* described the news of the "cold-blooded extermination of an unarmed people" as "facts that pass belief."[65] The magnitude of the horror certainly overwhelmed the imagination. Although this explanation may apply to the general public, and even to many members in the American Jewish community, it most certainly did not apply to the press corps, who had access to factual information. Nor did it apply to the higher officials in the government, the State Department, and Roosevelt himself, who had overwhelming evidence of what was actually happening by mid-1942.

There is no way of knowing whether the American people would have been roused to demand action if the press had made the issue more vital and important. Yet without such coverage, it was virtually assured that there would be no public outcry outside of the Jewish community. What efforts were made to bring the issue before the people generally were made not by the press but by the more radical, activist Jewish groups such as the Emergency Conference to Save the Jews of Europe and the Bergsonite

Emergency Committee. Numerous events were staged in 1943-44 by such groups to bring attention what was happening. Their task was extremely difficult because it was not reinforced by significant press attention. Though these organizations ultimately achieved some measure of success in publicizing the crisis, by then it was just too late.

The Role of Roosevelt

Roosevelt was viewed as the great humanitarian, the champion of the forgotten man, the innovative New Dealer whom American Jews believed in so strongly that they gave him 90 percent of their vote. Morgenthau said of Roosevelt, "He was keenly aware that America's historic tradition made it an asylum for the oppressed and for the homeless, a refuge for the victims of foreign tyranny."[66]

Yet Roosevelt's administrative style often led to overlapping agencies in perpetual conflict. Neither side knew where Roosevelt really stood–neither those who believed in the humanitarian roots of the New Deal, nor those who insisted that the refugees presented a threat to national security. There was no clear direction. As Feingold notes, "This absence of a specific mandate, which some observers see as the most typical aspect of Roosevelt's style of administration, was very apparent on the rescue question. Decision making was rarely clear cut."[67] Roosevelt also used the State Department as a foil, and therefore American Jewry rarely questioned his sincerity. He was in fact fully aware of what was happening on the rescue issue. Long wrote on 3 October 1940, "About noon I had a long satisfactory conversation with the President on the subject of refugees . . . the whole subject of immigration, visas, safety of the United States, procedures to be followed; and all that sort of thing was on the table. I found that he was 100 percent in accord with my ideas."[68]

For those who accepted the rhetoric of the New Deal, the evidence of indifference was difficult to accept. The cruelest lack of will was during the early period. Roosevelt knew well, of course, that the rescue of a foreign minority, in an era of continuing anti-Semitism, represented a distinct political risk. After January 1942, the Final Solution achieved a momentum of its own that would have taken tremendous energy and organization to affect, a commitment Roosevelt was unwilling or unable to make, a price he could not or would not pay. The irony is that while Jews venerated Roosevelt as their greatest friend and the highest representative of the humanitarian ideal, the rescue of the Jews never became a priority for the

Roosevelt administration. Winning the war was Roosevelt's top priority, and the controversial, complex situation of European Jewry was a matter of indifference by comparison. Any solutions were problematic at best, since two major factors were never under Allied control: Nazi determination to achieve the Final Solution, and physical control of the area where it was being carried out.

Nevertheless, having acknowledged Roosevelt's very real difficulties, there was action he could have taken. He could have acted to increase immigration into the United States, at least up to quota levels. If nothing else, if he had spoken out about the Final Solution, an aroused public might have backed some sort of rescue effort. Statements by the president might have brought the news out of the back pages of the newspapers and into the headlines. The result, at the very least, might have been the mobilization of public opinion, which was one of the major barriers American Jews could not seem to overcome.

Roosevelt also could have applied pressure on Axis satellites to release captive Jews, especially after the spring of 1943 when some of the satellites, convinced that the war was lost, were sending out feelers for favorable peace terms. This could have affected large numbers of Jews from Romania, Bulgaria, Hungary, and other areas. Had Roosevelt and his allies made public their awareness of the mass-murder program and their severe condemnation of it, and had they threatened punishment for these crimes, the Nazis might have stopped believing that the West did not care what they were doing to the Jews. Publicity and condemnation would also have warned European Jews of what was happening and that the deportation trains were leading not to labor camps but to crematoriums. None of these responses would have guaranteed significant results. Yet they involved little risk, both politically and in terms of the war effort. But Roosevelt had little to say about the problem, and instructed his staff to divert Jewish questions to the State Department. Years later, Emanuel Celler charged that Roosevelt, instead of providing even "some spark of courageous leadership," had been "silent, indifferent, and insensitive to the plight of the Jews."[69]

Conclusions

Taken together as an interest group, did Jewish organizations have the ability to have any real effect on American policy during the Holocaust? The historical context and the political environment within which Jewish activists had to operate was extremely negative. America was emerging from a decade of overt anti-Semitism. Depression-era American opinion overwhelmingly supported extreme restriction of immigration. State Department officials, especially Breckinridge Long and those working under him who controlled the immigration process, not only agreed with this position but also considered it their duty to execute policy to achieve its most extreme interpretation. The main avenue for any governmental action in the years before 1942 was obstructed constantly by Long and those working with him.

During the actual period of Hitler's final solution, the attention of the American people and government was absorbed by World War II. At this point, American Jews were trying to find a solution for a problem that was physically beyond their control. There was little possibility of rescuing appreciable numbers, and wartime priorities never included the rescue of a group of foreign people. The overwhelming problem was how to convince countries that were fighting for their own survival, and taking massive losses in a particularly cruel war, that the murder of Jewish men, women, and children deserved their special attention.

The American Jewish community was unable to get the facts accepted by the general public. Without "fellow travelers" any ethnic minority has little impact on the exercise of policy, particularly during wartime. Jewish rescue advocates never discovered a way to convince significant numbers of Americans that the Final Solution was taking place. Without a public response, the Roosevelt administration never felt a responsibility to take on the additional burden of action. Every means of public pressure, from delegations to the White House to giant public demonstrations, were tried but failed in this most critical task. Various points of access to decision-making processes, both in Congress and in the executive branch, were ineffective because American leaders were absorbed by the war and could not be convinced by one group that its problem required special attention. Roosevelt himself gave no priority at all to the problem.

Within this context, American Jewry seemed bound to fail. When their efforts did finally have some real results, it was simply too late. Hitler's determination to liquidate the Jews was greater than the willingness of a modern nation-state, in spite of the efforts of American Jews, to conduct a humanitarian mission during wartime to rescue a foreign minority for which it felt no responsibility. Even in a more normal environment there is only so much that a minority ethnic group can accomplish without the backing of public opinion. During wartime, without some presidential leadership, the task is virtually impossible. In spite of full knowledge of the facts, Roosevelt chose to ignore the situation. As Wyman states, "In the end, the era's most prominent symbol of humanitarianism turned away from one of history's most compelling moral challenges."[70]

Notes

1. David S. Wyman, *The Abandonment of the Jews* (New York: Pantheon Books, 1984), ix.

2. Henry Feingold, *A Midrash on American Jewish History* (Albany: State University of New York Press, 1982), 214.

3. Wyman, 5–9.

4. Ibid., 10–14.

5. Ibid., 6–8.

6. Herbert Stember, et al., *Jews in the Mind of America* (New York: Basic Books, 1966), 8.

7. Ibid., 8, 69.

8. Ibid., 8, 128, 137.

9. Ibid., 137.

10. Wyman, 12.

11. Henry Feingold, *The Politics of Rescue: The Roosevelt Administration and the Holocaust, 1938-1945* (New York: Holocaust Library, 1980), 127.

12. Wyman, x.

13. Deborah E. Lipstadt, *Beyond Belief* (New York: Macmillan, 1986), 128–129.

14. Feingold, 18.

15. Saul S. Friedman, *No Haven for the Oppressed: United States Policy Toward Jewish Refugees, 1938-1945* (Detroit: Wayne State University Press, 1973), 115–116.

16. Breckinridge Long, *The War Diary of Breckinridge Long: Selections from the Years 1939-1944* (Lincoln: University of Nebraska Press, 1966), 216–217.

17. Ibid.

18. Ibid., 239

19. See David Wyman, *Paper Walls: American and the Refugee Crisis, 1926-1941* (Amherst: University of Massachusetts Press, 1968).

20. Feingold, *Midrash,* 126–127.

21. Feingold, *Politics,* 9.

22. Lee O'Brien, *American Jewish Organizations and Israel* (Washington, D.C.: Institute for Palestine Studies, 1986), 72, 84.

23. Feingold, *Politics,* 10.

24. Ibid., 13.

25. Wyman, 238.

26. Long, 336.

27. Wyman, 239.

28. A. James Reichley, "Religion and the Future of American Politics," *Political Science Quarterly* 101 (1986): 36.

29. Alan M. Fisher, "Realignment of the Jewish Vote?" *Political Science Quarterly* 94 (Spring 1979): 99.

30. Lawrence H. Fuchs, *The Political Behavior of American Jews* (Glencoe, IL: The Free Press, 1956), 74.
31. Henry Feingold, "Roosevelt and the Holocaust: Reflections on New Deal Humanism," *Judaism* 18 (Summer 1969): 260–226; Wyman, 312.
32. Feingold, *Midrash*, 219.
33. Feingold, "Roosevelt and the Holocaust," 267.
34. Wyman, 330.
35. Friedman, 56.
36. Ibid., 27.
37. Ibid., 32.
38. Feingold, "Roosevelt," 260–266.
39. Feingold, *Politics*, 67–78.
40. Ibid.
41. Friedman, 90.
42. Feingold, "Roosevelt and the Holocaust," 265–266.
43. Feingold, *Midrash*, 208–209.
44. Lucy S. Dawidowicz, "American Jews and the Holocaust," *New York Times Magazine*, 18 April 1982, 48.
45. Long, 161, 216.
46. Feingold, *Politics*, 137–139.
47. Wyman, 42, 6 1.
48. Dawidowicz, 102.
49. Ibid.; Henry L. Feingold, *A Time For Searching, Entering the Mainstream, 1920-1945* (Baltimore: Johns Hopkins University Press, 1992), 232–233.
50. Lipstadt, 199–201.
51. Wyman, 107–108.
52. Dawidowicz, 110.
53. Ibid., 1
54. Ibid., 148.
55. Henry Morgenthau Jr., "The Morgenthau Diaries," *Colliers*, 11 November 1947, 63.
56. Wyman, 203.
57. Ibid., 204.
58. Ibid., 214–215.
59. Ibid., 330.
60. Morgenthau, 63.
61. Wyman, 285.
62. Morgenthau, 63.
63. David B. Truman, *The Governmental Process* (New York: Alfred A. Knopf, 1951), 214.
64. Stember, 145, 141.
65. Lipstadt, 273.
66. Morgenthau, 65.
67. Feingold, *Politics*, xii.
68. Long, 134.
69. Speech by Emanuel Celler, 23 October 1975, quoted in Wyman, 313.
70. Ibid., 3

FOREIGN AFFAIRS CHRONOLOGY

Jan 28–Mar 2	1932	Japanese troops land in Shanghai, intensifying Sino-Japanese crisis
Feb 2	1932	Meeting of Disarmament Conference at Geneva convened
Feb 3	1932	Secretary of State Stimson reiterates the Open Door Policy and asserts inviolability of Nine Power Treaty of 1922 respecting China's sovereignty and independence
Feb 18	1932	Independence of Manchukuo (Manchuria) under Japanese control
Jul 31	1932	National Socialists become strongest party in the German Reichstag
Sep 12	1932	Reichstag dissolved
Sep 15	1932	Protocol establishes Japanese Protectorate over Manchuria
Nov 8	1932	FDR wins presidential election with little said in campaign about foreign affairs
Dec 15	1932	Default of European governments in payment of war debts to the U.S.
Jan 30	1933	Hitler becomes German Chancellor
Feb 25	1933	League of Nations adopts Stimson formula for nonrecognition of Manchukuo
Feb 27	1933	Reichstag fire in Germany
Mar 4	1933	Inauguration of FDR as thirty-second president—his remarks on foreign affairs

limited to a "Good Neighbor Policy" to improve hemispheric relations.

May 28	1933	Free elections in Danzig
Jun 12–Jul 28	1933	World Economic Conference convenes in London to deal with the global depression
Jul 15	1933	Four Power Pact between Britain, France, Germany, and Italy—an abortive effort to create a major power bloc in the League
Jul 20	1933	Concordat signed between the Vatican and Nazi Germany
Oct 4	1933	Lytton Report condemning Japanese actions in Marchuria adopted by the League of Nations; Japan gives notice of its withdrawal from the League
Oct 14	1933	Germany announces its withdrawal from the disarmament conference and from the League
Nov 17	1933	Establishment of U.S. diplomatic relations with the Soviet Union
Dec	1933	Seventh Pan-American Conference in Uruguay; U.S. for the first time supports a resolution against unilateral intervention
Jan 26	1934	Polish-German Nonaggression Pact, the first break in the French alliance system
Feb 9	1934	Balkan Pact between Greece, Turkey, and Romania to protect Balkans from great power encroachment
Apr 4	1934	Soviet Nonaggression Pact with Poland and the Baltic states

Apr 13	1934	The Johnson Debt Default Act prohibits financial transactions with foreign governments in default of obligations to the U.S.
May 5	1934	Poles extend Nonaggression Pact with Soviets
May 29	1934	Disarmament Conference meets for a brief session without results because of uncompromising French position
May 31	1934	U.S.-Cuban Treaty abrogates the Platt Amendment
Jun 12	1934	Reciprocal Tariff Act authorizing FDR for a three-year period to negotiate trade agreements without advice and consent of Senate
Jun14–15	1934	First visit of Hitler to Italy; he and Mussolini have poor first impression of each other
Jun 30	1934	The "Great Blood Purge" of more radical social revolutionary wing of Nazi Party
Jul 25	1934	Attempted Nazi coup in Vienna
Aug 2	1934	Death of German President Paul von Hindenburg
Aug 6	1934	Withdrawal of U.S. Marines from Haiti
Aug 19	1934	Plebiscite gives Hitler total power and the title of Fuhrer
Sep 18	1934	Soviet Union joins League of Nations

Nov 10	1934	Italian Chamber of Fasces completes organization of the corporate state
Dec 19	1934	Japan renounces Naval Agreements of 1922 and 1930
Jan 7	1935	Franco-Italian Agreement
Jan 13	1935	Plebiscite in Saar Basin approves reunion with Germany
Jan 15–17	1935	Soviet leaders Zinoviev, Kamenev, and others tried for treason
Mar 16	1935	Germany formally renounces clauses of Versailles Treaty concerning disarmament
Apr 11	1935	Stresa Conference between England, France, and Italy
Apr 17	1935	League condemns German unilateral repudiation of the Versailles Treaty
May 2	1935	Franco-Soviet Alliance and Five-Year Pact
May 6	1935	Silver Jubilee of King George V
May 16	1935	Russo-Czech Pact of Mutual Assistance
Jun 7	1935	Stanley Baldwin becomes British Prime Minister
Jun 18	1935	Anglo-German Naval Agreement
Jul 11	1935	German-Austrian Agreement
Oct 3	1935	Italian invasion of Ethiopia

Oct 7	1935	League Council declares Italy the aggressor in Ethiopia
Oct 11	1935	League Assembly votes to impose sanctions on Italy
Nov 27	1935	Hoare–Laval Plan to appease Mussolini
Dec 2	1935	Anthony Eden becomes British Foreign Secretary
Jan 10	1936	King George V succeeded by Edward VIII
Jan 22	1936	Fall of Laval government in France
Jan 23	1936	Start of show trials in Moscow
Mar 7	1936	German reoccupation and remilitarization of the Rhineland
Mar 25	1936	London Naval Agreement
May 5	1936	Italian army occupies Addis Ababa
May 9	1936	Ethiopia formally annexed by Italy
Jul 18	1936	Start of Civil War in Spain
Sep 10	1936	Goebbels accuses Czechoslovakia of harboring Soviet planes
Sep 12	1936	Second Neutrality Act
Oct 1	1936	General Francisco Franco appointed Spanish head of state
Oct 25	1936	Berlin–Rome Axis proposed
Nov 14	1936	Germany denounces international control of her waterways

Nov 18	1936	Germany and Italy recognize Franco government
Nov 25	1936	Anti-Comintern Pact signed by Germany, Italy, and Japan
Dec 1	1936	Pan-American Conference on world peace convenes in Buenos Aires
Dec 10	1936	Abdication of Edward VIII and succession of George VI
Jan 2	1937	Anglo-German Agreement for mutual respect of interests in the Mediterranean
Jan 20	1937	Roosevelt inaugurated for a second term
Jan 23–30	1937	Further Soviet show trials
Feb 8	1937	Rebels in Spain capture Malaga
Mar 16	1937	Mussolini visits Libya
Mar 18	1937	Loyalist forces in Spain defeat Italian troops at Brihuega
Mar 25	1937	Italo-Yugoslavian Nonaggression Pact
May	1937	U.S. Neutrality Acts debated, reaffirmed, and expanded
May 28	1937	Neville Chamberlain becomes British Prime Minister and pursues policy of appeasement
May 31	1937	German warships bomb Almeria in Spain
Jun 18	1937	Bilbao falls to rebels

Jul 7	1937	Outbreak of hostilities between Japan and China
Aug 8	1937	Japanese take Beijing
Aug 25	1937	Japanese naval blockade
Sep 10	1937	Nyon Conference to deal with Mediterranean piracy in connection with Spanish Civil War
Sep 25–28	1937	Visit of Mussolini to Berlin
Oct 5	1937	Roosevelt delivers "Quarantine Speech" ambiguously proposing broader American involvement in international affairs
Oct 5–6	1937	League and U.S. condemn actions of Japan in China
Oct 13	1937	Germany guarantees integrity of Belgium
Oct 16	1937	Sudeten Germans demand autonomy in Czechoslovakia
Nov 2–24	1937	Brussels Conference seeks means of ending Sino-Japanese conflict
Nov 9	1937	Japanese capture Shanghai
Nov 29	1937	Sudeten German delegates leave Czech parliament
Dec 11	1937	Italy withdraws from League
Dec 12	1937	The "*Panay* incident," attack of Japanese bombers on American and British ships near Nanking
Dec 13	1937	Fall of Nanking to Japan

Dec 19	1937	Lord Halifax visits Hitler
Dec 24	1937	Japanese take Hangchow
Jan	1938	Roosevelt proposes plan to British for a conference of leading powers to discuss turmoil in Europe
Feb 4	1938	Subordination of German army and foreign services to Nazi Party
Feb 12	1938	Chancellor Schuschnigg of Austria meets with Hitler at Berchtesgaden
Feb 20	1938	Anthony Eden resigns as Foreign Secretary in opposition to appeasement policies; replaced by Lord Halifax
Mar 11–12	1938	German troops enter Austria, which is declared part of the Reich
Mar 26	1938	Passage of National Mobilization Bill in Japan
Mar 28	1938	Japanese install new government of the Republic of China at Nanking
Apr 15	1938	Mussolini withdraws some troops from Spain
Apr 16	1938	Anglo-Italian Pact in which British recognize Italian sovereignty over Ethiopia
May 3–9	1938	Visit of Hitler to Rome
May 26	1938	Military officers take preeminence in Japanese cabinet

Jul 19–21	1938	State visit of King George VI and Queen Elizabeth to Paris
Aug 3	1938	Italian government introduces racial programs directed at Jews
Aug 21–23	1938	Meeting of Little Entente representatives
Sep 12	1938	Hitler demands that Sudeten Germans be granted autonomy
Sep 15	1938	Chamberlain flies to meet with Hitler at Berchtesgaden
Sep 22–23	1938	Chamberlain's second visit to Hitler at Godesburg
Sep 24–29	1938	Czech government orders full mobilization; Chamberlain appeals to Hitler for a conference
Sep 29	1938	Polish note sent to Czechoslovakia demanding cession of Techen region
Oct 5	1938	Resignation of President Benes
Oct 21	1938	Japanese take Canton
Oct 23	1938	Japanese take Hankow
Nov 17	1938	Conclusion of trade agreements between Britain, Canada, and the U.S.
Dec 1	1938	Start of national register for military service in Britain
Dec 23	1938	Beginning of insurgent drive into Catalonia

Dec 24	1938	Declaration of Lima adopted by twenty-one American states affirming solidarity and opposition to foreign intervention
Jan 26	1939	Barcelona taken by Franco's troops
Feb 27	1939	Britain and France recognize Franco government
Mar	1939	Annihilation of Czechoslovakia and demonstration of Hitler's plans to extend claims beyond German ethnic areas
Mar 2	1939	Pious XII elected pope
Mar 21	1939	German annexation of Memel
Mar 28	1939	End of Spanish Civil War with surrender of Madrid
Mar 31	1939	Anglo-French aid pledged to Poland
Apr 7	1939	Italian invasion and conquest of Albania
Apr 13	1939	Anglo-French pledge extended to Romania and Greece
Apr 15	1939	Letter from Roosevelt to Hitler and Mussolini asking for assurances against attack on thirty-one listed nations; Hitler rejects with contempt
Apr 27	1939	British introduce conscription
May 3	1939	Molotov appointed Commissar for Foreign Affairs
May 12	1939	Announcement of Anglo-Turkish mutual assistance pact

May 22	1939	Conclusion of military and political alliance between Germany and Italy—full development of Rome–Berlin Axis
Jun 8–11	1939	King George VI and Queen Elizabeth on state visit to the United States
Aug 20–Sep 1	1939	Danzig-Polish Crisis
Aug 22	1939	British government restates its pledge to Poland
Aug 23	1939	Nazi-Soviet Nonaggression Pact signed in Moscow
Aug 24	1939	Roosevelt appeals to Victor Emmanuel II, to Hitler, and to President Moscicki of Poland suggesting direct negotiations between Germany and Poland; Britain and France sign pact of mutual assistance
Aug 25	1939	Hitler renews demands for free hand against Poland—Roosevelt again appeals to Hitler for a peaceful solution
Aug 26	1939	Premier Daladier of France appeals to Hitler
Aug 28	1939	British government urges Hitler to agree to a truce; Germany announces emergency rationing
Aug 29	1939	Hitler demands visit of a Polish plenipotentiary to Berlin within twenty-four hours
Aug 30	1939	Polish decree of partial mobilization
Aug 31	1939	German government publishes sixteen-point proposal to Poland but

communications cut; Supreme Soviet ratifies pact with Hitler

Sep 1	1939	Germany attacks Poland
Sep 3	1939	Britain and France declare war on Germany, thus initiating the Second World War
Sep 3	1939	Spain declares neutrality
Sep 5	1939	U.S. declares neutrality
Sep 29	1939	Germany and the USSR divide Poland between them
Oct 2	1939	Pan-American Conference proclaims safety zone in Western Hemisphere
Nov 3	1939	U.S. Neutrality Act amended to repeal embargo on arms to belligerents; exports to be on cash and carry basis only
Nov 30	1939	Soviet army invades Poland
Mar 20	1940	Paul Renaud becomes French Premier
Mar 30	1940	Japanese set up puppet Chinese government headed by Wang Ching-wei in Nanking
Apr 4	1940	Winston Churchill given general direction over British defense program
Apr 9	1940	German forces occupy Denmark and invade Norway
May 10	1940	Germans invade Belgium, the Netherlands, and Luxembourg;

		Chamberlain resigns and Churchill becomes Prime Minister
May 28	1940	Leopold III of Belgium orders his army to cease fighting
June	1940	Fall of France, British evacuation from Dunkirk, and start of Battle of Britain
Jun 10	1940	Italy declares war on France and Great Britain
Jun 13	1940	Germans occupy Paris; Marshall Petain named French head of state
Jun 22	1940	France and Germany conclude armistice; Vichy government created
Jun 28	1940	Wendell Willkie nominated as Republican candidate for president
Jul 5	1940	Vichy government severs relations with Britain
Jul 12	1940	Petain names Pierre Laval as Vice-Premier
Jul 18	1940	Roosevelt nominated for a third term by Democratic convention
Jul 20	1940	Roosevelt signs bill providing for a two-ocean navy
Jul 21	1940	Lithuania, Latvia, and Estonia petition to become part of USSR
Jul 27	1940	Pan-American Conference at Havana adopts plans for joint trusteeship of European colonies in Western Hemisphere

Aug 17	1940	Germany declares total blockade of Britain
Aug 18	1940	Roosevelt and Prime Minister MacKenzie King of Canada agree to set up joint board of defense
Sep 16	1940	Selective Training and Service Act passes in Congress
Sep 22	1940	Japanese begin occupation of Indochina
Sep 26	1940	Roosevelt places embargo on export of scrap iron and steel
Sep 27	1940	Germany, Italy, and Japan conclude Three Powers Act at Berlin
Oct 10	1940	Intense bombing of London by Luftwaffe
Oct 11	1940	Romania passes under German control
Oct 22	1940	Hitler and Mussolini meet at Florence—Italian forces launch attack on Greece
Nov 2	1940	Hungary endorses Rome–Berlin–Tokyo Axis
Nov 5	1940	Roosevelt elected for third term
Nov 10	1940	Coventry bombed
Nov 20	1940	Britain and the U.S. agree to partial standardization of military weapons and equipment
Dec 20	1940	Roosevelt names four-member Defense Board

Dec 23	1940	Anthony Eden becomes British Foreign Secretary; Lord Halifax named British Ambassador to the U.S.
Jan 6	1941	The "Four Freedoms" speech—Roosevelt's State of the Union address defines his conception of America's role in the world conflict and the fundamental purposes of American democracy
Jan 8	1941	Roosevelt appoints four-member Office of Production Management
Feb 28	1941	Churchill given unanimous vote of confidence by Parliament
Mar 11	1941	Congress passes Lend-Lease Act, a skillfully devised method of wartime aid originally conceived by Roosevelt to assist Britain without breaking domestic or international law
Apr 6	1941	German invasion of Yugoslavia
Apr 13	1941	The USSR and Japan conclude Neutrality Treaty
May 27	1941	Roosevelt proclaims unlimited state of national emergency
Jun 16	1941	U.S. orders German consulates closed throughout country
Jun 22	1941	Germany invades Soviet Union
Jun 23	1941	Vichy government gives Japan control of French Indochina
Jul 13	1941	Britain and Soviet Union conclude mutual aid treaty

Aug 9–12	1941	Atlantic Conference, the first of many wartime meetings between Roosevelt and Churchill, aboard naval vessels off coast of Newfoundland—the Atlantic Charter, a purposefully vague statement of Anglo-American goals, issued and made a public display of Anglo-American cooperation
Aug 18	1941	FDR signs bill permitting U.S. Army to keep men in service one month longer; Reich commission in Netherlands suppresses all representative bodies
Aug 25–29	1941	British and Soviet forces invade Iran
Sep 20	1941	U.S. revenue measure provides for defense expenditures
Sep 24	1941	Fifteen governments endorse Atlantic Charter
Oct 17	1941	Pro-Axis General Tojo becomes Japanese Premier and Minister of War
Nov 6	1941	U.S. extends $1 million Lend-Lease credit to Soviet Union
Nov 25	1941	Bulgaria joins Axis
Nov 26	1941	Tojo declares goal of eliminating British and American influence in Asia
Dec 2	1941	Roosevelt asks Japan to state its aims in Indochina
Dec 6	1941	Roosevelt appeals to Emperor Hirohito to help preserve peace
Dec 7	1941	Japanese launch surprise air attack on U.S. fleet at Pearl Harbor, Hawaii, preparatory

		to other attacks on Guam, the Philippines, Midway, Hong Kong, and Malaya
Dec 8	1941	U.S. declares war on Japan
Dec 15	1941	Congress passes appropriation of over $800 million for defense and Lend-Lease
Dec 20	1941	Admiral Earnest King becomes commander of U.S. fleet
Dec 21	1941	Treaty of Alliance between Thailand and Japan
Dec 23	1941	Free French take possession of St. Pierre and Miguelon off coast of Newfoundland
Dec 25	1941	Hong Kong captured by Japanese
Dec–Jan	1941	Arcadia Conference between Roosevelt and Churchill; decision made to establish combined Chiefs of Staff to coordinate Anglo-American strategy, logistics, and operations
Jan 12	1942	U-boat offensive off Cape Cod; two hundred ships sunk by April
Jan 15	1942	Pan-American Conference begins at Rio de Janeiro
Jan 16	1942	Roosevelt establishes War Production Board with direct responsibility for mobilizing wartime economy
Jan 29	1942	USSR and U.S. recognize Iranian sovereignty
Jan 30	1942	FDR signs Price Control Act to limit inflation

Jan 31	1942	Britain recognizes independence of Ethiopia
Feb 1	1942	Vidkun Quisling named head of Nazi puppet government in Norway
Feb 2	1942	Roosevelt signs Executive Order 9066 authorizing military to exclude "any or all persons" from areas of U.S. mainland designated as "military zones"
Mar 8	1942	Japanese occupy Rangoon in Burma; U.S. and Britain name General Stillwell to command army in Burma
Mar 9	1942	Conquest of Java by Japanese
Apr 4	1942	U.S. War Production Board halts all nonessential building
Apr 14	1942	Petain forced by Germany to reinstate Laval to French Governing Council in Vichy
Apr 18	1942	Blackouts called on East and West coasts of the U.S.
Apr 27	1942	Roosevelt proposes seven-point program to fight inflation
May 5	1942	British forces land at Madagascar
May 6	1942	General Wainwright surrenders on Corregidor
May 7	1942	Battle of Coral Sea
May 26	1942	Churchill and Molotov negotiate twenty-year mutual aid treaty

Jun 4–7	1942	Attack by Japanese on Midway
Jun 9	1942	U.S. and Britain agree to pool all resources of food and production
Jun 18	1942	Roosevelt and Churchill begin meetings in Washington; disagreement on first Allied offensive
Jun 30	1942	U.S. Congress appropriate $42 million for defense
Jul 6	1942	Argentina declares neutrality
Jul 16	1942	War Labor Board decrees wage stabilization plan
Jul 25	1942	Churchill and Roosevelt agree on invasion of North Africa; Eisenhower named commander in charge
Aug 7	1942	U.S. Marines land in Solomans
Aug 12	1942	Churchill visits Moscow to discuss a Second Front with Stalin
Aug 30	1942	Germany announces annexation of Luxembourg
Oct 1	1942	Germany annexes Slovenia
Oct 12	1942	U.S. Attorney General announces that unnaturalized Italians are no longer classed as enemy aliens
Nov 8	1942	U.S. forces land in French North Africa
Nov 11	1942	German forces move into unoccupied France

Nov 12	1942	Naval battle in Solomans ends in U.S. victory
Nov 17	1942	Petain appoints Laval his successor in Vichy
Dec 1	1942	With U.S. and British approval, Admiral Darlan appointed head of state in French North Africa
Dec 16	1942	Seventy-seventh Congress adjourns as longest sitting in U.S. history
Dec 24	1942	Admiral Darlan assassinated
Jan 1–18	1943	German disasters in the USSR begin; Soviet divisions relieve Leningrad
Jan 14–24	1943	Casablanca Conference between Roosevelt and Churchill resulting in agreement to continue heavy bombing offensive against Germany, to demand unconditional surrender, and to plan for a major cross-channel invasion
Feb 6	1943	Mussolini dismisses cabinet and assumes control of foreign affairs
Feb 7	1943	General Dwight Eisenhower appointed to command separate Allied Theater in North Africa
Feb 15	1943	Japanese take Singapore
Mar 12	1943	Congress extends Lend-Lease program for another year
Apr 27	1943	Soviet government severs relations with Polish government in exile

May 12	1943	Churchill and Roosevelt meet in Washington to prepare for a Second Front in Europe
May 29	1943	Roosevelt announces that Office of War Management is supreme agency for prosecution of the war
Jun 4	1943	French Committee of National Liberation formed including De Gaulle and Henri Giraud
Jul 1	1943	Opening of concerted Allied offensive in South Pacific
Jul 2	1943	Allies capture Rendova Island in South Pacific
Jul 10	1943	U.S., British, and Canadian forces invade Sicily under Eisenhower's command
Jul 16	1943	Roosevelt establishes Office of Economic Warfare
Jul 19	1943	Allied bombing of Naples
Jul 25	1943	Mussolini forced to resign
Aug 11–24	1943	First Quebec Conference—Churchill and Roosevelt meet and French Committee of National Liberation recognized by the U.S., Canada, and Britain
Sep 2	1943	British and American forces cross Straits of Messina into southern Italy
Sep 13	1943	Chiang Kai-shek elected president of Chinese Republic

Sep 15	1943	Mussolini rescued by Germans, who also seize several major cities, including Rome
Oct 1	1943	After landing at Salerno, American troops enter Naples
Oct 9	1943	Yugoslav guerrilla forces under Marshall Tito open offensive against Axis troops in Trieste region
Oct 31	1943	Allied forces land at Bougainville
Nov 9	1943	United Nations Relief and Rehabilitation Administration organized in Washington
Nov 22	1943	U.S. forces land in Gilbert Islands
Nov 22–26	1943	Cairo Conference attended by FDR, Churchill, and Chiang Kai-Shek to enhance symbolic importance of China and meet Churchill's desire for U.S.-British talks before the Teheran Conference with Stalin
Nov 28	1943	Teheran Conference, first meeting of the "Big Three," Roosevelt, Churchill, and Stalin, resulting in decision to begin cross-channel invasion in May 1944 in conjunction with invasion from southern France and Soviet drive from the East
Dec 27–29	1943	Army takes possession of all U.S. railroads to avert strike
Jan 22	1944	Allied forces land at Anzio in Italy
Jan 27	1944	Argentina severs relations with Germany and Japan after discovery of espionage plot

Feb 2	1944	Invasion of Marshall Islands by U.S. troops
Mar 11	1944	Ireland refuses to close German and Japanese ministries in Dublin to curb Axis espionage
Mar 15	1944	Allied forces launch attack on Cassino
Mar 22	1944	German troops occupy Hungary
Apr 20–May 1	1944	German troops in Italy capitulate
Apr 28	1944	Mussolini seized and shot without trial while attempting escape to Switzerland
May 3	1944	Spanish government agrees to limit shipments of minerals to Germany and to curb Axis espionage
May 18	1944	Cassino falls to Allies
Jun 4	1944	U.S. Fifth Army enters Rome, first European capital liberated
Jun 6	1944	Normandy Invasion begins
Jun 16	1944	U.S. bombing raids on Japanese island of Kyushu
Jun 17	1944	Germany sends pilotless planes to bomb British cities
Jun 20	1944	Soviet offensive against Finland begins
Jun 27	1944	Cherbourg taken by Allies
Jul 9	1944	British and Canadian troops capture Caen

Jul 11	1944	U.S. recognizes French Committee of National Liberation headed by Charles de Gaulle
Jul 18	1944	General Tojo and his cabinet resign
Jul 21	1944	Roosevelt nominated for fourth term by Democratic Convention
Jul 24	1944	Soviet forces drive Germans from Pskov, last important Soviet city
Jul 27	1944	Soviets recognize Polish Committee of National Liberation in Moscow
Aug 11	1944	Recapture of Guam by U.S. forces
Aug12	1944	Florence taken by Allies
Aug 15	1944	Allied troops land on French Mediterranean coast
Aug 23–24	1944	Soviets capture Bucharest; German forces in Paris capitulate
Jul 11–Aug 10	1944	Open warfare breaks out between Soviet Union and Japan; Romanian government surrenders to Soviets
Aug 24	1944	Underground resistance in Paris rises up against retreating Germans
Sep 2	1944	Allies liberate Belgium
Sep 4	1944	Monganthau Plan for Germany completed
Sep 5	1944	Soviets declare war on Bulgaria
Sep 8	1944	Bulgaria accepts armistice conditions

Sep 11–16	1944	Second Quebec Conference; Churchill and Roosevelt discuss postwar policy toward Germany
Sep 12	1944	U.S. First Army crosses German frontier at Eupen and north of Trier
Sep 14	1944	American forces land on Molucca and Palau Islands in the Carolinas
Sep 29	1944	Roosevelt calls attention to Nazi influence in Argentina
Oct 2	1944	Polish forces that rose against Germans capitulate when Soviet aid does not arrive
Oct 13	1944	Athens occupied by Allied forces
Oct 19	1944	General Douglas MacArthur and U.S. troops land at Leyte
Oct 20	1944	Belgrade occupied by Soviet and Yugoslav forces
Oct 21–22	1944	Second Battle of the Philippines Sea
Nov 7	1944	Roosevelt elected for a fourth term
Nov 26	1944	American B-29s begin raids on Japan
Nov 27	1944	Edward Stettinius succeeds Cordell Hull as Secretary of State
Dec 10	1944	Franco-Soviet Treaty negotiated by De Gaulle
Dec 24	1944	Churchill and Eden arrive in Athens to negotiate settlement in Greek Civil War
Jan 1	1945	France joins United Nations in full partnership

Jan 6	1945	Turkish government breaks diplomatic relations with Japan
Jan 11	1945	Greek Civil War ends
Jan 12	1945	Soviets take Warsaw
Feb 4–12	1945	Crimean Conference at Yalta, last of the wartime conference of the original members of the Grand Alliance; issues discussed include treatment of postwar Germany, the future of Poland and Eastern Europe, the future of Japanese-occupied East Asia, and structure of the new United Nations
Feb 19–Mar 17	1945	Battle of Iwo Jima gives U.S. airbase 750 miles from Yokohama
Feb 21	1945	Pan-American Conference in Mexico City
Mar 2	1945	Americans enter Trier
Mar 3	1945	Finland declares war on Germany
Mar 5	1945	American troops enter Cologne
Mar 21	1945	U.S. carrier aircraft attack key units of Japanese fleet
Mar 23	1945	American forces cross Rhine at Remagen
Mar 27	1945	Argentina declares war on Germany and Japan
Apr 1	1945	U.S. Marines and Army invade Okinawa
Apr 5	1945	Soviets renounce five-year Nonaggression Pact with Japan

Apr 11	1945	Ninth Army reaches the Elbe
Apr 12	1945	President Roosevelt dies at Warm Springs in Georgia; Harry Truman succeeds to presidency
Apr 30	1945	Hitler commits suicide in Berlin as Soviet forces capture city
May 8	1945	Terms of unconditional surrender signed at Rheims on previous day become effective, ending European phase of the Second World War
May–August	1945	Greatest air offensive in history as U.S. aircraft destroy Japanese navy, industry, and sea communications
Aug 6	1945	Atomic bomb dropped by U.S. on Hiroshima, destroying more than half the city
Aug 9	1945	Second atomic bomb dropped on Nagasaki
Sep 2	1945	Signing of Japanese unconditional surrender aboard the USS *Missouri*

BIOGRAPHICAL DIGEST

Arnold, Henry Harley ("Hap") (1886-1950). Commanding General, U.S. Army Air Forces, 1938-46.

Attlee, Clement (1883-1967). Leader of the British Labor Party, he served in Churchill's War Cabinet. In the general election of 1945, he replaced Churchill as Prime Minister.

Baldwin, Stanley (1867-1947). British Prime Minister and First Lord of the Treasury, 1923-24, 1924-29, 1935-37; Lord President of the Council, 1931-35. He worked with Roosevelt on various foreign policy concerns such as the Spanish Civil War.

Barnes, Harry Elmer (1889-1948). Historian and isolationist critic of Franklin Roosevelt. He opposed Roosevelt's foreign policies before and during World War II, when he wrote several pamphlets arguing against U.S. involvement.

Baruch, Bernard Mannes (1870-1965). Financial speculator, head of the War Industries Board in World War I, and unofficial economic advisor to Roosevelt after 1933.

Batista, Fulgencio (1910-1973). Cuban soldier and political leader, he was President of Cuba, 1940-44, 1952-59.

Beard, Charles A. (1874-1948). Prominent American historian and isolationist critic of FDR's foreign policies.

Benes, Eduard (1884-1948). Elected president of Czechoslovakia in 1935, he resigned in October 1938 upon German occupation of the Sudetenland. President of the Czech government in exile in London during the war.

Berle, Adolph Augustus, Jr. (1895-1971). Advisor to FDR during the 1932 campaign and long-serving member of the New Deal Brain Trust; Assistant Secretary of State, 1938-44; Ambassador to Brazil, 1945.

Bonnet, Georges (1889-1973). French Foreign Minister at the time of the Munich Conference in 1938.

Borah, William Edgar (1965-1940). Progressive Republican senator from Idaho and Chair of the Senate Foreign Relations Committee. He strongly opposed entrance of the United States into the League of Nations, and advocated a noninterventionist foreign policy.

Brooke, Sir Alan (1883-1963). Lieutenant, 2d Army Corps, British Expeditionary Force, 1939-40; Commander in Chief of Home Forces, 1940-41; succeeded Sir John Dill as Chief of the Imperial General Staff in 1941; accompanied Churchill at international conferences, 1942-43.

Bullitt, William C. (1891-1967). Sometime special representative for Roosevelt on diplomatic missions. Negotiated talks leading to recognition of the Soviet Union in 1933; first American ambassador in Moscow.

Byrnes, James ("Jimmy") Francis (1879-1972). Roosevelt's "assistant president," he served as Head of the Office of Economic Stabilization and as foreign policy lobbyist with Congress.

Cárdenas, Lázaro (1895-1970). President of Mexico, 1934-1940. His administration was marked by plans for redistribution of land, industrial development, renewal of struggles with the Catholic Church, and expropriation of foreign-owned oil properties.

Chamberlain, Neville (1869-1940). British Prime Minister, 1937-45. He pursued a policy of appeasement of the dictators until failure of the Munich Conference in 1938.

Chennault, Claire Lee (1890-1958). Leader of the Flying Tigers and Commanding General, 14th Army Air Corps during World War II. He convinced FDR to authorize the purchase of P-40 fighters and to permit American military aviators to leave active duty to serve with China.

Chiang Kai-shek (1887-1975). Leader of Chinese Nationalist forces during the years of the Roosevelt presidency. FDR attempted to strengthen Nationalist China as the dominant Asian power.

Churchill, Winston S. (1874-1965). British Prime Minister, 1940-45. A critic of the policy of appeasement during the 1930s, he developed a close wartime partnership with FDR.

Ciano, Count Galeazzo (1903-1944). Italian Secretary of State for Press and Propaganda (1935); served in Italian Air Corps during Ethiopian War, 1935-36; Minister of Foreign Affairs, 1936-43.

Cooke, Charles Maynard, Jr. (1886-1971). Principal strategic planner for the Chief of Naval Operations in World War II.

Coughlin, Charles Edward (1891-1979). Catholic priest, radio personality, and political dissident; prominent as an early ally and later strong antagonist of FDR.

Daniels, Josephus (1862-1948). Editor, southern reformer, cabinet member, and diplomat. Roosevelt was his Assistant Secretary of the Navy in the Wilson administration.

Darlan, Jean (1881-1942). During the Vichy regime Admiral of the Fleet, Vice-Premier, and Minister of Defense. In August 1941 he assumed command of all armed forces. He agreed in November 1942, after the Allied invasion of North Africa, to the end of opposition there. A useful but embarrassing ally until his assassination in December.

Davies, Joseph E. (1876-1958). U.S. Ambassador to the USSR 1930-38, Belgium 1938-39. In January 1937 Roosevelt sent him to Moscow to win the confidence of Stalin. He made a systematic effort to be conciliatory by overlooking arbitrary Soviet actions.

De Gaulle, Charles (1890-1970). Leader of the Free French during World War II. Roosevelt refused to recognize the Free French and maintained relations with the Vichy regime to prevent naval vessels and strategic overseas territory from falling into Axis hands.

Dern, George Henry (1872-1936). Secretary of War, 1933-36.

Detzer, Dorothy (1893-1971). National Executive Secretary of the Women's International League for Peace and Freedom (1924-46), she led a successful campaign for a Senate investigation of the American munitions industry, 1933-36.

Doenitz, Admiral Karl (1891-1980). Commander of German submarine fleet, 1936; Grand Admiral, 1943. As Reich President after Hitler's death he signed the unconditional surrender to the Allies on 7 May 1945.

Douglas, Lewis William (1894-1974). Budget Director, New Deal critic, and deputy administrator for the War Shipping Administration.

Early, Stephen Tyrel (1889-1951). Roosevelt's press secretary, 1933-1945.

Eden, Anthony (1897-1977). British Foreign Secretary, 1935-38, he resigned from the Chamberlain government after the Munich Conference. Secretary for War, 1940; Foreign Secretary, 1940-45.

Eisenhower, Dwight David (1890-1969). European theater commander in World War II.

Forrestal, James Vincent (1892-1949). Undersecretary of the Navy, 1940-44; Secretary of the Navy, 1944-47.

Franco, Francisco (1892-1975). A general on the Nationalist side in the Spanish Civil War, he received aid from Germany and Italy, and indirectly from other Western powers through their "nonintervention" policy that enabled the insurgents to buy war supplies. Dictator of Spain after the end of the conflict, he maintained neutrality during World War II.

Garner, John Nance (1868-1967). Vice-President of the United States, 1933-41.

Hacha, Emil (1872-1945). Third President of Czechoslovakia, 1938-39; President of the German "Protectorate of Bohemia and Moravia," 1939-45. He died in jail awaiting trial as a war criminal.

Halifax, Lord Edwin Frederick (1881-1959). Secretary for War, 1935; Lord Privy Seal, 1935-37; leader of the House of Lords, 1935-38; Lord President of the Council 1937-38; Foreign Secretary, 1938-40; Ambassador to U.S., 1941-46.

Halsey, William Frederick, Jr. (1882-1959). Commander of U.S. Third Fleet in World War II.

Harriman, William Averell (1891-1986). Regarded as the pivotal person in FDR's foreign affairs circle. He attended the Atlantic Meeting in 1941, headed the Lend-Lease mission to the Soviet Union, and returned there with Churchill in 1942 to ease Stalin's concerns about the absence of a Second Front. Ambassador in Moscow, 1943-46, he was at FDR's side at the Cairo, Teheran, and Yalta Conferences.

Hassett, William D. (1880-1960). Correspondence secretary and sometimes press secretary to FDR, 1935-45.

Hirohito (1901-1989). Emperor of Japan, 1926-1989.

Hitler, Adolph (1889-1945). German Chancellor, 1933-45. His contempt for Roosevelt and the United States led him to declare war on the U.S. after Pearl Harbor, thus paving the way for American entry into the European war.

Hoare, Sir Samuel (1880-1959). British Secretary of State for Air, 1922-24, 1924-29, 1940, for India, 1931-35, for Foreign Affairs, 1935; First Lord of the Admiralty, 1936-37; Home Secretary, 1937-39. He is associated primarily with the policy of appeasement toward Mussolini.

Holcomb, Thomas (1879-1965). Roosevelt's World War II Commandant of the Marine Corps, he prepared his service to meet the test of amphibious combat in the Pacific.

Hopkins, Harry L. (1890-1946). Roosevelt's confidant and frequent personal diplomat. In 1941 he became head of Lend-Lease, the nation's great effort to provide supplies and equipment to countries fighting the Axis powers.

Hull, Cordell (1871-1955). Secretary of State, 1933-1945. He was often slighted by Roosevelt's brand of personal politics.

Kennan, George (1904-   ). State Department expert on the Soviet Union who began in the 1930s to express concerns about the threat of communism. In 1947 he set forth the concept of communist containment in a famous article in *Foreign Affairs*.

Keynes, John Maynard (1883-1946). British economist and principal representative of the Treasury at the Paris Peace Conference in 1919. During World War II he contributed a great deal to the working out of economic strategy for the postwar world.

King, Admiral Earnest J. (1878-1956). After the attack on Pearl Harbor, Roosevelt named him Commander in Chief of the U.S. Fleet.

Knox, William Franklin (1874-1944). Secretary of the Navy, 1940-44. He publicly advocated stronger measures against the Axis Powers before World War II.

Konoye, Prince Fuminaro (1891-1945). Japanese Premier, 1937-39; Foreign Minister, 1938; responsible for much of Japanese policy in the Sino-Japanese War, 1937.

Laval, Pierre (1883-1945). French Minister of Labor, 1932, of Colonies, 1934, of Foreign Affairs, 1935-36. Vice-Premier in Vichy government, July–December, 1940. As Premier from April 1943 he pursued a policy of collaboration with Germany; later executed for treason.

Leahy, William (1875-1959). Admiral of the Fleet and principal military assistant to the President during most of the war. He served as a conduit of information between the President and the Joint Chiefs of Staff and played a vital role in the coordination of political purpose and military strategy during wartime.

Lindbergh, Charles A. (1902-1974). Noted aviator and, as leader of the America First Movement, the most prominent opponent of American entry into World War II.

Lindsey, Sir Ronald (1877-1945). Undersecretary at British Foreign Office 1921-24; Ambassador to Germany, 1926-28, and to United States, 1930-39.

Litvinov, Maksim (1876-1951). After Soviet Revolution he represented the Soviet government in London, headed the Soviet delegation at disarmament commissions in 1927, 1928, and 1929. People's Commissar for Foreign Affairs, 1930-39; Soviet Ambassador to the U.S, 1941-43; Deputy Commissar for Foreign Affairs, 1943-46.

Lothian, Lord Philip Henry (1882-1941). British Ambassador to the U.S., 1938-41. He publicly requested financial support from the Roosevelt administration at the outset of war in 1939.

MacArthur, Douglas (1880-1964). Army Chief of Staff and Pacific theater commander. He challenged the strategic priorities of Roosevelt and the Joint Chiefs. He argued that operations against the Japanese were neglected in favor of the war in Europe.

McCormick, Robert Rutherford (1880-1955). Publisher and editor of the *Chicago Tribune* and one of the most vehement opponents of Franklin Roosevelt.

MacDonald, James Ramsay (1866-1937). British Prime Minister 1924, 1929-35, he worked with Roosevelt to try to establish a monetary and economic agreement between the U.S. and Britain.

McIntyre, Marvin Hunter (1878-1943). Assistant secretary and, after 1937, secretary to the President until his death. With Louis Howe, Steve Early, and Missy Lehand, "Mac" McIntyre was one of the key administration insiders.

Mahan, Alfred Thayer (1840-1914). He served as FDR's naval advisor, influencing him deeply. They met and corresponded, and Roosevelt kept well-read copies of Mahan's books in his libraries. He often quoted Mahan with great precision and, despite his disdain for doctrine, adhered to Mahan's principles throughout World War II.

Marshall, George Catlett (1880-1959). Chief of Staff of the U.S. Army, including army air forces, under Roosevelt. He accompanied FDR to many important conferences and represented him at others. A strong supporter of Roosevelt's Europe first strategy and the cross-channel invasion concept, Marshall was a forceful advocate in Allied councils.

Masaryk, Jan Garrique (1868-1948). Czech Ambassador to Britain, 1925-38; lectured in U.S., 1939-40; Foreign Minister 1940-48 and Vice-Premier 1941-45. Head of Czech provisional government in London.

Masaryk, Thomas Garrigue (1850-1937). Founding President of Czechoslovakia (1918-1935).

Moley, Raymond (1886-1975). Assistant Secretary of State in 1933 and member of the Brain Trust, an informal group to whom the President turned from time to time.

Molotov, General Vyachheslev Mikhailovich (1890-1986). President and later Vice-Chair of the Council of People's Commissars, 1941; Commissar of Foreign Affairs, 1939; member of State Committee of Defense, 1930-41. He presided at the Anglo-Soviet conference in Moscow, September 1941, and other conferences in Britain and the U.S. in 1942. He was a delegate to the first United Nations meeting.

Morgenthau, Jr., Henry T. (1891-1967). Secretary of the Treasury, 1934-35. He involved Treasury in several key wartime issues. He opposed the incarceration of Japanese Americans in early 1942. In 1943–44, he played a major role in publicizing Hitler's Final Solution and helped establish the War Refugee Board. He directed preparation of the draconian "Morgenthau plan" for dealing with Germany after the war.

Mussolini, Benito (1883-1945). Italian Premier, 1922-1945. He entered the war on the German side despite Roosevelt's pleas to remain neutral.

Nagano, Admiral (1888-1947). Japanese admiral; Minister of the Navy, 1937-37; Commander in Chief of Japanese fleet, 1937; Chief of Naval General Staff, 1941; Fleet Marshal, 1943.

Nimitz, Chester William (1885-1966). American naval officer and Commander of the Pacific Fleet in World War II. On 2 September 1945, aboard the battleship *Missouri*, he signed the instrument of Japanese surrender as representative of the United States.

Nye, Senator Gerald P. (1892-1971). Progressive Republican senator from North Dakota who took the lead in supporting the Neutrality Acts in an effort to keep the U.S. out of the European war. He headed the Senate investigation of manufacturers and distributors of armaments, who were widely believed to be instrumental in provoking nations to war.

Petain, Henri (1856-1951). World War I hero who became Premier of Vichy France, 1940-44. His life was spared by General de Gaulle after the war.

Ribbentrop, Joachim von (1893-1946). German Ambassador to Britain, 1941-45; negotiated the Anglo-German Naval Agreement in 1936, the Soviet-German Nonaggression Pact in 1939, and the Axis Alliance in 1940. He was hanged as a war criminal.

Roosevelt, Anna Eleanor (1884-1962). Wife of Franklin Roosevelt. Increasingly an international figure in her own right, she often counseled FDR on important issues.

Sherwood, Robert Emmit (1896-1955). Speechwriter for FDR and Director of Overseas Division, Office of War Information, 1942-44.

Simon, Sir John (1873-1954). British Home Secretary 1915-18; Foreign Secretary, 1931-33; Home Secretary and deputy leader of the House of Commons, 1935-37; Chancellor of the Exchequer, 1937-1949; Lord Chancellor, 1940-45.

Spark, Harold Raynesford (1880-1972). Admiral U.S. Navy; Chief of Naval Operations, 1939-1942. He was stripped of responsibilities after Pearl Harbor.

Stalin, Joseph V. (1879-1953). Soviet Premier, 1927-1953. After the Nazi invasion of the Soviet Union in 1941, he became one of the wartime Big Three. Although wary of his intentions, Roosevelt believed he could persuade him to cooperate during and after the war.

Steinhardt, Lawrence (1982-1950). U.S. Minister to Sweden, 1933-37; Ambassador to Peru, the USSR, 1939-41, Turkey, 1942-44, Czechoslovakia, 1944-48.

Stettinius, Edward R. (1900-1949). Industrialist, New Deal advisor, and Secretary of State, 1944-45. In the summer of 1941, Roosevelt appointed him head of the Lend-Lease Administration. As Secretary of State, his main contribution lay in his role in the organization of the United Nations.

Stillwell, Joseph Warren (1883-1946). Commander, China-Burma-India theater, 1942-44. A constant thorn in the side of Chiang Kai-shek, he was recalled after complaints from the Nationalist Chinese government. Later he became a martyr for those who questioned Roosevelt's close wartime alliance with Chiang.

Stimson, Henry L. (1867-1950). Secretary of War 1940-45. He supported Japanese internment and promoted development of the atomic bomb.

Tojo, General Hideki (1885-1945). Japanese Minister of War in the Konoye government, 1937-40. Prime Minister, 1941-44, he was eventually hanged as a war criminal.

Vandenberg, Arthur H. (1884-1951). Republican senator who pushed for an isolationist stance. He favored the Neutrality Acts of the 1930s and protested the Lend-Lease Act.

Wallace, Henry A. (1888-1965). Vice-President of the United States, 1945-45; head of the Economic Defense Board, 1941; Secretary of Commerce, 1946.

Watson, Edwin Martin (1883-1945). Military aide to President Roosevelt throughout his presidency and from 1939 his secretary.

Welles, Benjamin Sumner (1892-1961). Assistant Secretary and Undersecretary of State, Ambassador to Cuba as well as personal friend and advisor of FDR. He is credited with originating the term "Good Neighbor Policy."

Woodring, Harry Hines (1890-1967). Secretary of War, 1936-40. He opposed U.S. involvement in a European war.

SELECTED BIBLIOGRAPHY

Beasley, Maurine, Holly C. Shulman, and Henry R. Beasley, eds. *The Eleanor Roosevelt Encyclopedia*. Westport, CT: Greenwood Press, 2001.

Berger, Jason. *A New Deal for the World: Eleanor Roosevelt and American Foreign Policy, 1920-1962*. New York: Columbia University Press, 1981.

Berthon, Simon. *Allies at War: The Bitter Rivalry Among Churchill, Roosevelt and De Gaulle*. New York: Carroll and Graf, 2001.

Black, Alida M. *Casting Her Own Shadow: Eleanor Roosevelt and the Shaping of Postwar Liberalism*. New York: Columbia University Press, 1996.

Brinkley, Alan. *The End of Reform: New Deal Liberalism in Recession and War*. New York: Alfred A. Knopf, 1995.

Buhite, Russell D., and David W. Levy, eds. *FDR's Fireside Chats*. Norman: University of Oklahoma Press, 1992.

Burns, James M. *Roosevelt: Lion and the Fox*. New York: Harcourt, Brace, 1956.

——. *Roosevelt: Soldier of Freedom*. New York: Harcourt Brace Jovanovich, 1970.

Burns, James M., and Susan Dunn. *The Three Roosevelts: Patrician Leaders Who Transformed America*. New York: Atlantic Monthly Press, 2001.

Caroli, Betty. *The Roosevelt Women*. New York: Basic Books, 1998.

Casey, Steven. *Cautious Crusade: Franklin D. Roosevelt, American Public Opinion and the War Against Nazi Germany*. New York: Oxford University Press, 2001.

Cashman, Sean D. *America, Roosevelt and World War II*. New York: New York University Press, 1989.

Cole, Wayne. *Determinism and American Foreign Policy*. Lanham: University Press of America, 1995.

Collier, Peter, and David Horowitz. *The Roosevelts: An American Saga*. New York: Simon and Schuster, 1994.

Cook, Blanche W. *Eleanor Roosevelt: 1884-1933*. vol. 1; *Eleanor Roosevelt, 1933-1938*, vol. 2, New York: Viking Penguin, 1993, 1999.

Curtis, Sandra R. *Alice and Eleanor: A Contrast in Style and Purpose*. Bowling Green, OH: Bowling Green University Popular Press, 1994.

Dallek, Robert. *Franklin D. Roosevelt and American Foreign Policy, 1932-1945*. New York: Oxford University Press, 1979.

———. *Franklin D. Roosevelt as a World Leader*. New York: Oxford University Press, 1995.

Davis, Kenneth S. *FDR. The New Deal Years, 1933-1937*. New York: Random House, 1986.

———. *FDR, Into the Storm, 1937–1940*. New York: Random House, 1993.

———. *FDR, The War President, 1940–1943*. New York: Random House, 2000.

Daynes, Byron, William Pederson, and Michael Riccards, eds. *The New Deal and Public Policy*. New York: St. Martin's Press, 1998.

Dickinson, Matthew J. *Bitter Harvest: FDR, Presidential Power and Growth of the Presidential Branch*. New York: Cambridge University Press, 1996.

Divine, Robert A. *Roosevelt and World War II*. Baltimore: Johns Hopkins Press, 1969.

Doenecke, Justus D. *Storm on the Horizon: The Challenge to American Intervention, 1939-1941*. Lanham, MO: Rowman and Littlefield, 2000.

Donn, Linda. *The Roosevelt Cousins*. New York: Random House, 2001.

Dunn, Dennis J. *Caught Between Roosevelt and Stalin: America's Ambassadors to Moscow*. Lexington: University Press of Kentucky, 1998.

Edens, John A. *Eleanor Roosevelt: A Comprehensive Bibliography*. Westport: CT: Greenwood Press, 1994.

Farnham, Barbara R. *Roosevelt and the Munich Crisis: A Study of Political Decision Making*. Princeton: Princeton University Press, 1997.

Feis, Herbert. *Roosevelt, Churchill, Stalin: The War They Fought and the Peace They Sought*. Princeton: Princeton University Press, 1957.

Ferrell, Robert H. *The Dying President: Franklin D. Roosevelt, 1944-1945*. Columbia: University of Missouri Press, 1998.

Fleming, Thomas. *The New Dealers' War: FDR and the War Within World War II*. New York: Basic Books, 2001.

Flynn, George Q. *Roosevelt and Romanism: Catholics and American Diplomacy, 1937-1945*. Westport: CT: Greenwood Press, 1976.

Fried, Albert. *FDR and His Enemies*. New York: St. Martin's, 1999.

Freidel, Frank. *Franklin D. Roosevelt: A Rendezvous with Destiny*. Boston: Little, Brown, 1990.

Gallagher, Hugh. *FDR's Splendid Deception*. Arlington, VA: Vandamere Press, 1994.

Glenden, Mary Ann. *A World Made New: Eleanor Roosevelt and the Universal Declaration of Human Rights*. New York: Random House, 2001.

Goodwin, Doris K. *No Ordinary Time. Franklin and Eleanor Roosevelt: The Home Front in World War II*. New York: Simon and Schuster, 1994.

Graham, Otis L., Jr., and Megan R. Wander, eds. *Franklin D. Roosevelt, His Life and Times: An Encyclopedic View*. New York: Macmillan, 1985.

Gurewitsch, Edna P. *Kindred Souls: The Friendship of Eleanor Roosevelt and David Gurewitsch*. New York: St. Martin's Press, 2002.

Harper, John L. *American Visions of Europe: Franklin D. Roosevelt, George F. Kennan and Dean G. Acheson*. New York: Cambridge University Press, 1994.

Hearden, Patrick. *Roosevelt Confronts Hitler: America's Entry into World War II*. DeKalb: North Illinois University Press, 1987.

Herzstein, Robert E. *Roosevelt and Hitler: Prelude to War*. New York: Wiley, 1994.

Hoopes, Townsend, and Douglas Brinkley. *FDR and the Creation of the United Nations*. New Haven: Yale University Press, 1997.

Kennedy, David. *Freedom from Fear: The American People in Depression and War, 1929-1945*. New York: Oxford University Press, 1999.

Kimball, Warren F. *Forged in War: Roosevelt, Churchill, and the Second World War*. New York: William Morrow, 1997.

Kinsella, William E., Jr. *Leadership in Isolation: FDR and the Origins of the Second World War*. Rochester, VT: Schenkman Books, 1970.

Klein, Jonas. *Beloved Island: Franklin and Eleanor and the Legacy of Campobello*. Forest Dale, VT: Eriksson, 2000.

Langer, William A. *The Undeclared War, 1940-41*. New York: Harper, 1953.

Larrabee, Eric. *Commander in Chief—Franklin D. Roosevelt: His Lieutenants and Their War*. New York: Harper and Row, 1987.

Leuchtenburg, William E. *Franklin D. Roosevelt and the New Deal, 1932-40*. New York: Harper and Row, 1963.

——. *In the Shadow of FDR: From Harry Truman to Bill Clinton*. Ithaca, NY: Cornell University Press, 1993.

——. *The FDR Years. On Roosevelt and His Legacy*. New York: Columbia University Press, 1995.

McJimsey, George. *The Presidency of Franklin Delano Roosevelt*. Lawrence: University Press of Kansas, 2000.

Maney, Patrick J. *The Roosevelt Presence: A Biography of Franklin Delano Roosevelt*. New York: Twayne, 1992.

Marks, Frederick W. *Wind over Sand. The Diplomacy of Franklin Roosevelt*. Athens: University of Georgia Press, 1988.

Merolda, Edward J. *FDR and the U.S. Navy*. New York: St. Martin's, 1998.

Miller, Dwight, and Timothy M. Welch, eds. *Herbet Hoover and Franklin D. Roosevelt: A Documentary History*. Wesport, CT: Greenwood Press, 1998.

Morgan, Ted. *FDR: A Biography*. New York: Simon and Schuster, 1985.

Newton, Verne W., ed. *FDR and the Holocaust*. New York: St. Martin's Press, 1996.

Olson, James S., ed. *Historical Dictionary of the New Deal: From Inauguaration to Preparation for War*. Wesport, CT: Greenwood Press, 1985.

O'Neill, William L. *A Democracy at War: America's Fight at Home and Abroad in World War II*. New York: Free Press, 1993.

Perlmutter, Amos. *FDR and Stalin: A Not So Grand Alliance, 1943-1945*. Columbia: University of Missouri Press, 1993.

Perras, Galen R. *Franklin D. Roosevelt and the Origins of the Canadian-American Security Alliance, 1933-1945: Necessary, but not Necessary Enough*. Wesport, CT: Praeger, 1998.

Persico, Joseph E. *Roosevelt's Secret War: FDR and World War II Espionage*. New York: Random House, 2001.

Pike, Frederick B. *FDR's Good Neighbor Policy: Sixty Years of Generally Gentle Chaos*. Austin: University of Texas Press, 1995.

Polenberg, Richard. *The Era of Franklin D. Roosevelt, 1933-1945: A Brief History with Documents*. New York: St. Martin's, 2000.

Robinson, Greg. *By Order of the President: FDR and the Internment of Japanese Americans*. Cambridge: Harvard University Press, 2001.

Rosenbaum, Herbert D., and Elizabeth Bartelme, eds. *Franklin D. Roosevelt: The Man, the Myth and the Era, 1882-1945*. Wesport, CT: Greenwood Press, 1987.

Rossi, Mario. *Roosevelt and the French*. Wesport, CT: Praeger, 1993.

Rubinstein, William D. *The Myth of Rescue: Why the Democracies Could Not Have Saved More Jews from the Nazis*. New York: Routledge, 1997.

Ryan, Halford R. *Franklin Roosevelt's Rhetorical Presidency*. Wesport, CT: Greenwood Press, 1988.

Sainsbury, Keith. *Churchill and Roosevelt at War: The War They Fought and the Peace They Hoped to Make*. New York: New York University Press, 1994.

Savage, Sean J. *Roosevelt: The Party Leader, 1932-1945*. Lexington: University Press of Kentucky, 1991.

Schlesinger, Arthur M., Jr. *The Age of Roosevelt: The Politics of Upheaval*. Boston: Houghton Mifflin, 1960.

Sears, John F., ed. *Franklin D. Roosevelt and the Future of Liberalism*. Wesport, CT: Greenwood Press, 1990.

Stinnett, Robert B. *Day of Deceit: The Truth About FDR and Pearl Harbor*. New York: The Free Press, 1999.

Szalay, Michael. *New Deal Modernism: American Literature and the Invention of the Welfare State*. Durham, NC: Duke University Press, 2000.

Underhill, Robert. *FDR and Harry: Unparalleled Lives*. Wesport, CT: Praeger, 1996

Van Minnen, Cornelis A. *FDR and His Contemporaries: Foreign Perceptions of an American President*. New York: St. Martin's, 1992.

Ward, Geoffrey C. *A First-Class Temperament: The Emergence of Franklin Roosevelt*. New York: Harper and Row, 1989.

Weiss, Stuart L. *The President's Man: Leo Crowley and Franklin Roosevelt in Peace and War*. Carbondale: Southern Illinois University Press, 1996.

Winfield, Betty H. *FDR and the News Media*. Champaign: University of Illinois Press, 1991.

Wolf, Thomas, William Pederson, and Bryon Daynes, eds. *Franklin D. Roosevelt and Congress: The New Deal and Its Aftermath*. Armonk, NY: M.E. Sharpe, 2001.

Young, Nancy, William Pederson, and Bryon Daynes, eds. *Franklin D. Roosevelt and the Shaping of American Political Culture*. Armonk, NY: M.E. Sharpe, 2001.

LIST OF CONTRIBUTORS

Stephen G. Bunch taught history at Eastern Illinois University after completing doctoral studies at the University of Illinois. He now works for the federal government in Washington.

Elizabeth R.B. Elliott-Meisel teaches history at Creighton University in Nebraska. Since she completed her doctoral work at Duke University, her research and publications have focused on Canadian-American relations and, most recently, Canadian historiography.

David M. Esposito teaches history at Penn State Altoona and recently was a Senior Fulbright Fellow in Indonesia. He has written extensively on American political and diplomatic history, including a book on Woodrow Wilson and American war aims in World War I.

Calvin W. Hines teaches diplomatic and military history at Stephen F. Austin University in Texas. He has published numerous works on Franco-American relations and French naval history.

Thomas C. Howard teaches history at Virginia Tech. His research and publications are mainly in modern British and African history, and on Anglo-American relations in the twentieth century.

William E. Kinsella, Jr. has taught at Georgetown and John Carroll Universities and is now a professor of history at Northern Virginia Community College. He has published extensively on American history, including a book on Franklin Roosevelt and the origins of World War II.

Manfred Landecker taught political science at Southern Illinois University until his recent retirement. His research and publications have mainly focused on United States foreign relations, especially the relationships between foreign policy and public opinion.

Maris A. Mantenieks is presently with NASA's Lewis Research Center in Ohio. His primary research interests and publications deal with the history of the Baltic states and Soviet relations with the Baltic region.

William D. Pederson teaches political science and is director of the International Lincoln Center for American Studies at Louisiana State University in Shreveport. His numerous books include several on the American presidency.

Julia M. Siebel is now a Development Research Analyst at Scripps College, Claremont, California. Since completion of her doctoral studies at the University of Southern California, her research and publications have continued to concentrate on the impact of World War II on American society and politics.

Carol Silverman is a financial consultant in Charlottesville, Virginia. Her graduate research at the University of Virginia focused on American responses to the Holocaust, a subject that she continues to pursue.

Chris Van Aller teaches political science at Winthrop University in South Carolina. His publications concentrate on civil-military relations, defense restructuring, and political culture and the environment.

INDEX

254